Sponge Bag
TEA
Night Gown
BIBLES
TRACTS
Revolvers
Whiskey
herds of Game.
Boiled Missionary
Cannibals enjoying a hearty meal
Beautiful Savage maiden with eyes like the Sea.
Strong Native, unaccustomed to Englishman's shooting.

OUT IN THE NOONDAY SUN

Valerie Pakenham

OUT IN THE NOONDAY SUN

Edwardians in the Tropics

RANDOM HOUSE
NEW YORK

Published in the United States
by Random House, Inc., New York.
Originally published in Great Britain
as *The Noonday Sun* by Methuen London Ltd., London.

Library of Congress Cataloging in Publication Data
Pakenham, Valerie.
Out in the noonday sun.
Includes index.
1. Great Britain – Colonies – History – Anecdotes, facetiae, satire, etc. I. Title.
JV1011.P34 1985 325'.341'09 84-45759
ISBN 0-394-52256-7

2 3 4 5 6 7 8 9
First American Edition

CONTENTS

Preface		7
1	Pillars	9
2	Rulers	23
3	Builders	43
4	Settlers	69
5	Preachers	91
6	Traders	115
7	Hunters	141
8	Players	167
9	Soldiers	189
10	Winners/Losers	217
Map		236
Biographical Notes		238
Photographic Credits		246
Select Bibliography		247
Notes to the Text		247
Index		251

TO THOMAS

PREFACE

My first encounter with the lost world of the Edwardians in the tropics was in the billiard-room of the house where I now live in Ireland. There, ranged along one wall between the estate records and the billiard cues, are the splendid collection of sporting and travel books amassed by my husband's great-uncle Bingo who spent his winters here during his long tenure as Master of the Westmeath Hounds. What thrilling reading they must have made for him in this damp and chilly corner of the British Empire (as Ireland still was): *Rifle and Romance in the Indian Jungle, Days in the Torrid Sudan, Hunting and Shooting in Ceylon, A Picnic Party in Wildest Africa*. For the Edwardian sportsman it must at times have seemed as if the whole tropical world had been invented for his delectation.

Judging by his books, Uncle Bingo's interests extended to more serious aspects of empire too. Here, for instance, is Sir Harry Johnston's mammoth study of *The Uganda Protectorate* (two volumes, 1,018 pages), covering its history, anthropology, geology, meteorology and linguistics. Or Curzon's study of *Russia in Central Asia* and Sven Hedin's journey (*Overland to India*) through the mountains, where the Great Game against the Russians was still in full swing. Or a well-thumbed copy of Slatin Pasha's *Fire and Sword in the Sudan*, translated by Major F. R. Wingate, which probably did more than any other book to fire the British conviction that they must reconquer the Sudan (of which Wingate was to become in due course a model Governor-General).

Starting like Uncle Bingo as a fireside traveller, I have dipped a little further into the vast pool of memoirs, diaries and letters left by the Edwardians who went out, in one capacity or another, to brave the tropical sun when England's belief in her mission 'to rule the earth' was at its zenith. In my narrow cross-section of empire, I have tried to recreate what it felt like for them, avoiding as far as possible the far more complex and thorny question of the effect of the British Empire on those they 'ruled'. I have also tried to show, without making too much of it, some of the many tensions inside the Edwardian Empire among Englishmen themselves: administrators against traders, settlers against administrators, soldiers against civilians – and almost everyone, it seems, against the missionaries.

The original conception of this book belongs entirely to my publisher, Christopher Falkus, who has never failed, during its writing, with kindness and encouragement.

Of the many experts, relations and friends who also helped with advice, time and material I would like especially to thank the following: Charles Allen, Alexander Antrim (who allowed me to see his great-uncle Sir Schomberg McDonnell's papers), Alan Bell, Timothy Best of Rowland Ward, Rachel Billington, Janet Carleton, Hugh Cecil, Dr Mary Cumpston, Lord Delamere (who showed me his grandfather's farm at Soysambu), James de Vere Allen, Gila Falkus, James Foster,

Martin Gilbert, Mark Girouard, Faith Hart, Max Hastings, Ann Holmpatrick, Elspeth Huxley, John and Jean Johnson (who made it possible for me to explore the missionary settlements on Lake Malawi), Anthony Kirk-Greene, Heather Laughton, Alan Lodge, Frank and Elizabeth Longford, Sir Charles Markham, Dr Peter Marsh, Angus McIntyre, Nigel McNair Scott, Michael Pakenham, Antonia and Harold Pinter, Julian Platt, Andrew Roberts, Pam Scott (who allowed me to see her mother Lady Eileen Elliot's scrapbooks), Xan Smiley, Greta Soggot, James Spooner, Dr Anthony Stockwell, Dr J. L. Sturgis, and Gillian and Ivor Williams. Two 'China hands' who allowed me to interview them – Jock Swire and Commander Charles Drage – have, alas, since died but I would like to record their kindness.

I am also deeply indebted to the staff of the following libraries: the Bodleian, the Indian Institute and Rhodes House in Oxford, the Foreign and Commonwealth Office Library, the Imperial War Museum, the India Office Library, the London Library, the National Army Museum, the School of Oriental and African Studies, the Royal Commonwealth Society (especially for their many dusty journeys of exploration into the basement on my behalf), and the United Society for the Propagation of the Gospel and their archivist, the Rev. Ian Pearson.

On photographs, my chief debt is to John Falconer of the Royal Commonwealth Society, who first introduced me to many of the more fascinating characters of the Edwardian Empire. My thanks also to Mrs Pippa Boyle, Miss Louise Bush of UAC, Lord Cranworth, Dr Peter Davies, Maggie Keswick, Robin Bruce Lockhart, my father Ronald McNair Scott, Alan Morkill, Adrian Swire, Miss Maureen Stanniforth of Unilever, and the Theosophical Society for providing me with pictures from private or company archives. And last but not least to Richard Coward who made superb photographic prints from many faded originals.

For permission to quote from manuscripts, I would like to thank the following: Robin Bruce Lockhart (for allowing me to reproduce extracts from works by Robert Bruce Lockhart), Mrs Dan Davin (for Joyce Cary's letters), Mrs Ian Parsons (for Leonard Woolf's papers), the London School of Economics (for E. D. Morel's papers), and the National Trust and Macmillan London Ltd (for permission to reproduce extracts from Rudyard Kipling's poetry).

Finally, my thanks to those who have had to bear the burden of empire at close quarters for months if not years: my children, my sister Linda Kelly, Dorothy Girouard who designed the book and helped at all stages with professional advice, Alex Bennion who skilfully edited it and my husband Thomas who has provided indispensable aid with everything from sources to the mysterious workings of his word processor.

Opposite King Edward VII inherits his Empire, January 1901.

We, as fast as we acquire new territory and develop it, develop it as trustees of civilization in the interests of the world.
Joseph Chamberlain, 1902

1

PILLARS

Noël Coward wrote his famous song celebrating 'Mad dogs and Englishmen' in 1932 when the sun was already low in the imperial sky. The four great 'white' colonies of settlement – Canada, Australia, New Zealand and South Africa – were already virtually independent as dominions. India, the cornerstone of England's tropical empire, was bent on following their lead. Within a generation, the terms 'colony' and 'empire' would become anachronisms, like the imperial breed who had once ruled nearly a quarter of the globe.

This book is about an earlier generation of English men and women – the Edwardians – who went out to the tropics at the imperial high noon, unclouded by doubts about their mission to 'rule the earth', or at least to sort out its dark untidy places into some kind of decent order. In 1900, as the old century ended, there seemed to be more than ever before to sort out. England had just come to an end of a frenetic round of imperial expansion – largely triggered by fear of losing out in the race for territory between the other European powers, the so-called Scramble for Africa. In twenty years she had added nearly five million square miles to her already vast tropical Empire, leaving even the most enthusiastic of imperial expansionists slightly out of breath. It was time for a pause, to digest what seemed to have been so impulsively acquired. 'It is easier,' as Joseph Chamberlain told a huge banquet attended by his colonial officials in June 1900, 'to conquer an Empire than it is to keep it.'[1] Once acquired, the new territories must be governed, defended, paid for – prayed for. The real scramble – between Englishmen themselves – was, many people sensed, just about to begin.

In the feverish excitement of the '90s, imperial conquests had been fuelled by an intoxicating mixture of motives.

'What enterprise,' asked the young Winston Churchill, who had ridden with Kitchener to Khartoum and already fought in several of Queen Victoria's 'little wars',

> is more noble and more profitable than the reclamation from barbarism of fertile regions and large populations? To give peace to warring tribes, to administer justice where all was violence, to strike the chains from the slave, to draw the richness from the soil, to plant the earliest seeds of commerce and learning, to increase in whole peoples their capacities for pleasure and diminish their chances of pain – what more beautiful ideal or more valuable reward can inspire human effort? The act is virtuous, the exercise invigorating and the result often extremely profitable.

'Besides,' he added, on a less elevated note, 'all the vigorous nations of the earth have sought and are seeking to conquer.... The instinct may not be wise but it is apparently healthy.'

Yet even as he wrote this, Churchill had also reflected on the 'inevitable gap between conquest and dominion ... filled with the figures of the greedy trader, the inopportune missionary, the ambitious soldier and the lying speculator....'[2] By the end of 1900 the gap had visibly widened, for England had just annexed by force its last and most valuable slice of Africa – the two Boer republics in the south – and was rather ingloriously and expensively engaged in rounding up the last of the Boers on the South African veldt. The war had revealed not only that the British Empire was alarmingly over-extended – 'the vast inland frontiers which our Navy cannot reach'[3] – but also that its motives might not be as impeccable as it usually claimed. Many high-minded Englishmen found it difficult not to suspect that the English would never have set out to bring the 'civilising mission' to the Boers (who were after all Christian and white) if it had not been for the glittering gold reefs of the Rand.

All this happened at a time when the English were about to lose their greatest imperial asset: their Queen. By 1900 Queen Victoria had ruled England for sixty-

Queen Victoria at Osborne in 1900 with an Indian attendant. Even in her eighties, she carefully read her boxes of Indian and Colonial dispatches.

three years, longer than the vast majority of her subjects had lived. For the last twenty-five of them, since Disraeli had given her the idea by creating her Empress of India, she had played with gusto the role of Great White Queen. And though she had certainly enjoyed the power and the glory of empire, she had also personified its gentler side, showing genuine concern and kindness for her duskier subjects, often preferring them to those who were white. Her courtiers were exasperated by her reliance in old age on her 'Munshi', an Indian clerk whom she had elevated to be a kind of personal guru. Even in her eighties, half blind, she had spent many hours perusing colonial and Indian dispatches and admonishing her imperial representatives to strive to be 'liked and beloved by high and low', not merely respected. Nothing, she warned Lord Curzon as he was about to set off to take up his post as Viceroy in 1898, would do more to undermine British rule in India than 'the snobbish and vulgar, overbearing and offensive behaviour of our Civil and Political Agents'.[4]

Though her son Edward VII, who succeeded her in January 1901, shared this dislike ('Because a man has a black face and a different religion from our own, there is no reason why he should be treated like a brute'),[5] he was never to command either the same affection or respect. The more sophisticated of his far-flung subjects sensed rightly that his interests and pleasures were European. The royal yacht never bore Edward himself east of Suez once he became king, though he dutifully dispatched his son, the future George V, thither in his stead. At home, one of the first tasks of the new Edwardian Court was to clear out some of the lumber of Empire accumulated during his mother's reign. A huge pile of elephant tusks –

annual tribute from an African chief – was packed off to the London auction rooms; the Munshi was turned out of his sinecure at Frogmore Cottage and sent back to India; likewise the Indian attendants in St John's Tower at Windsor who had once cooked the royal curries. Osborne, with its splendid Durbar room designed by Kipling's father, was given to the country by the King to make a convalescent home for officers wounded in what he and almost everyone else devoutly hoped would be the last of England's imperial wars.

But if the Empire's figurehead had lost some of its potency and the Empire's virtue was already rather tarnished, the main structure at the onset of the Edwardian age was still felt to be remarkably sound. *Blackwoods*, the most imperially minded of the literary reviews, reminded its readers in its 'Reflections on the King's Accession', that 'it was the qualities of race' that had brought England her great possessions, 'its energy, its spirit of adventure, its capacity to colonise, to rule subject-races, to vindicate its liberties ...'[6] (That there was any contradiction between 'ruling subject races' and vindicating liberties, *Blackwoods* did not pause to consider. By 1901 most imperial pundits had concluded, more or less regretfully, that some English liberties were not exportable. You could no more carry English democracy to India, for instance, than ice in your luggage.)

Still the chief pillar of state was the venerable Lord Salisbury, now very old and bowed and apt to fall asleep in Cabinet meetings, but considered generally the wisest statesman of his day. For most of the last twenty years, until the recent election, he had combined the role of Prime Minister and Foreign Secretary; and it was his quiet diplomatic pressure in the chancelleries of Europe – backed when necessary by British boats and troops – which had secured for England the lion's share in the Scramble, three times more than any other European power. Not that Salisbury himself had often shown much enthusiasm for these new additions. Salisbury's political views had been formed in the '70s, when, as he often reminded the public, England had been free to trade wherever she chose without undertaking 'the inconvenience of protectorates'. It was only, he claimed, the harsh new facts of international rivalry in the tropics that had made him change course. In private he seldom ceased to doubt if the change had not been for the worse. If only England's Empire could have been left to the old informal methods, relying on the initiative of English adventurers and arrangements with native chiefs; so much 'cheaper, simpler and less wounding to [the natives'] self-esteem',[7] as he wrote to the Chancellor of the Exchequer, Sir Michael Hicks-Beach. Like the old Queen, Salisbury deplored the

Right Joseph Chamberlain, the Colonial Secretary, caricatured in the Liberal *Westminster Gazette*, by Carruthers Gould.

Opposite Lord Salisbury, the Prime Minister, in old age.

'damned nigger' attitudes east of Suez which so often provoked unnecessary and expensive wars. By 1900, his distaste for jingo emotions had made him sound almost Gladstonian. To estimate the real worth of Empire, he told the Tory faithful sternly, you must divide victories by taxation.

Salisbury's cutting style had always acted as a much needed antidote to the rosier imperial language of the Tory press – 'frantic boast and foolish word'[8] – as even Kipling had been moved to call it three years before. But for the last six years, the Tories had also been able to rely on a more inspiring imperial message from Joseph

Dr Ronald Ross pursues the mosquito. His discovery in 1898 of the malarial parasite in the stomach of the dapple-winged mosquito and his work on the prevention of malaria (despite Chamberlain) were to transform life in the tropics in the new century.

Chamberlain, the Colonial Secretary. Chamberlain was the odd man out in Salisbury's aristocratic government. 'Joe, though we all love him dearly, does not form a chemical combination with us,'[9] as Arthur Balfour, Salisbury's nephew and political heir once felinely observed. Chamberlain was an ex-Radical, a screw-manufacturer from Birmingham who had made his name in municipal politics and had gone on to become the rising star of the Liberal party before he split with Gladstone over Irish Home Rule. Still anathema to the Liberals, he had surprised even the Tories by his genuine enthusiasm for Empire in all its aspects when he finally joined them in 1895. He saw the huge ragbag of tropical colonies in his charge as a vast slum, waiting, like Birmingham, to be 'improved'; or, using language more appropriate to his new Tory colleagues, as 'undeveloped estates' which, he claimed, with proper investment and management could bring their owners unbounded wealth.

Chamberlain's call for a new *constructive* imperial policy instead of the traditional one of stumbling along at the least possible cost had impressed even Salisbury and the dour Sir Michael Hicks-Beach; until they were sharply called to order by the Treasury's permanent officials, who embodied what Chamberlain bitterly called the 'departmental mildew'. Chamberlain was forced to look elsewhere to finance his 'improvement programme' – largely unsuccessfully. Business magnates like the King's friend, Sir Thomas Lipton, proved no keener than the Treasury to invest in Chamberlain's tropical slums. Finally, a Colonial Loans Stocks Bill was devised, which Chamberlain hoped might solve his financial impasse.

By 1901 however 'Treasury mildew' had dampened even Chamberlain's enthusiasm for 'undeveloped estates'. The Boer War was still proving a hideous financial drain and the stock market had been unresponsive to the new Colonial stocks. Chamberlain had to persuade the Bank of England to buy them in even to finance the schemes on which he had already embarked. Dr Ronald Ross, the man who had discovered that mosquitoes were the carriers for the malarial parasite three years before, arrived in Chamberlain's office at Whitehall in March with an ambitious new scheme for malarial control, only to be blasted out of the room on the grounds of its prohibitive cost. By now Chamberlain sometimes wondered whether some of his tropical slums even *merited* improvement. 'I have an idea,' he minuted on one West Indian file, 'that we press sanitation and civilisation too strongly on these backward communities. If they like bad water or insufficient water, it might be as well to let them find it out for themselves.'[10] Inside the Birmingham non-conformist lingered the old Victorian horror of subsidising the undeserving poor.

The politician in Chamberlain had also switched his hopes to a more rewarding kind of empire – the great white colonies which had so loyally volunteered troops for Britain's aid in the South African War. Chamberlain had always dreamed of some kind of Greater Britain – a great imperial federation of Anglo-Saxons. (Where and how India, for instance – which the viceroy, Lord Curzon, bitterly pointed out was by far the Empire's largest component – fitted into this scheme Chamberlain never fully explained.) In two years he would leave the Colonial Office and pursue this chimera via what he called the 'Tradesman's Entrance' (Tariff Reform), shattering the Tory party in the process. But for the moment he was the most exciting man in English politics and a focus of hope for Empire-builders out in the field who often felt that no one in government really cared.

In London, at his house in Prince's Gate, or at Highbury, his splendid red-brick villa outside Birmingham with its fine collection of tropical orchids, he was a generous and bracing host to colonial officers on leave. 'He made one feel how entirely he trusted to one's discretion,' wrote Frederick Lugard, back from governing the huge new protectorate of Northern Nigeria. 'After dinner,' recalled another old hand long after,

> when the port had gone round, Joe would take his glass and sit down by the youngest member of the Colonial Service in the room. 'Got an axe to grind?' he would say, and the man, if he was wise, would bring out some darling scheme for the welfare of the tribe he governed, which an unsympathetic secretariat had shelved. Joe would listen carefully and if he thought there was something in it, he would do something about it. Ah yes, Joe was a great man. . . .[11]

After he left the Colonial Office in 1903, 'men on the spot' felt things were never quite the same.

The most permanent pillar of the imperial structure was of course neither Chamberlain nor Salisbury (who would resign in 1902 as soon as the peace with the Boers was signed and hand over the leadership to his nephew Arthur Balfour) but the Civil Service in Whitehall.

'*We* are always here,' as one Foreign Office mandarin grimly reminded Lord Salisbury's protégé, Sir Harry Johnston, when he returned very full of himself in 1899 from a weekend at Hatfield with an appointment as the new High Commissioner for Uganda.[12] Harry Johnston, a squeaky-voiced ex-art student of five foot nothing with a gift for linguistics, mimicry and comic verse, might have annexed large portions of tropical Africa for the British Empire almost singlehanded in the days of the Scramble, but he was not their idea of a suitable proconsul in a more sober imperial age; and with Lord Salisbury's departure from office he was never to be given another post. Many another career that, it seemed, would carry all before it out under the noonday sun was to wither in the colder, greyer climate of Whitehall.

In 1901 the administration of England's vast Empire was divided between three departments of state, all housed in one massive block built round a courtyard on the south side of Downing Street. Designed in the 1860s by Sir George Gilbert Scott in what Lord Palmerston had insisted was a suitably imperial style (Italian Renaissance), its interior revealed subtle variations of grandeur and style.

The grandest section was the Foreign Office with a superb double staircase overlooked by a large fresco of Britannia embracing the sea traders – a high Victorian concept of empire which Lord Salisbury would probably have preferred to retain. By 1901, however, the Foreign Office was responsible for nearly all the new African protectorates Salisbury had acquired during the late '80s and '90s: British Central Africa (soon to be Nyasaland), British East Africa (later Kenya), Uganda and Somaliland; and found them all, Harry Johnston reported, 'a horrid bore, dontcha know'. They would be handed over to the Colonial Office in instalments from 1903. Then there was the Sudan, nominally, in Lord Cromer's tactful phrase, an Anglo-Egyptian condominium since Kitchener had reconquered it three years before. And of course there was Egypt itself, popularly known as the 'veiled protectorate', which was not legally part of the Empire at all. The British had gone there in 1882 to sort out the bankrupt Khedive, and remained there ever since; and all negotiations were now conducted with the so-called British Agent, Lord Cromer.

In the south-west corner of the building, sharing the ravishing view over St James's Park, was the India Office, which had almost as grand a staircase, ornamented with life-size statues of heroes of the Raj; and its own internal Durbar courtyard decorated with majolica ware. The staff reflected in microcosm the vast apparatus of the Viceroy's government in Calcutta, which in April migrated lock, stock and barrel to Simla and the cool of the Himalayas. But it was a controlling microcosm. Once a week, a Council made up of retired Indian Civil Servants and Indian Army officers met to veto or approve the Viceroy's proposals, a system which the Viceroy, Lord Curzon, exasperatedly compared to Chamberlain or Salisbury having to submit proposals to a committee in Ottawa. Still, even Curzon deferred to the Permanent Under Secretary, Sir Arthur Godley, like himself a brilliant product of Dr Jowett's Balliol, who had been at the India Office since 1885. Sir Arthur, Curzon liked to remark, had made him understand the true meaning of a 'Godley, righteous and sober life'.[13] Sir Arthur's clever young men conducted relations not only with so-called British India, but also with the 600 or so nominally independent princely states and Burma, annexed by the British in 1881 after a series of 'little wars'. Secure in its revenues and in its army, the India Office took a lofty view of almost everyone else, and even Lord Salisbury's under secretaries ventured as seldom as possible through the only interconnecting door on the first floor.

Compared with these two prestigious departments, the Colonial Office had always been a poor relation: a labyrinth of odd-shaped rooms with smoky chimneys and lifts that did not work. Chamberlain had done his best to smarten it up with new paint and electric light, and had even offered to divide his own handsome office on the first floor to improve his staff's cramped quarters. By 1900 its staff was

Right The grand staircase at the India Office, Whitehall, decorated with tropical foliage for Edward VII's coronation, 1902.

Below Joseph Chamberlain's room in the Colonial Office. By 1900, his staff were so cramped for space that he had offered to divide it.

still astonishingly small: just over a hundred clerks who divided up the huge ragbag of the colonial Empire between five departments – for the West Indies, West Africa, South Africa and Asia, and one for Canada and Australia (who were already granted quasi-diplomatic status).

Socially the Colonial Office was not quite so pukka as the Foreign Office, and intellectually it was no match for the India Office or Chamberlain's enemies, the Treasury clerks. But it got through an enormous variety of business without fuss and suffered less than the haughty India Office from Queen Victoria's abomination – 'red tape'. Its ethos was paternalistic and evangelical. Cecil Rhodes had denounced it for being run by missionaries, philanthropists and Jews, and it was suspicious of what New Imperialists like Rhodes stood for: aggressive commercial interests, land-hungry white colonists and would-be concessionaires. But on the whole they had responded loyally to Chamberlain's call for an 'improvement' programme and, like the colonial officers abroad (to whom they rather condescended), they were genuinely grateful at last to have in Chamberlain a man to fight their causes in the Cabinet and at Westminster. The previous Colonial Secretary, Lord Knutsford, had been known irreverently by the office as Peter Woggy (in charge of all those 'Wogs') and had been known to dread the annual Colonial Debate. Chamberlain, reported *The Times*'s famous colonial correspondent, Miss Flora Shaw, they called the Master. But even the Master found the officials tactfully impervious to many of his views. One senior clerk simply took home and left there the files of which he did not approve.

The most unreliable, and to some Edwardian empire-builders the most dangerous, element in the imperial structure was the British people themselves. As the Edwardian age began, it was true, imperialists could feel reasonably safe. The 'Khaki election', pushed through by Chamberlain in the autumn of 1900, when patriotic fervour was at its height, had just returned another large Tory majority. And by now most of the Liberals were committed imperialists too, though they liked to distinguish between their kind of imperialism, based on 'Christian principles and common sense' and the false kind, exemplified by Chamberlain: aggression and territorial greed. But no twentieth-century politician could feel entirely secure for long, given the unpredictable nature of the new mass electorate.

Only nine months before the election, at the worst moment of the Boer War, Chamberlain had feared that the government might fall. And Lord Salisbury had made it a principle never to embark on any major imperial venture except at the start of a Ministry. He had seen too many swings of the political pendulum in Gladstone's time. Politicians and civil servants often envied their proconsuls' 'benevolent despotism' abroad with its relative immunity from Press or Opposition sniping. When Lord Curzon complained to Sir Arthur Godley about the Council of India's interference with his plans, Godley pointed out sharply that Curzon was lucky not to have to deal with the House of Commons direct. And even when the Opposition were quiescent, powerful pressure groups like the great missionary societies or the Society for the Protection of the Aborigines could

Two imperial issues which lost the Tories votes: the use of Chinese labour in the Rand goldmines, and Chamberlain's call for 'protective' tariffs on food.

suddenly stir things up. It was the 'system', 'that mob at Westminster' which Sir Alfred Milner, the High Commissioner in South Africa, believed would make the Empire impossible to run. Even a great man like Joe could do nothing with it.

Ironically, Milner's gloom at the incompatibility of the party political system at home and Empire-building abroad was echoed by the rump of radicals and Gladstonian liberals still left. How could one teach good government when the British government itself operated like 'something between a see-saw and a game of chance'?[14] Radicals also feared, more seriously, that all that 'benevolent despotism' abroad might corrupt English democracy at its source, and that men like Milner or Curzon would sacrifice the English working man or soldier to 'empire-building', given half a chance. The tremendous row that was to blow up over 'Chinese slavery' (the use of indentured Chinese coolies in the Rand gold mines after the Boer War, sanctioned by Milner) was not so much a protest against the way the coolies were treated, but at the use of cheap foreign labour rather than offering the English miner a decent wage. When Kipling exhorted the English to know that:

> ... ye are the People – your throne is above the King's
> Whoso speaks in your presence must say acceptable things[15]

he was more accurate than he knew. The people were never wholly convinced that there was much in empire for them even at this period. And when the Liberals gleefully pointed out that Chamberlain's Tariff Reforms meant dearer food, the voters deserted the imperial party in droves. Some things were not acceptable, however eloquently put. And the working man felt that the white man's burden at home was hard enough as it was.

The most frequent charge levelled against the Edwardian Empire was a Victorian one, first coined by James Mill: that it was all a vast system of outdoor relief for the younger sons of the aristocracy. Though the New Imperialists openly admitted that they were looking for markets for 'those superfluous articles – our boys' as well as for British goods, few of the Englishmen who appear in this book would fit strictly into this category. Aristocrats, even younger sons, seldom bothered with Chamberlain's 'tropical estates' except as soldiers or to shoot game. Lord Salisbury's daughter, Lady Maud Cecil, saw the Empire as a very middle-class affair. 'Of course the best class of English don't come out to the colonies and those that do are apt to be bounders.'[16] And Raymond Asquith, the cleverest of young Edwardians,

Two stages in the advance of empire. *Opposite* the military occupation of Perak after the murder of a British 'adviser', 1876. Frank Swettenham, a future proconsul, in white (*far left*). *Above Pax Britannica* firmly in the saddle twenty years on. Swettenham (*standing left of palm tree*) and Hugh Clifford (*fifth right on elephant*), Perak, 1897.

saw the whole thing as rather vulgar. 'The day of the clever cad is at hand,' he wrote to John Buchan just after the Boer War. 'I have always felt it would come to this if we once let ourselves in for an empire. . . . A gentleman may make a large fortune but only a cad can look after it.'[17] Even India in his view did not deserve a Curzon as Viceroy (a view with which many Indians and Anglo-Indians would come to agree!) 'It is scandalous the way we lavish the flower of our race on this dull provincial empire of ours.'

Regardless of this urban disdain, most Edwardian Englishmen in the tropical Empire saw themselves as 'gentlemen', and did their best to exclude those who were not. Out under the tropical sun, as Leonard Woolf – the most critical observer of imperial *mores* – noted, the English usually became rather grander in manner than they were at home. In the East, with its caste-conscious hierarchies of servants, the rituals of upper-class Edwardian life became accentuated, and were to remain frozen long after they had begun to melt away in England itself; Anglo-Indians really did change for dinner in the jungle. It was in Africa that Lady Maud Cecil's verdict often proved nearer the truth. East Africa especially soon became a notorious magnet for 'bounders', who arrived in droves, noted Bishop Tucker of Uganda regretfully, as soon as the Uganda Railway was opened. West Africa could be used to solve the problem of the family black sheep permanently. 'Dear Uncle Henry may talk lugubriously of the burden of Empire,' says the hero of Saki's novel, *The Unbearable Bassington*, bitterly just before he is dispatched to the Gold Coast, 'but he evidently recognises its uses as a refuse container.' He is dead from fever within a few weeks.

But the Empire also supplied a field for more admirable kinds of aristocratic export: a sense of service or chivalry. What was the White Man's Burden as defined by Kipling in 1897 but a new version of *noblesse oblige* which was finding itself increasingly without a home in industrial England? Many of the famous Edwardian proconsuls described their early adventures in terms which read like pages from Malory or Walter Scott. Frederick Lugard, a child of Anglo-Indian missionaries, left the Indian Army in despair after an unrequited love affair and went off to Africa to fight the Arab slave-traders – 'I can think of no juster cause in which a soldier may draw his sword.'[18] Frank Swettenham, son of a highly eccentric Scottish attorney, and Hugh Clifford, who *did* come from a very old and aristocratic Catholic west-country family, charged about the Malay jungles like King Arthur's knights – mounted on rafts or elephants rather than horses – rescuing maidens, freeing slaves, toppling tyrants.

The result was nearly always the same: a further extension of the British Empire and the installation of a different kind of tyrant – the British Resident or High Commissioner. Which leads one to another definition of the word 'bounder' once given by Lord Curzon to a puzzled foreign enquirer. 'A bounder, Madam, is one who succeeds in life by leaps and bounds.'[19] Many Edwardians in the tropics were bounders in this sense, like the Victorian empire-builders before them. The expansionist urge on the frontiers was often as strong as ever, and would burst out again dramatically after the First World War.

Opposite Lord Curzon in his vice-regal robes, 1899.

They that dig foundations deep,
Fit for realms to rise upon,
Little honour do they reap
Of their generation
Any more than mountains gain
Stature till we reach the plain.
Rudyard Kipling, 'The Pro-Consuls', 1906

2

RULERS

In 1892 when Cecil Rhodes was explaining to Gladstone the special capacity of the English for ruling the darker-skinned races, the old man interrupted him with a sigh, 'That's all very well, but I am at my wit's end to find a man competent to be Viceroy of India.'[1]

Ten years later the age of proconsuls seemed in its prime. In India Lord Curzon – lord of 300 million souls – was planning the last details of his great Coronation Durbar – the 'Curzonation' the wags called it. In Egypt, the second brightest star in the imperial sky, the veil of the 'veiled protectorate' had grown so thin the English almost ignored it. Lord Cromer had run the country for twenty years. When he drove

Left Lord Curzon and his wife arrive for the Coronation Durbar at Delhi, 1903. The irreverent called it the 'Curzonation'.

Right The Durbar held at Singapore for the Malay sultans, 1903. Sir Frank Swettenham (*seated, centre*) talks to Sultan Idris of Perak.

out from the British Agency in Cairo in his grey frock coat and hat, syces ran to clear the way for 'El-Lord'. He was as permanent as the sphinx, as comforting as a rock to lean on. 'It is fortunate for us,' wrote Lord Salisbury just after his retirement to Curzon, that, as menacing forces drew more closely round England, 'the satraps of the Empire were never more conspicuous for intelligence and force than they are now – yourself, Cromer, Milner, Kitchener.'[2]

Kitchener, like the Queen of Spades, had been passed on from one proconsul after another. Cromer had sighed with relief when he went to South Africa, after his victory at Khartoum, to deal with the Boers early in 1900; Lord Milner, the High Commissioner in South Africa, was soon begging the Cabinet to tell him that he was urgently needed in India. And Curzon, sublimely confident, was now looking forward to his arrival to help him lick the Indian Army into shape. He would make the soldiers squirm, but that would do no harm, Curzon told Salisbury's old secretary, Sir Schomberg McDonnell. Reforms could get nowhere with the 'present decayed old rip, who kisses girls behind settees'. In November 1902 Kitchener at last arrived and was, reported Curzon, 'mad keen about everything'. But there were soon ominous signs. 'I have never met so concentrated a man,' wrote Curzon to McDonnell. 'He has an argument. You answer him. He repeats it. You ... demolish him. He repeats it without alteration a third time. But he is as agreeable as he is obstinate and everyone enjoys his dinners and his gold plate immensely.'[3]

In the new parts of the tropical empire, lesser satraps had emerged. In Malaya, Sir Frank Swettenham had created his own proconsulship as first Resident-General of the Malay States. Swettenham had been one of the first and most successful of the British Residents sent in the 1870s to 'advise' the Malay sultans – 'advice' which, as the Colonial Office blandly admitted, 'could not be disregarded'. Now, with the proliferation of roads, railways, and rubber plantations, it seemed only sensible to 'federate' the states under a new central control. In theory, overall command of British Malaya remained with the High Commissioner at Singapore. In practice, Swettenham at Kuala Lumpur outflanked his overlord Sir Charles Mitchell as suavely as he had once outflanked the Malay sultans whom he had been sent to 'advise' as a young man. Sir Charles died in 1899, exhausted from trying to control him.

Swettenham's elder brother, Sir James, the next High Commissioner, succeeded no better in controlling Frank. A dragon of public virtue, he disapproved of Frank's plan for leasing land alongside the Selangor railway to English developers at highly favourable rates. In 1901 James was removed to the West Indies and Frank got the job of High Commissioner himself.

In 1903 he had held his second Durbar for the Malay sultans in Singapore. Despite the splendid reception, there were some mutterings from his guests. It was not, complained Sultan Idris of Perak (the English *beau idéal* of a progressive native ruler) what the British had originally promised when they persuaded the Malay sultans to join the Federation. Now all power had devolved on Singapore. If only,

Right Sir Frank Swettenham, about to resign 'after thirty-three years in an enervating climate' talks to another Singapore veteran, Admiral Keppel.

Opposite Punch's view of Sir Harry Johnston's triumphal progress through Uganda, 1902.

countered Swettenham, the Malays would seize the splendid opportunities opening up for their country instead of leaving them to the Chinese. In October 1903, to everyone's surprise, he resigned. He was, he told the Colonial Office, anxious to leave Malaya before he became a burden on the country 'after thirty-three years in an enervating climate'.[4]

Enervated or not, retirement certainly gave Swettenham a new lease of life. He became director of a dozen new rubber companies with what *The Times* found rather 'indecent haste' and was to live another forty-two years on full pension.

Even darkest Africa now offered a respectable proconsular career. In the old days, men hardly survived long enough to make their mark. No one, Gladstone had told John Bright gloomily, who was anybody would go as governor to Africa. And one governor who asked if the Colonial Office would pay his return voyage was told the question had never arisen. The health hazards were still formidable. The diminutive Sir Harry Johnston, who had served as consul in West Africa, Central Africa and was now busily engaged on a grand scientific tour of the Ruwenzori mountains in the new Protectorate of Uganda, had barely survived his fourth dose of blackwater fever a few months before. When he got back to England in 1901, his luggage bulging with new species of flora and fauna, it was clear he could not make another tour in Africa; and the Foreign Office declined to open healthier doors.

Forcibly retired aged forty-three, Sir Harry turned his hand to politics. His

"One of the mightiest factors yet introduced into Central Africa."
(Sir H-rry J-hnst-n, K.C.B.)

attempts to win a Liberal seat were ruined by the same irrepressible humour which had disturbed the Foreign Office mandarins. The part-Irish electorate of Rochester did not like his evolutionary jokes about the 'interesting ape-like colonists of post-glacial Ireland'. A Nonconformist Sunday school audience were alarmed when he projected by mistake a slide of a huge naked Ugandan tribesman. 'Praise the Lord,' said the minister hurriedly. 'Praise *all* his wondrous works.'[5]

For Johnston's exact contemporary and friend, Frederick Lugard, the Edwardian age had brought an upswing of fortune. Lugard had spent the last fifteen years fighting in person or in print most of the great battles of the Scramble for Africa – first against the Arab slave-traders in the south; then quelling (or exacerbating as his enemies claimed) the civil wars in Uganda; finally fighting off the French for Chamberlain along the shores of the Niger. Now, only a year after he had raised the British flag in a newly cleared patch of bush beside the confluence of the Niger and Benue rivers, he had already started building his new 'empire' in earnest.

Disregarding the Colonial Office's instructions to 'avoid collisions', he moved towards the end of 1902 against the great northern emirates of Kano and Sokoto, which, he claimed, had defied the new British rule, and by April 1903 he could claim the whole of Northern Nigeria to be effectively 'settled'. The Colonial Office was left quivering with apprehension, disapproval and relief. They were in an 'insane funk re Kano' wrote Lugard to his brother; 'if we'd messed it I should have been broke'.[6] But he now at least had a powerful ally back in England to put public opinion right. For in 1902, much to London's amazement, the small cadaverous 43-year-old High Commissioner had married the famous Flora Shaw, ex-colonial editor of *The Times*. 'If it be *the* Flora Shaw, I congratulate you,' wrote Curzon from India. 'If it be another, may she be equally brilliant and no less charming.' (His own beautiful Mary, an American heiress, was charming, but in a far less formidable vein.)

Frederick Lugard

At first Flora had loyally intended to share her husband's work in Nigeria. But a few months at Lugard's headquarters at Lokoja were too much for her – both the tedium and the climate made her ill. 'The days as they pass at present are absolutely without incident,' she wrote. Fred worked from six in the morning till just before dinner – when they went for a 'tearing walk' together. She scarcely saw him otherwise. She did her best to use her time, by sending long detailed descriptions of Fred's work to Chamberlain and inviting him to visit them, 'You will find not lions but orchids in the woods.'[7] But to relatives she confessed herself 'somewhat dull and depressed'.

After three months she returned to London to work in the 'sphere of influence' she knew best: the London political scene. When Chamberlain resigned, much to both the Lugards' regret, she turned her persuasive powers on his successor, Alfred Lyttleton. She and Fred had thought out a way to make his great work in Northern Nigeria go forward even more effectively – 'continuous administration'. Lugard would spend six months 'on the spot' in Nigeria, six months directing it from the Colonial Office in London, working out long-term administrative policy in a climate where he could recuperate and think – and incidentally be at Flora's side. It was, after all, not so very different, as a clever young journalist Leo Amery pointed out to her at a London dinner, from what the Viceroy did in India – seven months governing from Simla, five months down in Calcutta. London would be Fred's Simla.

Curzon, had he heard the plan, would certainly not have seen the parallel. In 1903 he had accepted the chance of a second term as Viceroy, but returned to find it as frustrating as the first had been exhilarating. Simla, he wrote to his friends, was a desert – like dining every day with the butler in the housekeeper's room. There was no society, no relaxation, no conversation, no amusements. Kitchener was increasingly difficult; the Indian press blamed the Viceroy for every disaster that occurred and he was not able to defend himself. He was as helpless as a monarch and had all and more of the responsibility of a prime minister. No one in the Cabinet in England seemed to care about the problems of India, where the real work of empire was to be done; everything was done for the colonies. In vain McDonnell urged him to return – to run for a bigger race, the Tory leadership. If he started his run now, nothing could stop him becoming the next Tory prime minister – and the whole policy of the Empire would be his to dictate.

McDonnell sensed what Curzon still failed to grasp – that Kitchener was not only difficult, but a dangerous rival who was conducting covert sapper operations in England via his friends at Hatfield. A stream of boyish confidences and doubts about Curzon were being sent by Kitchener to his devoted admirer, Lady Salisbury, who passed them on to her cousin, Arthur Balfour. Balfour, stung by the vice-regal tone of Curzon's letters, was sympathetic. So too, was the new Secretary of State for India, St John Brodrick, once Curzon's closest friend.

Lord Kitchener

The power struggle came out into the open early in 1905. Kitchener threatened to resign if he did not get full control of the army. The Cabinet backed him, with a feeble attempt to patch over the quarrel – Balfour's shaky government could lose a viceroy but not the national hero. Curzon resigned and came home in November after an angry exchange of letters to a sparse reception at St Pancras station. Both Balfour and St John Brodrick had discovered other pressing engagements. In fact Balfour's government fell the next day – and, by coincidence, the roof of St Pancras. 'How like St John to bring it off one day too late,' wrote Mary Curzon bitterly.[8]

Curzon's own bitterness increased beyond measure when he found he was not even to receive the usual proconsul's peerage. McDonnell, his most long-suffering friend, was deluged with reproachful letters. Seven years of his life given to India, his health, his career, and now his heart sacrificed (for poor Mary Curzon died, her health broken by India, shortly after their return) and meanwhile Milner and Cromer went from honour to honour. It is a measure of Curzon's paranoia that he wrote this just after Milner had suffered a humiliating vote of censure by the new Liberal House of Commons for licensing Chinese labour in the Rand mines.

The Liberal landslide in the 1906 general election shook half of Balfour's Cabinet out of their seats – including Balfour himself and Alfred Lyttleton. Would it shake even that paragon of proconsuls, Lord Cromer? It seemed not – Campbell-Bannerman, the new Liberal Prime Minister, even offered him the Foreign Office, but Cromer refused. As Lord Salisbury had remarked years before, 'If the world were falling to pieces before his eyes and Egypt was left intact, Lord Cromer would not ask for more.'[9] After his second marriage in 1901 to Lady Katherine Thynne, he seemed rejuvenated, sounder than ever. The stream of English visitors to Cairo – Liberal and Tory – continued to sing his praises. The hospitality at the Agency (Cromer's residence) was excellent; over dinner Cromer would sometimes regale guests with stories of the dissolute insolvent days of the Khedive Ismael's banquets when a huge pie containing a naked dancing girl would be the last course. It was quite sickening, noted Wilfrid Scawen Blunt in his diary, the way even the Liberal press lapped up everything Cromer said when he explained the benefits of British rule.

Lord Cromer, the most admired of Edwardian proconsuls.

Blunt, an odd mixture of poet, Sussex squire and political agitator, was notorious for his anti-imperialist views. He had lived on and off in Egypt almost as long as Cromer, breeding Arab horses, and prided himself on being the Radical thorn in Cromer's flesh. Cromer's staff at the Agency dismissed him as a tiresome poseur, who liked to refer to his home in the Cairo suburbs as 'my house in the desert', lived in studied discomfort, wearing Bedouin dress, and put on an elaborate ritual when English visitors called. He would have a bowl of camel's milk brought in to him and explain he drank nothing else. His championship of Arab nationalism was seen as another pose – copied from Byron, whose granddaughter he had married. No one in Egypt, wrote Rennell Rodd, took any notice of the 'mad Englishman', though of course he was excellent company. Cromer, even more tolerant, rescued the middle-aged Radical when his boat was shipwrecked, gave away his daughter in marriage for him and lectured him about irrigation and the fellahin.

By 1900 even Blunt seemed to be won over to Cromer. 'He certainly is a great man in his official way,' he noted after a visit to the Agency, adding characteristically, 'after 74 days at Sheykh Obeid [the famous 'house in the desert'] I felt strange

Wilfrid Scawen Blunt, seen by Cromer's staff as a tiresome poseur.

and naked in European clothes.'[10] In July 1901, though, Blunt's blood was brought back to the boil – eight English officers chased a fox into his walled garden and were set on by his indignant servants with staves. The servants were arrested for assault and sentenced to three to six months' imprisonment. Blunt sent a torrent of protest to the press attacking Cromer personally. ('In big game shooting,' he told Schomberg McDonnell, once again acting as go-between, 'it is safest to go straight for the rhinoceros.')[11] The rhinoceros failed to charge, however. Unperturbed, Cromer sent word that Blunt should keep his garden wall in better repair. There was no mending social fences after that.

Five years later, Blunt got his chance. In June 1906 there was a grand replay of the Sheykh Obeid affair. This time it was British officers out shooting who provoked an attack at a village called Denshawai. The game birds proved to be the villagers' tame pigeons. In the fracas, one officer died of concussion and sunstroke. Cromer called a military tribunal and went on leave to England. The savage sentences meted out on the villagers (four hanged, seventeen sentenced to prison or flogging) brought an uproar in Egypt and England – with Blunt orchestrating the Liberal

Lord Minto (Curzon's successor) at a gymkhana in Simla, 1907. Curzon's reported comment on hearing of his appointment was, 'Fancy sending to succeed *me* a gentleman who jumps hedges.'

press. So much for English justice and talk of 'civilising' Egypt. Cromer, overwhelmed, resigned the following year – claiming failing health. Blunt was jubilant – *his* sport was up at last. He had Cromer's brush in his pocket and 'the mask of the ancient red fox dangling from his saddle'.

Unlike Milner and Curzon, Cromer enjoyed a triumphant return to London. All the Liberal ministers turned out to meet him at the station. In the Commons debate on the extent of the nation's gratitude, each party claimed him for their side, with odd results. He was, Campbell-Bannerman claimed, the best type of Liberal administrator – profoundly respectful of the Egyptian race, convinced Egypt could only be regenerated by the Egyptians. Cromer, Balfour countered, had raised Egypt from the lowest pitch of social and economic degradation, carrying out a great civilising work among a people who could not rise to it themselves.

The debate neatly highlighted the Liberals' dilemma in governing their empire. Could proconsuls be Liberals at all? As *Blackwoods* magazine had once smugly put it, good administrators become Tories, Tories become good administrators. Certainly the Liberal landslide had filled colonial ranks with foreboding. It had returned, wrote Sir Hugh Clifford from Trinidad to his old friend, Frank Swettenham, an 'appalling collection of extremists, cranks, faddists, false sentimentalists and haters of their country. Thank God for the House of Lords.' (Clifford, like Swettenham, had spent years as a British Resident in the Malay States, where *Pax Britannica* had been at its most successful, and was an ardent exponent of imperial trusteeship in the pages of the literary reviews.) 'It was all disgusting,' agreed

Swettenham; he had heard that any follower of Joe Chamberlain or Lyttleton was now to be thrown out.[12]

It soon became clear however that neither jobs nor the Empire were in danger. Even the old Gladstonian John Morley, installed in the India Office, was now talking of the Empire as a wonderful thing. ('No one means to give anything away.') He did his best to find common ground with the new Viceroy, Lord Minto, a conscientious Tory peer famed in youth as a dashing steeplechase rider. As for the Colonial Office, it now had an ex-Viceroy, Lord Elgin, for Secretary of State.

A notoriously inarticulate Scottish peer of fifty (Queen Victoria had found him 'painfully shy'), Elgin was an unknown quantity to Flora Lugard, who had been carefully cultivating the sympathetic Liberal imperialists she knew. She rushed to enquire and was told he was four-foot broad, four-foot high and stuffed four-foot full of commonsense. But he eluded her when she tried to track him down to explain the famous scheme for 'continuous administration' in Northern Nigeria which she believed Lyttleton had agreed to. Lord Elgin did not go out to political dinners – he was happiest, like Gladstone, chopping down trees. 'A splendid afternoon's exercise,' he wrote to his wife just after his appointment, 'cutting down trees by the secret path from lunch to tea. Then digging on the road for an hour. Topping up with a big bath (hot).'[13]

His new job, however, had one physical obstacle which could not be so easily dealt with: the young Winston Churchill as Under Secretary. It was Churchill's first ministerial post; but at thirty-one he had already made himself a reputation throughout the Empire as brilliant, brash and ambitious. The Colonial Office, like Elgin, viewed the appointment with distaste. 'He is most tiresome to deal with and, I fear, will give trouble – as his father did,' wrote Sir Francis Hopwood, the Permanent Head.[14] Flora Lugard, who managed to obtain an interview with him, was, however, impressed by his quick grasp of affairs – and his praise for her husband's work. She noted Churchill talked all the time as if he and not Elgin were Secretary of State.

The honeymoon of mutual admiration was short-lived. Both Elgin and Churchill put thumbs down on the Lugards' scheme for 'continuous administration' – there was no reason, wrote Churchill in one of his sonorous phrases, why the labours of the Colonial Office should be increased by being made into a 'Pantheon for proconsuls' on leave. Responsibility for administration must remain with the 'man on the spot'. The Colonial Office were soon to eat their words; for in late January 1906, Lugard 'on the spot' in Nigeria once again forced them into backing a military expedition against a rebellious tribe. It ended with the massacre of about 2,000 peasants armed with hoes and axes, precisely the sort of unpleasant 'punitive expedition' which the Liberal Cabinet wished to avoid. Parliament and public opinion would never stand it. The public might have been more shocked if they could have read Churchill's minute to Elgin suggesting withdrawal from large parts of Nigeria altogether to curb Lugard's 'administrative ambition.... I see no reason why savage tribes should not be allowed to eat each other without restraint....' Elgin calmly dismissed the minute.[15]

Right Punch's view of Winston Churchill's departure for East Africa, 1907.

Opposite The eleven-year-old King Daudi Chwa of Uganda, and his letter to the Governor, Hesketh Bell.

The problem of controlling Lugard in Nigeria was luckily solved by his own resignation. After a summer back in England on leave, he could not bear to return to Nigeria without his Flora, whose health was too frail for the climate. The Colonial Office had a happy solution. Lugard was offered the governorship of Hong Kong, where Flora could go with him – and where Lugard would be firmly under the thumb of a well-oiled colonial bureaucracy.

Thanks largely to the Lugards, Northern Nigeria had now become a prestigious posting. Lugard's Annual Reports were published in full in Flora's old paper, *The Times*, every year. And in 1906 a monumental book on Nigeria entitled *A Tropical Dependency*, by Flora herself, appeared. Northern Nigeria could now take its place, she suggested, as a model of successful English autocratic rule in the tropics beside India and Egypt. She described in detail her husband's pioneering method of indirect rule which retained the native authority of the emirs in partnership with their British rulers. Even Wilfrid Blunt was reported to have been impressed. ('One likes to hear of people of the wrong way of thinking who can read it with sympathy,' wrote Flora to her husband.)[16]

Old Malay hands like Swettenham and Clifford must have snorted – they believed they had pioneered the method twenty years before. But there was a freedom left in Africa lost in the older tropical colonies like Malaya where telegraphs and good roads had banished the romantic independence of the early Residents. Hugh Clifford, who had loved his early days in the Muslim courts of the Malay sultans, applied to succeed Lugard but was refused; though the Colonial Office noted, with approval, that he was one of the few men in the service with 'a real and responsive insight into the genius of alien races'.[17] Instead he was sent to Ceylon, where in 1908 as acting governor he impressed Leonard Woolf with his 'formidable' personality and his prowess as a 'ladies' man'. Northern Nigeria

UGANDA.

MENGO,
UGANDA.
26-3-07

Dear Mr Hesketh Bell,

I am sending you a fortogruf th of me. I heard that you shot two alyfunts. I am very glad to hear that you came back. I am shooting my rifle. On march 25, I went to Gayaza to see the little girls and the Kati-kiro gave them their prises. I hope you are well; when will you come to Nakasero?

I am your friend,
Daudi Cwa.

Letter from the little King of Uganda, aged 11.

received a military expert instead – Sir Percy Girouard, the brilliant young engineer who had laid the line to Khartoum for Kitchener. He was reputed to be the only officer ever to have dared contradict Kitchener to his face.

It was Churchill who was to switch public attention dramatically to benevolent despotism in action on the other side of Africa. In the summer recess of 1907 he set off on a sporting holiday to East Africa with Elgin's enthusiastic blessing ('Parting is such sweet sorrow', read *Punch*'s cartoon). The kindly Campbell-Bannerman begged Churchill to relax and 'not to overdo it'. They both should have known their Churchill better by now. The sporting holiday, to Elgin's dismay, became in no time a kind of dazzling official progress recounted at length by Churchill in a spate of dispatches to the Colonial Office and a series of articles in the *Strand Magazine*. From Mombasa he caught the famous Uganda Railway and, seated by the Governor, Sir James Hayes Sadler, on the cowcatcher in front, recorded the spectacular scenery of the Highlands for his readers: rugged gorges, struggling young plantations of rubber, fibre and cotton ('the beginnings of those inexhaustible supplies which will one day meet the yet unmeasured demand of Europe . . .') and above all 'plains crowded with wild animals'.[18] He got out at Simba to shoot a few. From Nairobi he went on to Elmentaita to go pig-sticking with Lord Delamere, the leader of the English settlers. Then on to the railhead at Kisimu and by steamer across Lake Victoria to Entebbe and the Uganda Protectorate. And here in the heart of Africa, he told his readers, he found a fairy tale; a tropical feudal kingdom inhabited – not by naked savages like the East African Highlands but by an 'amiable, clothed, polite and intelligent race'.

Nominal king of the fairy tale was the young Daudi Chwa – eleven-year-old son of King Mwanga of Buganda, whom the British had deposed after a rising in 1899, and packed off to exile in the Seychelles. The child king, wrote Churchill grandiosely, was now being reared 'under the shelter of the British Flag to a temperate and instructed maturity'.[19] (Alas for his hopes – Daudi Chwa, like many another English-educated experiment, turned out to have acquired some very English vices and died partly of drink aged only forty-three.) The real ruler, fleshly embodiment of the British flag, who now greeted Churchill was Henry Hesketh Bell – 'Juju' Bell to his friends.

Of all the Edwardian proconsuls, none except Sir Hugh Clifford was to have so long and varied a gubernatorial career as Hesketh Bell; and few were more delightfully eccentric. His diaries, kept throughout his official life ('for want, I suppose,' he once wrote 'of a pal of a wife'), read like a real-life Mr Pooter, transported from Holloway to the tropics; and his scrapbooks reveal that he was also an indefatigable amateur inventor (patent collar studs, tropical chest-protectors, water-closet guards, telescopic caravan extensions). Born in the West Indies, he joined the Colonial Service as a clerk and in 1890 was sent to the Gold Coast for four years. He described it luridly in his short stories, published by the indispensable *Blackwoods*, as the land of the '3 Ds' – drunks, destitutes and desperadoes. (One of them begins: '"What brought you to this cursed hole, Jervis?" asked the governor, knocking out his pipe. "Was it a girl, the Jews or the gee-gees?"' In fact the hero – who dies of fever – is trying to support his poor young mother.)[20]

His diary entries, however, remain remarkably cheerful between the bouts of fever and deaths of his colleagues. There are rampageous evenings playing 'bumps' ('we all took it in turn sitting on each others' laps'),[21] and amateur concerts at which he sings 'Mandalay' with éclat. After a return to the West Indies, he met Neville Chamberlain who was running his father's sisal plantation there, and in 1899 with great excitement made a weekend visit to Highbury, where he did his best to catch the great man's eye. He succeeded, for in 1899 Chamberlain made him Administrator of Dominica, a tiny tropical paradise in the Windward Islands. He threw himself with true Chamberlain fervour into developing his 'tropical estate' and soon Dominica was one of the most prosperous of the West Indian islands, thanks to its trade in grapefruit – for which, wrote Bell, American demand was inexhaustible since American women had heard grapefruit prevented babies. In 1905, much to his surprise, he was offered the post of High Commissioner of Uganda by Lord Elgin. It was Joe's last leg-up for his protégé – he had picked him out for the job before he resigned in 1903.

After 'poor little Dominica' it was indeed a leg-up. Uganda was the size of Spain with a population of three and a half million. And like Churchill later, Bell was bowled over by the charm and sophistication of his kingdom. Entebbe – laid out by Sir Harry Johnston with an artist's eye – was the prettiest of garden suburbs. (The red-roofed houses reminded Bell of Hampshire.) The white population were of the best sort (all 'sahibs'), the ladies pretty and smart, the musical evenings superb – Bell's 'Mandalay' was soon in great demand. The natives were wonderfully intelligent and polite, though he noted they saw English rule as a 'necessary evil'

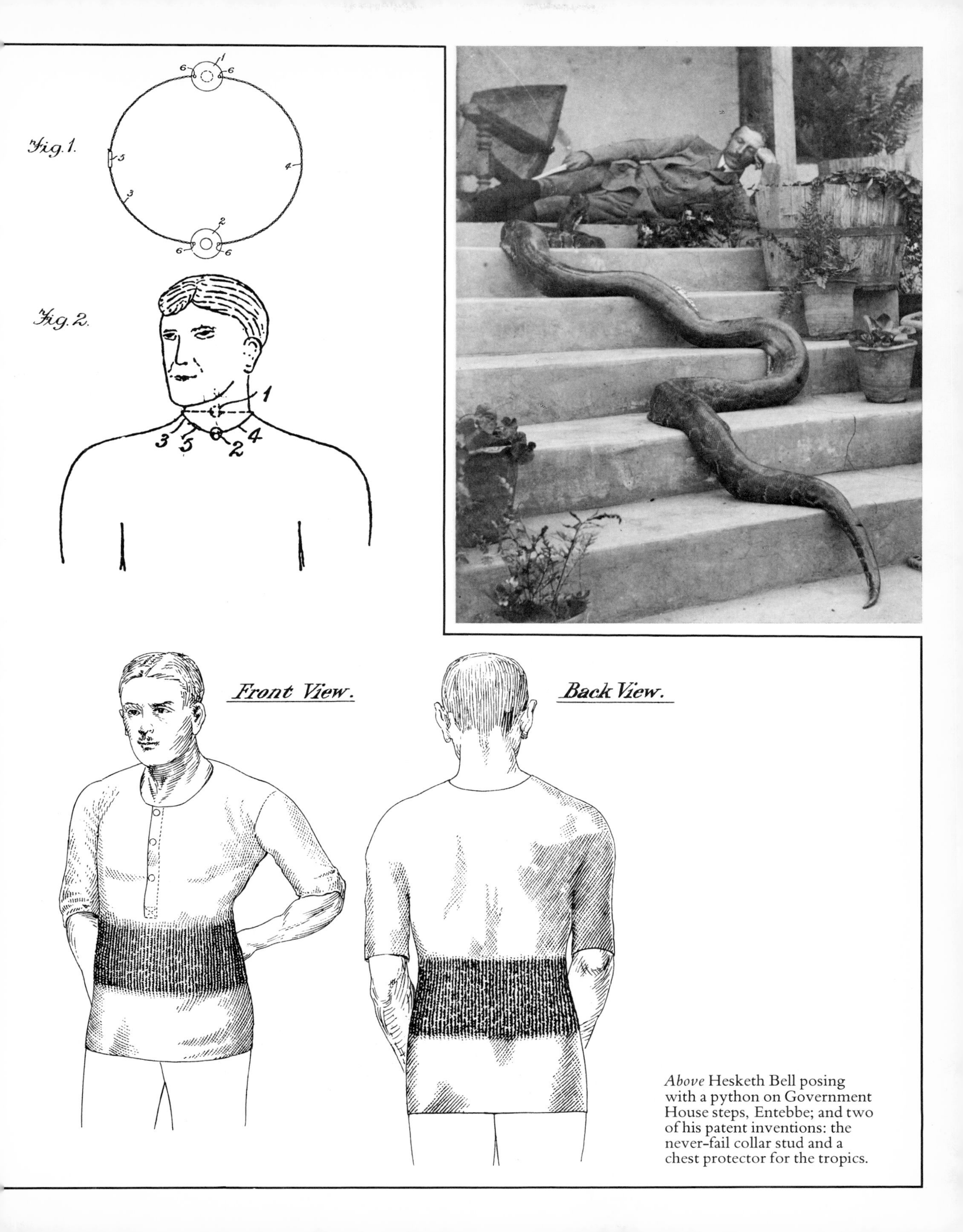

Above Hesketh Bell posing with a python on Government House steps, Entebbe; and two of his patent inventions: the never-fail collar stud and a chest protector for the tropics.

Hesketh Bell outside his new house, with Entebbe's English community, 'all sahibs'.

without much enthusiasm. The servants were excellent: though the 'small boy' or 'toto' rapidly proved his superior intelligence, Bell wrote home, by stealing all his silk underclothes.

Only Government House left much to be desired. Harry Johnston (who had preferred to share meals with his baby elephant) had had a snake pit put near the door to deter official visitors. The doorways were so narrow that at one of Bell's first parties, two officials' wives got jammed together racing to establish precedence. He eventually sold the house to a Mr Goldman, who planned to turn it into a hotel and told him flatteringly how much he reminded him of the great Lord Milner. Bell built himself a handsome new villa on the hill overlooking the new golf course and Lake Victoria. The new drawing-room doors were framed with a magnificent pair of tusks shot by the governor. The first big dinner here was a splendid affair. The *pièce de résistance* was Poulet de Brobdignag – roast ostrich. To the strains of a lively march, the huge bird was trundled round the table in a bathtub balanced on top of a pram – only to tip over and send a cascade of ostrich gravy over one unfortunate officer's scarlet mess jacket.

Churchill, who landed at Entebbe in November 1907 in a white uniform glittering with medals, proved a master at eluding the duller guests at the gala dinner in his honour. But Bell got on well with him, and on the way to Kampala by rickshaw enjoyed a great 'pow-wow' in which Churchill told him about his early adventures.

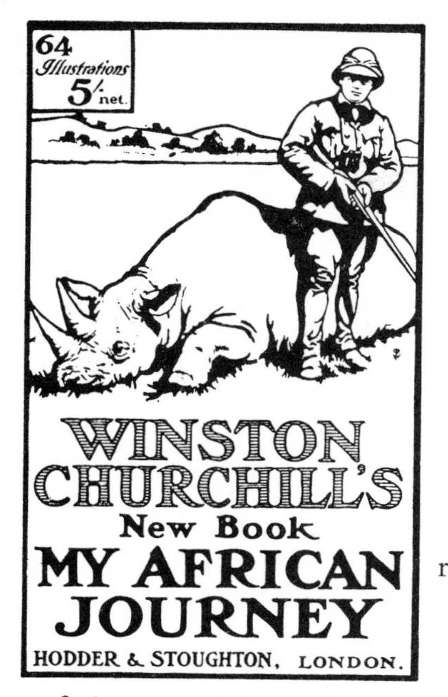

Bell, who prided himself at being at forty-three the youngest governor in the service, was rather taken aback when Churchill looked at him as if he were Methuselah and announced that he would be prime minister by that age. He got his own back when he explained in a speech to the assembled chiefs at Kampala Churchill's exact position in the Empire. A cousin of the Kabaka's translated the speech into homely but graphic terms. The King of England, he said, had many servants to run his vast property – Churchill was the 'toto' of the servant in charge of Uganda – a 'toto' being, Bell gleefully recorded, the small black urchin who helps the cook and is rewarded by pickings from his master's table.[22]

After a week on tour with Bell and his officials, Churchill left to shoot rhino *en route* for the Sudan. He sent the Colonial Office a cheerful telegram: 'So fari so goodi.' By then he was an even more thorough convert to 'constructive' imperialism and to Bell's improvement schemes. A year later he published *My African Journey* – based on his *Strand Magazine* articles – with a glowing testimonial to Bell's work. 'Concentrate upon Uganda,' Churchill urged his readers. There was almost no limit to its possibilities. Rubber, sisal, cotton, cinnamon, cocoa, sugar, coffee – everything could grow in its fertile soil though cotton alone could make Uganda's fortune. 'All the best qualities of cotton are to be found in the highest perfection,' and there were 'a hundred thousand intelligent landowners occupying 20,000 square miles of suitable soil' to grow it. Nowhere else would investment repay so well – not in East Africa with its 'expensive white settlers' or barren Somaliland with its dangerous inhabitants. Uganda offered a chance of a 'practical experiment in state socialism'.[23]

Though Bell may not have liked the last phrase, he must have been delighted at the effect of his carefully arranged tours of cotton gins and plant stations and 'pow-wows' over dinner. The next year's colonial estimates, including the money for his new railway, went through without a hitch. In June 1908 he heard he had been created a K.C.M.G. 'I dare say by this time next month it will seem to me I have never been anything else but "Sir Henry",' he wrote to his aunt in England. At this rate he should be promoted to a really big colony and a G.C.M.G. before he retired.[24] The initials stood, went a hoary civil service joke, for 'Kindly Call Me God' and 'God Calls Me God'.

The next year he tried out his most esoteric improvement scheme yet. How wonderful it would be if African elephants could be caught and trained for transport purposes instead of being slaughtered for their ivory. To test the possibilities, he imported a 'ready-made' female elephant from India. The experiment soon ran into trouble. 'Fukti', as she was called, had come accompanied by her mahout who now demanded extortionate wages for staying with her. Then he announced she could not be used for transport – she was a shikari elephant, trained for shooting tigers. Bell firmly ordered her to be harnessed to a wagon. There was a sound like rifle fire as, at a word from her mahout, Fukti suddenly swelled out her belly and burst all the newly made harness. At a second attempt, this time harnessed with chains, she zigzagged off at top speed down the avenue and tore down the gateposts of Bell's new Government House. After a further increase in the mahout's wages she was restored to a docile state, and was soon placidly browsing outside Bell's office window while the triumphant mahout anointed her toenails with ghee. In January Bell set off on a 'grand tour' of the province, but by the time they returned, it was clear that Fukti was a 'white elephant'. Her running costs in food were enormous, and Bell was relieved to sell her to a circus agent from Ceylon. But at least she had given him some enjoyably Curzonian moments. The natives, unmoved hitherto by the wonders of English telephones, telegrams, bicycles or even Bell's motor car, had also been impressed at last. 'Whatever reputation on other counts I may have gained here,' wrote Bell, 'I shall always be remembered as the Governor who rode an elephant.'[25]

Poor Bell. After riding an elephant he was soon, in one observer's phrase, to find himself 'tied to a tiger'.[26] For in August 1909 one of the Colonial Office's periodic reshuffles took place. Girouard was sent to East Africa to deal with the settlers who had proved too much for Sir James Hayes Sadler. Hesketh Bell was offered Northern Nigeria (£3,000 a year and a letter 'couched in very gratifying terms'.) The tiger waiting for him was Charles Temple, Girouard's chief of staff and close friend. Temple, who later wrote one of the most fascinating attempts to explain Indirect Rule, taking the theory far beyond Lugard, was the son of a distinguished Indian Civil Servant and had joined Lugard's staff in 1901 after years in Brazil. Fanatically protective of the Muslim emirates he ruled, he had refused to allow any missionary activity which might undermine the Native Authority. Bell, who had been impressed by the missionaries in Uganda, gave permission in an unguarded moment to the Church Missionary Society to open a station outside Kano; and suddenly found himself the target of Temple's powerful guns. Charles Strachey in the Colonial Office was one of Temple's closest friends. From the dizzy heights of High Commissioner of Northern Nigeria, Bell plummeted to a third-class governorship of the Leeward Isles. It was almost back to square one – the same faces, the same surroundings, the same scandals.

'Everything,' he wrote sadly the day after he arrived, 'seems so small and unimportant after the great problems that occupied me in Uganda and N. Nigeria. I don't feel I can ever adjust to such a come-down.'[27] But two days later he gave an 'At Home' for two hundred people at Government House and recovered his spirits. He was to serve another two spells as governor after that, in the beautiful tropical island of Mauritius. After his retirement he devoted himself to writing an official survey of the colonial empires in the East, and became a theosophist.

It was Lugard who, much to his surprise and joy, was now offered his old kingdom – and more. For the Colonial Office, who had long despaired of making Northern Nigeria solvent, moved to amalgamate it with the profitable south. The

Lugard makes a triumphal entry at Duala, 1916, German Cameroons.

Liberal doubts about Lugard had almost evaporated. It was only Sir Frederick who could undertake this great work, announced Sir Lewis Harcourt, the Colonial Secretary, to the Commons. But the triumphant return of 1912 was soon to turn sour. The fall of 'poor Bell', as Lugard called him, had been a premonition. To Lugard's surprise when he arrived at Government House at Zungeru, Charles Temple, now Acting Governor of Northern Nigeria, showed an extraordinary inability to understand that Lugard was now once again his overlord. He even failed to evacuate Government House – Lugard had to stay in the rear quarters, as he wrote to Flora, in 'a small bed with a tiny camp mosquito net on four stakes tied to it and the *necessary arrangements* were abominable'.[28]

The obstinacy and disloyalty in obeying Lugard's orders soon proved to have spread all over the Service. Even if he could have got rid of Temple, he could not have got rid of Temple's friends in the Colonial Office. Soon the old pattern of acrimonious exchanges was in full swing; while Flora, at home in London, put Lugard's case with charm and eloquence over tea to a mesmerised Lewis Harcourt. Pinned down there in 1914 by the war, Lugard struggled on, waging an almost continuous war of paper. He resigned his governorship in 1919 and left, commenting bitterly that the Colonial Office would be 'glad to see the last of him'.

Rival rulers, 1916. Lord Lugard (*centre*) with Sir Hugh Clifford (*left*), Governor of the Gold Coast, who was to succeed him in Nigeria. Clifford found Lugard 'a crashing bore'.

His successor was Hugh Clifford, who promptly denounced Lugard's system – or lack of it. The ruling ideas of Lugard's government, he reported to Lord Milner (who was now, with Curzon, miraculously reinstated in the affairs of Empire in the post-war government), were designed to perpetuate in Nigeria the 'medieval conditions which at present prevail!'[29]

A formidable proconsular battle followed between Flora and Clifford, conducted through the unlikely medium of the *Encyclopaedia Britannica*. In Flora's entry for Nigeria in 1911, Nigeria is the creation of one man, Sir Frederick Lugard (poor Hesketh Bell and Percy Girouard are almost ignored). In Clifford's entry for 1922, it became the achievement of many hands, and there was a strong hint that Lugard had made a mess of things.[30]

But Flora won, for by the time she wrote her last entry, Clifford was *hors de guerre*. He had suffered from strange manic attacks ever since his early days in Pahang. In his later governorships – on the Gold Coast, Nigeria and Ceylon – there were strange episodes when the Governor appeared at garden parties in native dress or, on one horrifying occasion, in no dress at all. In 1927 he was finally made governor of his beloved Malaya, which in his stories and novels he had never left. But it was too late; his periodic bouts of madness could no longer be concealed. He was retired on the official grounds of his wife's ill health. And, it is recounted, for years afterwards he would sometimes be found sitting in Malay dress, a huge bald half-naked figure on the steps of the Colonial Office, catching the nervous bowler-hatted officials by their coat tails as they went in and telling them stories of the Malay Courts long ago.

Opposite Eastern cadets in the Malay States, early 1900s.

So some of us chivvy the slaver,
And some of us cherish the black,
And some of us hunt on the Oil Coast,
And some on the Wallaby track:
And some of us drift to Sarawak,
And some of us drift up The Fly,
And some share our tucker with tigers,
And some with the gentle Masai.
Rudyard Kipling, 'The Lost Legion', 1895

3

BUILDERS

In July 1900, *Blackwoods* magazine carried a story by Hugh Clifford on a familiar theme for its readers. In the heart of the steaming jungles of Kalamantan, Gervase Fornier, a callow young Englishman, is crouched rigid with terror in a tiny stockade. Outside, the head-hunting Murut tribesmen beat their drums. He is the only white man for miles, with only a tiny police force of Dyaks to back him up. Suddenly the telephone rings (an unexpected jerk into the twentieth century): it is Tom Burnaby, the 'old hand', calling to reassure the new recruit. Night after night, the terrified youngster draws comfort from the disembodied English voice. Then one night he notices the voice is strangely faint – perhaps the batteries are running low. The scene shifts to Burnaby, lying

Right Shooting the rapids: Swettenham's pioneer days in the Malay jungles.

Opposite The calmer waters of colonial bureaucracy, Kota Bharu, early 1900s.

racked with fever in a long chair with a bamboo spear festering in his thigh. He has been up-country to settle a spot of trouble. He knows if he leaves to have the wound treated, Fornier will go to pieces. He stays, and with a last fevered phone call tells the youngster to keep his pecker up. An hour later, Fornier is rung to be told Tuan Burnaby is dead, and the accursed Muruts are threatening the village. 'Hath the Tuan any orders?'

> Then Gervase Fornier's new-found manhood came to his aid. His words rang down the wire firm and imperative and the Malay, recognising the tone of the master, listened humbly and never so much dreamed of disobeying. 'Bury the body within the walls of the blockhouse . . . and keep watch . . . over the grave until I come. In six days I shall be with you.'

Struggling through the jungle, Fornier reaches Burnaby's fort and fights off the Muruts. His new-found confidence 'is baptised in blood'. He never looks back – soon even the wild Muruts swear by the 'very toenails of Tuan Fornier'.

The Heart of Kalamantan – and Tom Burnaby – 'have turned a waster into a good officer'.

Like many of Clifford's stories, 'The Heart of Kalamantan' is partly an exercise in nostalgia – for the brave days when he and his friend Frank Swettenham were sent as untried youngsters into the Malay jungles, 'cast like a dog into the sea', as Swettenham put it, to sink or swim.[1] Swettenham's earliest days in Selangor had been spent in a mosquito-ridden stockade whose floor dissolved in mud whenever the river rose. Clifford had lived for a year as the only white man at the court of Pahang, where the 'solitude and monotony' ate into him like 'corrosive acid' until, he wrote, he learned to read 'The Great Book of Human Nature' all around him.[2] Like Fornier and Burnaby, they could see themselves as part of Kipling's 'Lost Legion',

Split in a thousand detachments
. . . breaking the ground for the rest.

By 1900, Clifford admitted, the ground in most of Malaya was all too well broken. In Perak and Selangor, the heel of the white man was so ground in that they were hardly 'Native States' at all. An official could spend weeks without coming into contact with an Asiatic except those who waited at his table or ironed his shirts. There was no effort to absorb the 'native point of view'. Colonial bureaucracy had taken over.[3]

It was a recurring cry throughout the Eastern tropics. Young empire-builders were not what they were. Even the prestigious Indian Civil Service was in decline, reported the Viceroy, Lord Curzon soon after his arrival in 1899. 'The average young Englishman who has been for ten years in this country no longer has the affection of the people or love of India his forerunner possessed in days gone by.' Partly it was the attitude of the natives (some of whom showed an irritating desire to govern themselves), partly the lack of great men to set an example, but most of all it was improved communications which were always 'drawing a man's heart back to England'. The electric telegraph might bind the Empire together, but it also undermined its spirit. Two years later Curzon was even more damning: the Indian Civil Service was turning out 'with increasing frequency some of the meanest and most malignant types of disappointed humanity whom it has been my fortune to meet'.[4]

Curzon's strictures can be taken with a pinch of salt; by 1904 he was himself a case of 'disappointed humanity'. There were plenty of devoted Englishmen out in the districts still living and working very much as their predecessors had thirty years before. But in the cities, the 'Heaven-born', faced with nothing but 'police, crime and sanitation', could turn sour.[5] 'We are not pleasant in India,' says Ronnie, the young city magistrate in E. M. Forster's *A Passage to India*, 'and we don't intend to be pleasant. We have something more important to do.'

Since 1858 the Indian Civil Service had been created by a highly competitive exam held every August; the result had been an intellectual élite that was still regarded as one of the wonders of the Empire, and ran India on well-oiled wheels.

By 1900 the principle of the Competition Wallah had been extended to England's other possessions in Asia. Burma, annexed by Lord Dufferin in 1886, was administered by the I.C.S., though the country, they found, was as different from India as England itself. There was no caste and no purdah and the Burmese girls walked and talked freely as they liked. The I.C.S. succumbed to them in droves, much to the apprehension of the government in Rangoon. Singapore, Hong Kong, Ceylon and the newly federated Malay States were sent yearly batches of Eastern Cadets who had passed lower down in the Civil Service exam. The ones who passed best usually chose Ceylon, the oldest and most delectable Crown Colony. The Malay States rated lowest – a state of affairs which produced a long and testy debate as to whether the Competition Wallah was required here at all. What was wanted, wrote the High Commissioner to the Colonial Office, were good energetic all-rounders 'of moderate attainments and if possible well brought up ... High scholarship (was) unnecessary.'[6]

Meanwhile some scholarly types slipped through the exam net. In 1902 the Malay States were appointed their eminent future historian, Richard Winstedt, who, fresh from Oxford and philosophy, was delighted on arriving at his first mosquito-ridden outpost to find a fellow district officer reading Hegel. Only later did he become aware that the man never turned the page. Ceylon in 1904 received an altogether pricklier Cambridge intellectual – Leonard Woolf. There has seldom been a more reluctant recruit to empire-building. Having chosen Ceylon as a less awful alternative to the Post Office or the Inland Revenue, which was all his Civil Service exam marks had rated, he left his Cambridge friends – the future Bloomsberries – and caught the boat from Tilbury in 'a horrible state of mind and complete despair', accompanied by ninety volumes of Voltaire and his fox terrier Charles.[7]

For the man who disliked exams, there was still one service in Asia that did not require them: Rajah Charles Brooke's in Sarawak. This remarkable old autocrat who had inherited his kingdom from his uncle, Rajah James, back in 1868, still ran it on feudal lines though it was now a British protectorate. He vetted all his recruits in person and had strong views on what was needed in Sarawak. Life in jungle out-stations was sedentary; there was no room for adventurous or sporting types. His own recipe for success forty years before had been 'a good book, even a novel, and profuse perspiration', but now any such easy notions about life in the jungle were out of place. 'We require good accountants ... with a knowledge of surveying and an idea of official routine' preferably 'gentlemen' and English or Scots. (Rajah Charles did not count the Irish as gentlemen after some unfortunate experiences and had grave doubts about Australians and Americans.)[8]

Unlike the High Commissioner in Malaya, he also had a weakness for scholars, men who could turn out an article on local Dyak customs, flora or fauna for the

Pioneering British administration in East Africa: Frederick Jackson makes treaties with Kikuyu chiefs, 1889.

Sarawak *Gazette*. On tour, Brooke's officers were expected to eat and sleep in the Dyak longhouses which gave them the opportunity to observe these at first hand. If you did not go to sleep at once, wrote one officer, the fleas and the noises of animals and human life made sleep impossible. Brooke disapproved of 'anglicisation' and those who tried to make the out-station an English home from home. Armchairs and other comforts had quickly to be hidden out of sight when he called on inspection tours. Liaisons with native women were positively encouraged (an excellent way, he believed, of breeding Sarawak's future Civil Service). English wives were taboo; not that his officers could have afforded one. Sarawak salaries were painfully low and the whole state was run on a shoestring. One recruit remembered being too poor even to buy whisky for his 'sundowners'. He had to make do with gin and water, 'a beastly drink'.

Vyner Brooke, the Rajah's heir, found life up-country equally austere. He was sent fresh from Cambridge to learn the ropes at a tiny out-station at Simanggang and found himself a kind of post office clerk, sticking on stamps and sorting files. Later he was promoted to doling out castor oil to the natives and vaccinating Dyak babies. His superior was a taciturn alcoholic who insisted that Vyner should shave him every morning since his own shaking hand would cut his chin.

If bureaucracy and autocracy seemed inescapable even in Sarawak by 1900, Africa offered wider and wilder shores. There were certainly no exams. Up to 1900, the Colonial Office had been hard put to it to find even moderately respectable recruits. Salaries were low (the Treasury had vetoed Chamberlain's efforts to bring them up to Asian standards) and the number of replacements needed alarmingly high.

Beware and take care of the Bight of Benin.
For one who comes out
There are forty go in . . .

ran the old rhyme. In West Africa, the most notorious 'white man's grave', the death rate for officials was eight per cent a year, and many more were invalided home after an almost fatal dose of blackwater fever, malaria or typhoid. Bankrupts, divorcees, cashiered army officers – all were grist to the mill. They did not even need to be gentlemen. 'Mr Rowland called today,' ran one Colonial Office memo. 'He seemed an energetic keen little chap, though he is not beautiful to look at (rather like a cheese-maggot) and drops his H's. He has made several trips to the (Gold) Coast and is not afraid of the climate.'[9]

East and Central Africa and Uganda, still under the Foreign Office wing in 1900, had almost as high a death rate and an even higher rate of eccentrics, since many of their officials were inherited from the old Charter Companies. Harry Johnston, an eccentric himself, listed the strange habits of some of his political officers in British Central Africa. One wore nothing but glasses and a bath towel; one he found planting his garden with canned peas and another insisted on bringing rhino dung to lunch at Government House. In the East African Protectorate (the future Kenya), Richard Meinertzhagen, a clever young officer seconded to the King's African Rifles, who arrived fresh from India in 1902, was shocked by the 'low class of men' appointed as officials.

> Few of them have had any education. . . . One can neither read nor write. . . . When such men are given unlimited power over uneducated and simple-minded natives it is not extraordinary that they should abuse their powers, suffer from megalomania and regard themselves as little tin gods.[10]

Perhaps he exaggerated – Meinertzhagen was hypercritical of most people he met and, as one future Kenyan shrewdly observed, 'When tin god meets tin god there is bound to be trouble.'[11] But there was no doubt that the rather rickety backbone of English administration in East Africa had been badly strained by the advent of the famous Uganda Railway with its hordes of Indian coolies, railway officials and demands for food. One pioneer administrator, Francis Hall, who had been living up in Kikiyu since 1895, reported indignantly that the coolies who were 'the scum of India' thought they could do what they liked with the 'jungli-wallahs', and were providing a shocking example to the natives.[12]

After the Indians came the white settlers – another plague for officials – demanding land and natives to work it. By 1906 when Churchill arrived on his East African tour, he found settlers and officials already at loggerheads. But Churchill, unlike Meinertzhagen, painted a glowing picture of the young English district officer in East Africa as defender and protector of his flock, and the scope offered for 'earnest and intelligent youth'.

> To him there come day by day the natives of the district with all their troubles, disputes and intrigues. Their growing appreciation of the impartial justice of

A plague for district officers – Indian coolies swarm up the Uganda Railway into Kikuyuland, 1899.

> the tribunal leads them increasingly to carry all sorts of cases to the District Commissioner's Court. When they are ill they come and ask for medicine. When they are wounded in their quarrels it is to the white man they go to have the injuries dressed. Disease and accident have to be combated without professional skill. Courts of justice and forms of legality must be maintained without lawyers. Taxes have to be collected by personal influence. Peace has to be kept with only a shadow of force.[13]

But despite his testimonial, East Africa always failed to rise very high in the Colonial Service popularity stakes. 'You'll find yourself bedevilled at every turn by the bloody settlers,' one new recruit was told on the boat to Mombasa. He later listed the gloomy fate of the officers he served under. One died of drink, two of blackwater fever, one was murdered, one committed suicide, one had D.T.s and one drowned himself in the Red Sea on his way home.[14]

Most parts of Africa could have returned pretty much the same statistics even without the settlers. Compared to the older Asian colonies with their clubs, hill-stations and polo-grounds, most African stations were hardship posts. Instead of a cool bungalow, a leaky hut; instead of appetising curries, scrawny native chicken and greasy soup. 'How I *hate* and *loathe* the sight of the filthy food,' wrote one recruit from an out-station in Northern Nigeria. '... The only thing that does not turn my stomach is the morning porridge.' Then there was the acute loneliness, which could produce the sudden outbursts of black rage known as *furor Africanus*.

Though Baden-Powell's handbook for empire-builders was soon exhorting girls to make 'some Englishman happy in an African hut', only the most intrepid as yet gave it a try; and the Colonial Office discouraged it. Far better for the young A.D.O. (Assistant District Officer) to get to know his tribes free from such encumbrances. The A.D.O. was, of course, expected to practise high-minded celibacy. In 1909 the Colonial Office circulated a confidential memorandum to colonial governors warning that 'cases of concubinage' with native women would be regarded as serious offences. The warning had to be hastily withdrawn when it was revealed how widespread the practice was. In Northern Rhodesia alone, almost the entire service would have had to be dismissed.

But probably the most serious drawback about Africa for many recruits was the tsetse fly, which made touring on horseback impossible in large areas. The bicycle was a practical but hardly companionable alternative. ('In the dry season the paths through the bush smoothed by the feet of natives afford an excellent surface,' wrote Churchill.) The two areas of Africa which shot to the top as prestige postings both owed it at least in part to the horse.

The first was the Sudan Political Service, set up in 1901 by Lord Cromer to take over from Kitchener's military administration. Soldiers, in Cromer's view, did not make good administrators. He gave recruitment a flying start by arranging for excellent salaries (paid for by Egypt) and three months' paid leave a year. Men left too long on the spot, he sensibly noted, lost their sense of proportion. 'A period of nine consecutive months is quite long enough for any European to remain in such a climate as the Sudan.'[15] Small wonder that the Sudan Politicals soon rivalled even the I.C.S. Recruiting, as for the rest of Africa, was by interview, and the Sudan Service soon emerged with a strong bias towards Oxford athletes, 'sound second- and third-class men'. Oars and cricket bats decorated many an officer's home, and Sudan passed into legend as the country where the 'Blues beat the Blacks'. Working in a vast terrain almost devoid of roads and telegraphs, the Sudan Politicals soon acquired too an enviable reputation for independence and lack of paperwork. The pattern had been set by the old military administrators who lingered on for years in the south. Known as the Bog Barons and ruling like thanes over the warlike tribes in their remote fever-ridden swamps, they refused to learn Arabic, the official administrative language, kept native mistresses and tended to leave in a cloud of dust at the approach of any official inspector. Compared to the Bog Barons, the new civilians were models of muscular Christianity and mostly lived up to the high moral tone set by the Sudan's admirable governor-general, Sir Reginald Wingate, and his wife during their sixteen years at Khartoum. News of any liaison reaching Lady Wingate's ears could mean the coldest of receptions at Government House.

The second most prestigious service in Africa was, predictably, Lugard's in Northern Nigeria – set up a year before Cromer's. Lugard had strong views on the 'class of men' he wanted, almost exactly the opposite of Cromer's brief. 'Boy-administrators' who thought they knew everything 'because they were BRITISH' were his bugbear (he had seen them operating with disastrous results elsewhere in Africa). He preferred 'selected army officers' like himself, 'an admirable class of

Lady Wingate at Khartoum with her pet stork. For sixteen years, she and her husband, Sir Reginald Wingate, set a strict moral tone for the Sudan Political Service.

The Old Coasters' day; designed to refute the Holy Northerners' view of them as hard-drinking slackers.

men' who he claimed were less likely to engage in punitive expeditions than civilians – not a view the suspicious Colonial Office shared.

Compared with the relaxed, hard-drinking 'Old Coasters' further south, the tone of the 'Holy Northerners', as they came to be called, was military and austere; they wore uniforms and social life centred around the mess. But perhaps only 'selected army officers' could have survived the pace at all. 'Sir Frederick has nearly killed himself and a fair proportion of his staff with overwork,' wrote Flora Lugard enthusiastically to Moberley Bell, her old editor at *The Times*, during her brief visit to Lokoja in 1902. 'Yet they like it. After all they are all working for an idea . . . the ruling of the world by its finest race – the best plan for the exercise of justice and liberty and individual effort which the world has seen.'[16]

The handful of early Residents – as they were called – strung out like tiny planets in the vast spaces of Northern Nigeria (by 1905 Lugard had seventy-five political officers in an area of 300,000 square miles), often found the 'idea' receding behind a haze of malaria and exhaustion. 'The only time off was when we had a go of fever,' recorded one,[17] though he remained devoted to the Chief. Sweltering by day, frozen by night (the temperature could drop 73 degrees) they were also showered with a tropical rainstorm of instructions. By 1906 the Chief's 'Political

A district officer on tour in Northern Nigeria, early 1900s, surveys the local produce.

Memoranda', as he called them, ran to 310 closely printed pages and – ominous sign – the chapter on office work listed thirty separate records to be kept or sent in.

The 'Memoranda', along with Lugard's Code of Law, were handed to new recruits as required reading ('I stuck nobly at it till 2 a.m.,' wrote one recruit fresh from Oxford.) But the earlier Residents took many of them with a pinch of salt and kicked against Lugard's frenetic attempts at centralisation. Rule soon became 'indirect' in more senses than he intended for, as in the Sudan, absence of roads or telegraphs – and his own absences by Flora's side in London – left his officers to evolve as best they could their strange symbiosis with the Fulani emirs, the old Muslim ruling caste, whom Lugard had enlisted in his administration, making a virtue of necessity; 'their ceremonial, coloured skins, mode of life and habits of thought', he explained in his Annual Report, being so much more appealing to the native population than 'the prosaic businesslike habits of the Anglo-Saxon'.

Many of the Anglo-Saxons found their partnership an uphill struggle and preferred dealing with the pagan tribes who did not come under 'indirect rule'. The Fulani, as Charles Temple, one of Lugard's most brilliant Residents, confessed after fifteen years of service, could run rings round even the most experienced political officer in argument, and few of the emirs showed much enthusiasm for Anglo-

Making camp: an attempt to beat the mosquitoes.

Saxon businesslike habits. Even attempts to mould the next generation seemed to get nowhere. 'I have so great a dislike for these erotic and feeble-minded youths that I feel I can do them no good,' wrote one disillusioned Resident instructed to give the emir's sons tutorials in good government.[18] Backing Fulani rule over a resentful Hausa peasantry could also seem, despite Lugard's optimism, a long way from the 'idea'. Another Resident wrote after six years in Nigeria:

> If [the Emir] is using me to oppress the people, how must they feel towards the government? An alien race, different in colour, ideas, character backing up the other alien race [Fulani] in oppression. . . . If I am merely an instrument of injustice and oppression, what is the use of my working myself to death in an unhealthy climate and intense discomfort and in exile from home and friends?[19]

Yet almost every 'Northerner' disliked even more what they saw as the consequence of trying to 'Europeanise' and 'Christianise' natives in the south and the older West African colonies. 'Northern Nigeria is paradise compared to those parts,' wrote Joyce Cary breezily to his wife in 1916. 'And the people are gentlemen. Not that slaves aren't seized up here and men eaten, but it is done in a polite manner – not obtrusively.'[20] The 'trousered black' from Lagos raised the same English hackles as the 'Westernised babu' in India. That was the trouble with the civilising mission – the young English administrator who embarked on it so often disliked the results. It was the same problem wherever he went, from the dry plains of upper India to the jungles of Ceylon and Malaya or the swampy delta of the Niger river.

'There is no such thing as a typical English colonial administration,' wrote one eminent historian of the Edwardian Empire, 'only a bewildering variety.'[21]

Yet it is impossible not to see a strong family resemblance developing between the new African and the older Asian services by the time the Liberals inherited Salisbury's and Chamberlain's huge tropical Empire. Everywhere the old Lost Legion were giving way to Churchill's 'earnest and intelligent youth', ex-public school, idealistic and steeped in Kipling. 'The time has passed,' wrote Sir Percy Girouard firmly from Nairobi, 'when we can recruit our staff from so-called pioneers and cowpunchers.'[22] By 1906 there were 20,000 colonial administrators in the field. Let us look more closely at two of them, both highly intelligent – one in Asia, one in Africa: Leonard Woolf and Joyce Cary. Both were to leave the colonial service in their early thirties, for other careers (Woolf was to become a political writer and Cary a novelist), but both testified that their colonial service 'made a man' of them; though in a more profound and happily less blood-stained sense than Clifford's hero who finds himself 'up against it' in the jungle. Woolf has already been glimpsed embarking gloomily for Ceylon in 1904; Cary was to leave ten years later, one of the last young men to join the Northern Nigerian Political Service before the outbreak of the First World War.

It is rather an odd experience to compare Woolf's letters to his friend Lytton Strachey with the cool detachment of his autobiography about Ceylon – written fifty years later on. The letters to Strachey are one long wail of despair. His fellow cadet on the voyage out is a dolt, a stone, a toad, a fool. The English in Colombo (where he spent the first few weeks) are hell, but the place and the people are absolutely beautiful – how they must despise the boorish English officials. His transfer to Jaffna in the extreme north of the island did little to cheer him up. There were fifteen Europeans who all quarrelled incessantly and spent their leisure playing tennis or bridge; the women were all hags or whores or missionaries or all three; the work he was given in the office was unutterably futile. There was no one to talk to; no time to read. He foresaw 'dry rot of everything'.[23]

In fact, as his autobiography makes clear, there were soon breaks in the cloud of misery. First, Woolf took a perverse pleasure in being accepted by his fellow colonials as a good fellow (thanks initially to his fox terrier Charles, who caught and killed a native cat and snake in a very imperial manner) while he continued to fulminate against Jaffna society in letters to Strachey. Second, after escaping from the initial drudgery of being the office 'fag', he admitted to Lytton that the work was at least not as bad as it would have been in a 'degraded London office'. He was soon applying the ethical principles of his friend and hero, the Cambridge philosopher G. E. Moore to Jaffna court work, with wonderful results; the Tamils much appreciated their subtlety. Then he was sent to a vast Pearl Fishery camp at

Leonard Woolf in Ceylon, 1906, with his fox terrier Charles.

Marichchukaddi where he found it quite natural to keep order over 40,000 Arab and Tamil divers with a loud voice and a walking stick; and on his return to Jaffna, he found for the first time a man worth talking to, the new government agent (or district commissioner) called Price. He was, he told Strachey admiringly, 'an absolutely pure cold intellect. I feel like a baby in his hands.'[24]

Price, although he gave Woolf a passion for efficient administration – and for efficient prose – which was to last him the rest of his life, was not in other ways an ideal mentor. He seems to have brought out a latent bullying streak in Woolf, who was soon writing to Strachey that people did not like his or Price's strong measures; and shortly after that they had lodged a complaint against him, or rather the Jaffna Association had, 'which consists of demi-Europeanised lawyers and schoolmasters' who were trying 'to ape the associations and agitations in India'.[25] At this stage, Woolf certainly seemed to have acquired many of the same attitudes as the Indian Civil Service. They were brought on more severely because he had just returned from a totally different kind of world – administering an arid sandy peninsula called Mannar which had a few jungle villages where he had been the only white man. He wrote:

> Out in the villages, out in the jungle it is different. You are still absolute; the villager still comes to you to settle his disputes and help him when his crop fails and your word is law. But the people are all coming into the towns and in the

towns it is becoming ... hell – everyone is educated with the worst form of education the world has ever produced. The boys are taught to hate us, not because we treat them as inferiors but because we treat them as inferiors and tell them that they are our equals.[26]

In March 1907 he denounced Price to Strachey for refusing to appoint him A.G.A. to Mannar. 'I should have liked it above everything.'

Luckily for Woolf, he was removed soon afterwards from over-educated protesting Jaffna to Kandy, the administrative capital, where his efficiency in speeding up the work of his office and in more social matters caught the attention of Sir Hugh Clifford, who promoted him within a year, the youngest assistant government agent in Ceylon, to a remote jungle district in the extreme south tip of the island – Hambantota.

A few years later in *Blackwoods*, reviewing the novel which Woolf wrote after he had left Ceylon, *The Village in the Jungle*, Clifford recalled – a shade patronisingly as an old hand – Woolf's 'rather pathetic' delight and gratitude on being appointed to his 'desolate district'. Woolf's letters – or rather the shortage of them – confirm the delight. At last removed from the irritations of his fellow sahibs, the only white man for a twenty-mile radius (with the exception of one Belgian missionary) in charge of 1,000 square miles and 100,000 people, he forgot Cambridge and Lytton and, by that strange kind of osmosis which affected so many Englishmen before and after, fell in love with the country, the people and the way of life which were 'entirely different from everything to which I had been born and bred'.

Sad to say, the love affair was not reciprocated, for, as Woolf admitted himself, his promotion increased his other passion – for efficiency – to dangerous proportions. For his two and a half years in Hambantota he worked and thought of nothing else but his district, how to increase its prosperity, diminish poverty and disease, start irrigation works, open schools. But the two most outstanding achievements he lists – increasing output from the local salt pans (a government monopoly in Ceylon as in India) and getting his census forms in before any other district – were more designed to appeal to his superiors in Colombo than the local villagers. And even when his efforts were entirely benevolent and altruistic, like the time, during the fight to stamp out a hideous epidemic of rinderpest, when he had to shoot a diseased buffalo, he found himself unable to convince them of the need to do so:

... they had less understanding of my ways, my intentions, my affection for them than the half-bred bitch walking at my heels. They were the nicest of people and I was very fond of them, but they would have thrown stones at me or shot me in the back ... had they dared.[27]

Woolf used this episode in his autobiography as 'a moral tale about imperialism – the absurdity of a people of one civilisation and mode of life trying to impose its rule upon an entirely different civilisation and mode of life'. But equally well it could illustrate one of Kipling's definitions of the White Man's Burden – 'the hate of those ye better'. And it is clear from Woolf's official diaries that he struggled on manfully with the burden. He tried to teach his villagers to plough with oxen to make up for the loss of their buffalo, he enforced attendance at his new primary school in Hambantota, and he wrestled with conservative headmen. ('They are hopeless,' he wrote, '... the entire male population of these parts consists of dismissed headmen. The next time ... I shall recommend the appointment of a woman.')[28] And he applied the law with such thoroughness that the authorities in Colombo were driven to ask why the percentage of fines and sentences was higher in his district than any other.

Perhaps it was just as well that in 1911, when Woolf came home on leave, he found himself to his surprise and relief still a 'native' of Cambridge, and fell in love with Virginia Stephen. In 1912 he asked for an extension of leave, and having refused with characteristic intransigence to give his reasons to a puzzled Colonial Office, resigned.

> I did not feel that I could explain to Mr Harcourt that I had come to dislike imperialism, that I did not want to become a Governor, that I wanted to marry Virginia Stephen and that if I didn't marry her I would like to continue to be a Ceylon Civil Servant provided they appoint me permanently Assistant Government Agent Hambantota.[29]

At least the last three reasons ring true; and Woolf's novel, written in the autumn of 1911, perhaps provides the key to the first. It is an exceptionally gloomy picture of the cycle of poverty, corruption and decay in a jungle village of Ceylon which the well-intentioned white district officer seems powerless to change. Woolf sent it to Lytton Strachey who shuddered and had to brace himself to write back. The psychology was certainly masterly, but wouldn't Leonard now attempt some whites.

> I did hope for one bright scene with some fetid white wife of a Governor ... Is it true that headmen behave so vilely; if so, surely it is a great scandal. Lord how horrible it all is. Fortunately there are other things in the world ... Whites, Whites, Whites![30]

Clifford by contrast gave it a glowing review, from far away in the governor's fort on the Gold Coast. It was the most true and understanding presentment of Oriental peasant life ever placed before Western readers by a European. And Mr Woolf, his junior, had understood the profound truth which had escaped him during all his years in the splendid luxuriant forests of the Malay Peninsula – the jungle always wins.[31]

Joyce Cary, who was also to serve under the ubiquitous Clifford, embarked from Liverpool for Nigeria early in the summer of 1914, cheerfully free of such reflections. Part Anglo-Irish, educated at Clifton – the most Empire-minded of English public schools – he had already spent two adventurous years serving in the

ambulance unit in the Montenegrin war and, despite a disastrous fourth at Oxford, had been picked as one of the six successful candidates (out of sixty-four) for service in the prestigious north. On arrival he escaped the usual 'fagging' at headquarters and was sent straight to Bauchi Province, one of the Muslim Northern Emirates. Unlike Woolf, he took immediately to his senior officer, H. S. Edwardes. Edwardes, a swashbuckling eccentric who wore Elizabethan boots and read Gibbon aloud, was already a legendary figure. His pamphlet on road-building – cunningly entitled 'The Improvement of Native Paths' (since roads were officially the business of the Public Works Department) was used by improving district officers all over Africa. (Edwardes appears as 'Old Sturdee' in Cary's most famous African novel, *Mister Johnston*.)[32] As for Bauchi province, it was, wrote Cary to his father, 'a place with a real Mohammedan Emir, harems, eunuchs, a headsman and practically fresh blood spilled on its market place'.

Cary was sent almost straight away to look after the easternmost corner on his own, 'a district bigger than Wales' where, he wrote confidently to his father, 'I shall be very busy'. His district officer was away tackling 'some rebellious villages in the South'.[33] *Pax Britannica* was still precarious in parts of Northern Nigeria.

The day after this letter, 3 August 1914, *Pax Britannica* was shaken to its foundations. The first signs reached Cary's station, Nafada, when a horseman galloped in with a bunch of telegrams, announcing that all the troops in Nigeria were converging there. Cary was bemused – was the whole province in a state of rebellion? His district officer returned hotfoot from the South to enlighten him: England and Germany were now at war. From now on Cary became very busy indeed, dealing with the less agreeable consequence of the scramble for Africa. Nigeria had a 300-mile frontier with the German Cameroons to defend. Cary had to organise the transit camp, enlist men and buy grain for the troops, which in a district already on the edge of famine was an almost impossible task. Next he struggled with a smallpox epidemic which was to haunt him for the rest of his life. He was as impressed by the extraordinary stoicism of the sufferers as he was appalled by their resignation.

Cary spent the next two years fighting in the Cameroons campaign and did not return to life as a district officer until early in 1917. By this time the focus of his life had changed dramatically. He had married the girl, Gertrude Ogilvie, whom he had joined the Colonial Service originally to impress. His daily letters to her over the next few years must be one of the fullest – a million and a half words – and most vivid accounts ever written of a district officer's life. They also provided an emotional and intellectual safety valve without which it is difficult to believe Cary's volatile Irish temperament could have weathered the next few years. The war had

Opposite Joyce Cary in Northern Nigeria, 1915, temporarily seconded to military duties.

Above Cary's drawing of his leaking rondavel at Bussa, from a letter to his wife, 1917.

stretched the thin white line of English administration even thinner than it was before, and almost immediately after Cary's arrival at Nafada he was told he was singlehandedly to take over Borgu on the west bank of the Niger, along the Dahomey frontier.

The prospect was daunting. Borgu was notoriously the poorest and most backward division in Northern Nigeria, much of it swampland with, Cary wrote, 'a wretched small population of pagans little removed from monkeys'. It had also just provided a case history of the shortcomings of Lugard's Indirect Rule. In 1912 both the reigning emirs had been deposed by Cary's predecessor and new ones instated. As the division was administered from the far side of the Niger, these new rulers had almost a free hand for extortion. The result was a popular rising a few months before Cary arrived which had been only partly quelled. 'I shall go for bush on Monday,' he wrote to his wife. 'I don't know what is in store for me, but I foresee a rough time.'[34]

Cary's long trek into Borgu did nothing to reassure him. He stopped on the way to nurse a colleague who was near death from blackwater fever and to pack up the belongings of another who had died. He reached Bussa, his new headquarters, at the start of the wet season and found his new home was an open rondavel with a roof that leaked like a sieve. The first few days they were also plagued by tornadoes.

'Darling, this really is a trying country,' he wrote. 'Imagine sitting in a house without any walls . . . with a forty-mile wind blowing. I had to dash round to rescue my property, papers, books, clothes, all blowing wildly about. . . . I have rigged up an old tent now over my bed, so that I hope to have a dry bed now in spite of the rain.'[35]

During the first few weeks Cary suffered from acute loneliness. His old station in Bauchi had had five or six other white officers, military and civil, and he had rather enjoyed the social life and gossip of the mess, even more the polo, played on half-wild native ponies. Here there was no white man nearer than ten days' trek away across the Niger.

> People who complain of the dullness of the country in small towns should try Borgu for a few months. To read the same books over and over again, to get papers six weeks old, to play the same tune on a degenerated accordion and never to see a friendly face at all or a human face either, except black caricatures. I daresay it would do 'em good or drive them to drink. It has driven a good many Nigerians to drink but though I would willingly amuse myself that way, it doesn't really amuse me.[36]

Musa.

Part of Cary's irritability stemmed from his acute anxiety about administering Borgu properly. He had almost no political experience; most of his last three years in Nigeria had been spent soldiering. His only adviser to his subjects' state of mind was the so-called political agent, Musa, a Hausa-speaking native, whose main job was to act as a liaison between Joyce and the local emirs. His information invariably contradicted that of the emirs' vizir, who called daily according to the protocol of Indirect Rule, to give an official report. Both implied 'deviously and resolutely that the other was a liar'. Years afterwards Cary described the appalling sense of blindness and distrust which took possession of him during those first few months. 'It was like a foreign intruder seizing on my mind. I would wake up at night and feel as if the dark itself were an immense black brain plotting behind its thick featureless countenance. . . .[37]

Cary was rescued from something very like a nervous breakdown by a chance meeting with his old chief, Edwardes, while on tour. Edwardes told him that he himself had found that the only way of making real contact with 'his people' was to sleep alone in the bush at night, as far as possible from his official entourage. Anyone with real grievances would come to find him there, braving the terrors of the bush at night, 'ghosts, lions, hyenas and so on'. As for himself, no lion however hungry would attack a mosquito net. The device worked. After a few days Cary was woken by voices whispering out of the dark, and though most of the grievances were trivial – one man kept him up half the night explaining the wrongful division of a deer – at least they gave him some rough barometer of his subjects' feelings.

By September Cary's own emotional barometer was showing signs of rapid improvement. Partly it was relief that he could cope with what he called 'the vegetable motions of administration – hearing petty cases, taking taxes, lecturing chiefs and so on'; partly his discovery that he could after all stand being alone.

> I haven't exchanged a word of rational conversation with a rational being since May, and when I do talk English I have to pick up the simplest words and repeat my meaning in two or three forms. Today I doubt if I have said more than a score of words altogether, and all those were Hausa words. All this makes it easy for me to understand the queer cases out here of fellows drinking themselves to death, getting homicidal mania, or breaking down into neurotic wrecks when in the back bush by themselves, though I myself am as fit as a flea and suffer no ill effects at all. Partly this is because I know what to guard against – nerves – drink – idleness, etc. and partly because I have always been able to extract a very high degree of pleasure out of books and almost companionship.[38]

Still it was with relief and some mock alarm that Cary received the news that he was to be relieved just before Christmas. Would the officer replacing him find him grown very eccentric? His clothes were in rags, rotted by the humidity, but he gave himself a drastic haircut. 'It was very long and I couldn't face Diggle. Now I look as if I had been eaten by rats. However, you won't mind what I look like if I come home, will you?'

Cary got back to Borgu six months later to find life considerably improved, thanks to Diggle. The headquarters had been moved from swampy Bussa to Kaiama in the hillier country to the south, and Diggle had planted a garden, now bursting with fresh vegetables. Though the house at Kaiama was scarcely less derelict than the one at Bussa – it had a huge hole in the upper floor – Cary grew quite fond of it. 'I could see from my bath down into the office and know at once what I was in for that morning.' Like Woolf in Hambantota, Cary had now discovered the positive aspects of his remote province. Just because it was so cut off and had no telegraph (that instrument to which Curzon had attributed the moral decay of the Indian Civil Service) he had been given leave 'to make quick decisions,

Steaming back to Borgu up the Niger.

in fact to do what I liked', and he could escape 'the endless minute-writing and form-filling of a big station in a rich province'.[39]

He spent much of the next few months on tour – it was the dry season – mapping the outlying areas of his kingdom as part of a detailed survey he intended to make of each district, and found himself warming unexpectedly to his pagan subjects.

> I have been through three small villages today . . . and made more acquaintances than for a long time past, and with a great deal of pleasure. I find lonely men in lonely huts working hard all the year to support one blind father and a child – or chiefs in old age still cheerful and undaunted, with nobody left in their tumbledown hamlet but a leper or so and one household . . . They respect and care for the old, they feed the sick and the poor – there are no cases here of people starved to death – they pet and spoil their children. What would be wrong with us is wrong to them. It is true that many things that are wrong to us are not wrong to them, but it is a question whether they are essentials.[40]

Cary also made his first attempts to alleviate Borgu's wretched poverty. He improvised bridges over some of the innumerable rivers which drowned dozens of travellers every year, and cut rough dirt roads through the bush. He had been struck by the prosperity of the border towns along the great trade route through Dahomey and hoped to channel some of it to the isolated villages of the interior. To encourage traders he built primitive rest houses or zungos on the loneliest stretches of road, charging a penny per traveller or a halfpenny for a woman or a goat. The authorities had refused the tiny capital needed for the zungos so Cary scraped it together from his allowance for 'native uniforms, miscellaneous and secret services'. The results were more dramatic than he could have hoped. The zungos repaid their cost in less than a year and within months the flow of trade to the villages along his roads had doubled and poverty visibly retreated a little: there was more demand for local goods, hides, dried fish, shea butter, not so many children with 'swollen bellies and skeleton faces'.[41] He noted with much cynicism that the new item on his district returns, 'zungo receipts', was accepted by the Northern Nigerian Treasury without comment. Like many district officers, Cary's genuine idealism had crystallised to bitterness at the sheer niggardliness of colonial practice. In Northern Nigeria

> ... a few hundred thousand on roads and bridges would be worth millions in a few years, but they won't do it. Instead of that the whole notion is to scrape a penny saving here and there ... The only way a governor can commend himself to the Secretary of State is by economies.[42]

Cary's opinion of the native authorities was hardly more flattering. The local emirs were 'hopeless'; the emir at Bussa had been 'too slack' to inspect a bridge twelve miles away which Cary wanted him to copy. In retrospect Cary could see the irony of expecting a highly conservative Muslim ruler to share his own enthusiasm for opening up Borgu to the outer world, which would almost certainly undermine further his own authority. The same paradox, as he was aware, underlay his own position. Half his pleasure in Borgu was feudal, though it did not take so negative a form.

bove Setting off on tour with the emir's official escort. *Below* Taking a bath before an admiring female audience.
ketches from Cary's letters to his wife from Borgu, 1917–19.)

> It is strange to live in such calm and in such a position. I walked out this evening two miles up the road by myself and the women I passed went down on one knee and the men bowed their heads literally to the dust, and cried out 'Lord'; even farmers a quarter of a mile away in the fields hailed me and salaamed, and I thought how strange it would look to our democratic Europe – and what a little person I am in reality. Who knows me at home – but 25,000 people here call me 'Baba' or father. Of course they call Diggle Baba too or anyone else who is sent, and they don't care tuppence for me really. There is no affection or loyalty – only respect. I think more of them than they do of me – like the czar and his people. Yet they run to me when they are in trouble, and they depend on me for much – for protection from tyranny and exploitation, and injustice. I could do more for them if I was allowed to spend a little more money – I want a vaccinator and a vet – I want an engineer and some bigger bridges that can be made with bush timber, I want some better roads – and a larger staff.[43]

It is revealing to compare Woolf's reaction to the same situation. He wrote in his autobiography that the flattery he received as 'father of his people' produced in him a growing political schizophrenia. He was 'an anti-imperialist who enjoyed the fleshpots of imperialism, loved the subject peoples and their way of life and knew from the inside how evil the system was beneath the surface for ordinary men and women'.[44] Woolf's claim that he was always subconsciously anti-imperialist was received with some scepticism later by his ex-subjects. But some of the violence of his reaction against the imperial system after he had left the Colonial Service may have been in part a puritan guilt for having succumbed earlier to the 'fleshpots'.

Cary's 'calm' was shattered the day after writing this letter by a sharp reminder of his other responsibilities. His wife understandably viewed his growing love affair with Borgu with increasing alarm. With two small children, she could hardly join him there. As Cary himself admitted, only the queerer sorts of missionaries tried to bring up white children in Nigeria and their children all died. Cary must resign from the service and find work in England or she could not answer for the future of their marriage.

Cary was so shattered that he did not reply for two days and then in terms that can hardly have cheered her, for they showed just how strongly he was now gripped by the service ethos. What could he do at home? His only special qualifications were for his job here. 'You would like me very much less as a failure at home – embittered, struggling and helpless . . . and I have done nearly a third of my time. In eighteen years' service I have to spend twelve in Africa. In three months I will have completed four years in this country'.[45]

Here he had work which could be respected, 'which is good and has been good for others. My children need not be ashamed of me if I am never more than an officer in this service. Indeed as an author, even as a great author, I might be less worthy of respect.'

One blow was rapidly succeeded by another. Cary was suddenly given orders to close down Borgu Division entirely and transfer himself to Zuru across the Niger. The officer there was, it transpired, Lady Randolph Churchill's latest husband, thirty years her junior, who was now required by his wife at home – not a role Churchill had probably ever envisaged for his 'earnest and intelligent young men'. The order sent Cary's opinion of the colonial authorities in general and Sir Hugh Clifford in particular to its lowest ebb. Everything would go to ruin, his mangoes, his garden, his work, Borgu itself. 'Last time they abandoned it they had a fight and fifty people were murdered, but Lady R ... an amorous old woman ... must have her husband.'

After ten days' trek through the rains to Kontagora with an immense caravan,

> Musa, the boys, Bawa the courier, Lafia the scribe, my fifty carriers and eight hammock men, Musa's eight carriers, nineteen police with twenty-seven carriers, four loads of office books and ten of money ... in all 132 people marching along in a row ...[46]

Cary was told that another replacement had been found for Zuru, and he was to go back to Borgu. He returned to find his garden, as predicted, a weed-choked ruin.

How soon Cary admitted to himself that he could not reconcile marriage and Borgu is unclear. In the last months before his leave he was still talking of his next tour and he used the dry season of 1919 to begin his most ambitious project yet: a grand trunk road south to link Kaiama with Lagos. It was to be 'a real road, cambered, with ditches and dead straight'. Cary was using his old chief Edwardes' pamphlet for his instruction manual. He walked out every evening to inspect its progress, feeling, he wrote, like 'a Roman engineer when he strolled down the long reaches of Watling Street'. Would the English too one day '... be recalled by the breaking of the Empire and shall some Blackman in the year 4000 trace my road for a paper in the Kaiama Archaeological Society and debate learnedly on the ancient greatness of Britain?'[47] If he could only push the work on far enough, his replacement must carry on with it, 'even if he swears'. He noted wryly that at last he and official policy were at one. 'It seems that I am in the fashion. Clifford has issued a big circular about roads.'

What finally made Cary's mind up was the news he received just before he went on leave that he had sold three stories to an American magazine at $200 apiece. If he could earn as much from three weeks' writing as in a year as an A.D.O., he could at last afford to resign.

Or so it seemed. In fact, Cary's next twelve years were to be a painful struggle to live by his pen – his first novel *Aissa Saved*, was not published until 1932 when he was forty-four. His difficulties as a writer were partly a result of his colonial experience. Leonard Woolf wrote in his autobiography that his years in Ceylon changed him from 'an aesthetic to a political animal'. Cary's in Nigeria made him, he wrote in 1944, into

> ... a man who, after ten years of active, thoughtless and various experience in the world, began rather late in youth to ask himself what it amounted to; to dig up all his foundations, to find out exactly what they were; who discovered then, as you might expect, that some of them were mud, some were hollow caves of

Right Hubert Berkeley, 'the uncrowned king of Upper Perak'.

Opposite Berkeley's stable of horses and some of his 'adopted daughters' at Grik, 1926. (Photo by Alan Morkill who succeeded him there as district officer.)

air, others sand; and who then slowly and painfully rebuilt them, as far as he could manage the task, as a coherent whole on which to find a new life and a new mind.[48]

Cary set all his early novels in colonial West Africa. They contain an extraordinary gallery of English district officers, most of whom are aspects of himself: Rackham, the swaggering Anglo-Irishman, more obsessed with polo than anything else; 'Monkey' Bewsher, who believes that only he can manage his pagans; Rudbeck, who becomes totally absorbed in building his road. But the character who haunted Cary's imagination, hero of a novel which he wrote and rewrote and never published, was the old patriarch, Cock Jarvis, going to seed among his pagans in the remote province he had conquered twenty years before, 'just before Lugard's time'. Now more than half-mad, firing off insulting letters to the 'base barnacles' at headquarters in Lagos, he is a compound of Lugard, Cary himself as he might have been, Edwardes and 'all the glorious band of pioneers' whom Cary met in his Nigerian days.

If Woolf had a hero among the white *hamadorus* of Ceylon, it was another relic of a bygone age: seventy-nine-year-old Sir William Twynam, who had ruled Jaffna as government agent for forty years and stayed on to live peacefully in an old Dutch house by the sea. If, Woolf wrote, he had not married Virginia, that was the kind of life he would have chosen, to immerse himself forever as district officer in Hambantota, married to a Singalese wife. It is an improbable vision, given what Woolf admitted himself was his ambitious nature. It is easier to imagine a steely blue-eyed Sir Leonard Woolf, KCMG issuing stern directives from the governor's

office. 'I would not have liked to be a minor colonial official when Leonard was a colonial administrator,' wrote his nephew. Anyway, the days when a jungli-wallah could be left alone for years to rule his own patch of jungle had gone. Or had they?

There was one famous twentieth-century survivor, even in Asia, of what many district officers saw as the golden age of benevolent paternalism: Hubert Berkeley, the 'uncrowned king' of Upper Perak. Berkeley was the younger son of a Catholic family who had owned land in Worcestershire since Norman times. Strongly Royalist, he regularly noted the date of the battle of Worcester in his diaries. According to legend he first saw Perak while a naval officer in the late '80s and was so fascinated by the beauty of the coast that he jumped ship and took a job on land with the Straits Settlement police. He transferred himself to the Perak Government Service in 1889 and two years later was sent to Upper Perak, the wildest part of the state. He remained there with brief interludes as district officer for the next thirty-five years, resisting all attempts to move him, and fathering, it is rumoured, a great number of half-Malay children.

The stories of Berkeley, especially of his high-handed treatment of the Secretariat, are legion. Trees blocked roads accidentally when high-up officials attempted to inspect his district. The chief secretary at Kuala Lumpur was foiled by a telegram reporting heavy rain and no bridge at the seventy-fifth mile. True enough, except that there had never been a bridge or a need for one at that particular place. Official circulars and queries from the Audit Office were thrown into the waste-paper basket or sent down for display in his famous double-barrelled lavatory down by the river. Visitors and junior officials were often invited, much to their confusion, to join him there, where he would recount his most successful battles against the authorities. One wall was decorated with a large picture of Sir Frank Swettenham which, Berkeley said, helped his bowel movements.

Unlike everywhere else in Malaya, office hours in Grik, Berkeley's station, were kept brief and flexible and were much enlivened by the spectacle of his elephants being loaded and unloaded at a large platform outside. He made all his journeys through his district either by elephant or by horse and boat, and successfully kept the district free of cars by not building suitable roads. Berkeley's passion was elephants and much of his official diary is devoted to them. 'It is with deep regret that I have to report the death of Kulop Chanda, which occurred this month', runs one entry, designed to tease the authorities. 'He had put in many years of faithful and devoted service and by his death a grievous loss has been suffered by the government of Perak.' The diaries show that the elephants were often expensive government servants. Damage by elephants is a frequent entry and tours of his district were ponderous and slow, since each elephant had to be carefully bathed morning and afternoon.

Berkeley's own bathing ritual was almost as elaborate. Twice a week he would drive in a landau to a hot sulphurous spring a few miles from his house to wallow in a shallow cement pool he had constructed there, followed by a cold plunge into a stream nearby. His dress on these occasions, recorded his junior, was a sarong 'of a highly variegated tartan pattern' and a straw boater with a ribbon inscribed 'HMS *Malaya*'.

Yet it would be wrong to write off Berkeley as merely a self-indulgent eccentric. By all accounts he was deeply beloved by the 'rayats' of his district and worked incessantly for their well-being, setting up irrigation schemes and rice mills. It was said that he knew the name of almost every family in Upper Perak and their life histories. At Christmas and Hari Raya, the feast that celebrates the end of Ramadan, he would invite the entire local population to take part in festivities provided at his own (or perhaps the government's) expense. The authorities at Taiping and Kuala Lumpur left him to his own devices, largely because he clearly ruled his district well. Luckily there was little official desire to 'develop' such a remote area in the interests of the Empire. For many officers of the Malay civil service, caught painfully between the demands of European and Chinese agents of 'economic progress' and their protective feelings and preference for the Malays, Berkeley's rule in Upper Perak represented the ideal. He was, wrote one officer from nearby Kuala Kangsar, 'a very great Englishman. . . . We shall not look on his like again'.[49] What Berkeley had recreated successfully in Malaya was the life of an eighteenth-century English squire, perhaps the dream of most district officers, both then and later.

In 1927, at the age of sixty-two, Berkeley finally went back to England, slipping easily, by all accounts, into the more conventional activities of a squire: farming, riding to hounds twice a week, and sitting on the Bench. He died soon after the fall of Singapore, heartbroken at the English failure to defend the Malay people.

Opposite Berkeley Cole and Lord Cranworth, two early settlers in East Africa.

Once the oxen are broken and the native taught, continuous manual labour in the sun *is no longer necessary.*
Lord Cranworth, *A Colony in the Making*, 1912

4

SETTLERS

The 'ordinary public school and 'varsity man,' advised an old hand in one of G. A. Henty's novels, 'if he has no interest (that is, no powerful family connection) and is not bent on entering the Army even as a private, should emigrate if he hasn't sufficient income to live on.'[1]

Henty – huge, hearty, bearded, the embodiment of Victorian virtues – died on his yacht at Weymouth in 1902, or he might have been pleased to note a useful new annual compendium, price two shillings and sixpence, called

The Settlers' Guide. Subtitled 'New Homes under the Old Flag', the cover itself was enough to cheer the would-be emigrant. Under the flag, gaily waving in a tropical breeze, a huge liner slips past a palm-covered spit of sand towards the harbour, reassuringly guarded by a naval gun. Inside, usefully indexed from 'A for Acquisition of land' to 'Z for Zanzibar', there were opportunities for English settlers 'of all classes', amply illustrated with maps and statistics. The fullest chapters, naturally enough, were devoted to the white dominions – Canada, Australia and New Zealand.

But for adventurous spirits, men with a modicum of capital and a sound constitution, there were plenty of more esoteric openings. Take Papua in the Pacific for instance – one of the newer adjuncts to the Empire, a country half as large again as England itself and climatologically, reported the *Guide*, 'much maligned'. At the slight risk of beri-beri or snake bite, you could rent up to five thousand acres of land at threepence an acre, suitable for rubber, coffee or coconuts, with seeds provided by government nurseries.

If Papua was too remote, you could try Fiji further north, consisting of 225 islands (80 of them inhabited) with Crown land at sixpence an acre, or ten shillings for sugar-growing land. Though the native Fijian was not a good worker (in his savage cannibal state, reported the *Guide*, he had extorted the 'unwilling admiration of the pioneer missionaries by persuading his victims to build their own ovens'), the government had now decided to allow the importation of Indian coolies for labour, at wages of one shilling per day without rations.

Further north again there was British North Borneo, with large tracts of fertile land available for the 'larger capitalist'; and British Malaya offered good prospects and good sport. Or, moving west, there were eleven new African protectorates to choose from, most of them vast. The *Guide* had good words to say of them all, except Somaliland, whose 68,000 miles of 'parched upland' were inhabited, it warned, by warlike nomad tribes who so far had resisted all efforts to establish *Pax Britannica*.

Westwards again across the Atlantic there was the older British Empire in the Caribbean – a 1,700 mile chain of tropical islands where the life of the planter still had much to recommend it: scenery, a healthy climate and pleasant, cultured society. Or you might prefer the South American mainland. There was British Guiana, 'the most neglected of colonies', which at four shillings and twopence an acre freehold or an annual rent of twopence halfpenny or less an acre, provided the cheapest Crown land in the Empire. The climate, though hot and moist, was healthy. Indeed there was no reason, in the *Guide*'s optimistic view, why almost anywhere in the tropics (except Somaliland) where the flag flew, could not offer to the man who followed the rules of tropical hygiene the prospect of a 'green old age'.

How splendid it all sounded for Henty's young men. Even Cecil Rhodes might have been satisfied. In the 1890s he had worked himself into a frenzy at the lack of English *Lebensraum*, prophesying bloody civil war if new lands for English settlers were not found. And he had certainly done his bit. Rhodesia, his namesake, where he lay buried in the Matopo Hills (he died the same year as Henty) was seen as one of

'Promise fulfilled' – Cecil Rhodes's favourite photograph of himself. He died in 1902, having secured, he believed, vast areas of Africa for English settlement.

the most promising of the new African colonies, with the sort of settlers the English approved of – hard-working, no-nonsense pioneers of yeoman stock. Rhodesia, the *Guide* hoped, would soon fall into line with 'our great democratic colonies'.

It was not like its neighbour further north, British East Africa, the future Kenya, which had already acquired a dangerous notoriety in Liberal circles. 'Just because it has advantages in natural resources, every sort of man from Peers downwards flocks there,' warned Lord Elgin to his successor at the Colonial Office, Lord Crewe, men 'quite unwilling or unable to work'.[2] Crewe, after a short spell in office, agreed. The settlers who had just marched up to Government House in Nairobi and insulted the governor, Sir James Hayes Sadler, with angry demands for more native labour, were a threat to good order – the kind of people who provoked expensive native risings and questions in the House. It might be cheaper to ship them all home.

The Colonial Office, from long experience, had never shared Rhodes's optimistic view that the more of the earth inhabited by the English the better for everyone concerned. And these new claims for White Man's Countries in territories where there were large indigenous black populations were clearly a formula for trouble. As Winston Churchill pointed out in his book after his visit to British East Africa in 1907, the last thing the settlers desired was that the Highlands should be denuded of their native inhabitants. White Man's Country in Africa meant black men's work.

The Settlers' Guide saw no problem beyond what it called 'the English government's misguided sense of fair play', and devoted one of its longest chapters to British East Africa. Here was a superb climate, fertile land, and an ample supply of intelligent native labour – essential to each and every enterprise. It was especially suited for settlement by the public schoolboy whose upbringing should fit him to control the natives. Here at last was a country in Africa where a higher white race might make a permanent home.

British East Africa was a cockpit of conflicting views from the beginning. It all began with that strangest of imperial ventures, the Uganda Railway.

> What it will cost, no words can express;
> What is its object no brain can suppose;
> Where it will start from no one can guess
> Where it is going to nobody knows.
> What is the use of it none can conjecture
> What it will carry there's none to define
> And in spite of George Curzon's superior lectures
> It clearly is nought but a lunatic line

mocked Labouchère's magazine *Truth* when the project was pushed through Parliament in the '90s against a barrage of Radical protest.

In fact its original purpose was largely military – to transport troops from Mombasa on the coast to Uganda and thence, it was planned, to conquer Sudan from the south and secure the vital source of the Nile. It was one of the few imperial schemes for which Lord Salisbury had shown positive enthusiasm. He followed its painful progress across the deserts and escarpments with what his daughter called feelings of 'militant paternity', bringing down photographs and stories to regale his family at Hatfield.

In the end the railway was too late for the Sudan campaign. It had cost the Treasury £5½ million and when it reached Kisimu on the shore of Lake Victoria in 1901, it all seemed odder than ever. There was no trade worth speaking of from Uganda and none from the land on the way. The grassy highlands which flanked the line were largely inhabited by fierce Masai tribesmen, whose only enterprise was to own large herds of cattle which they were not interested in selling. A few pioneers had walked up from Mombasa and settled in nearby Kikuyuland in the late '90s. The first white 'Kikuyu' baby had been born there in the Diamond Jubilee year, and coffee and everything the settlers had tried had grown like magic. The Brussels sprouts were ten feet high. But nobody was quite sure if Europeans could settle right on the Equator without long-term mental and physical deterioration, however bracing the highland air seemed. Lugard, who was there in the early '90s, believed it might be possible if you took off your hat only under a thick tree. Sir Harry Johnston, on his way back from Uganda in 1901, decided the Highlands were as healthy as England itself. The problem he foresaw was not the climate but the settlers themselves; in his experience in British Central Africa British settlers were the most disagreeable lot of people he had ever had to deal with. Joseph Chamberlain, who travelled up on the completed railway in 1902, was also deeply impressed

Opposite An elaborate photographic joke staged during the construction of the Uganda Railway.

Lord Delamere (*third left*) hunting in Somaliland, 1897, the year he stumbled into the Kenya highlands.

by the Highlands. The scenery reminded him of the Wiltshire downs. He decided they would make an excellent national home for the Jews. He made the offer to the Zionist leader, Theodore Herzl, when he returned to London, although he seemed to have forgotten quite where the Highlands were, noted Herzl, like the manager of a dry-goods store who is not quite sure 'whether some slightly uncommon article happened to be in stock'.[3] The offer was turned down by the Zionists, though not before an excited clamour from the few existing settlers. 'Is British taxpayer proprietor East Africa content that beautiful and valuable country be handed over to aliens ... Country being settled slowly surely by desirable British colonial settlers ...' cabled one of them, Lord Delamere.[4]

Delamere, a wild red-headed young man with large estates in Cheshire, had stumbled on the Highlands by chance in 1897 on a shooting trip from Somaliland, and had been so bowled over by the streams, cedar forests and waving grass of the Laikipia Plateau that he returned for good in January 1903 with his young wife, convinced that he could found another New Zealand here in the heart of Africa. But 'slow' rather than 'sure' settlement was the truth of the matter in 1903. No one except Delamere had arrived with any capital to invest seriously in farming the Highlands. The Foreign Office, who still ran the Protectorate, were only half-convinced that colonisation was a good idea and felt that perhaps East Africa might do better if Indians were allowed to settle rather than Englishmen. After all, there were already plenty of Indians there: the coolies who had helped build the railway and those who had settled on the coast. Delamere and the tiny Settlers' Association had, however, one fervent ally – Sir Charles Eliot, the new High Commissioner.

Eliot was as odd a phenomenon to find in Africa as the railway itself. He was a dapper Balliol scholar, who had been consul in Persia, had written one book on the Ottoman Empire and another – for relaxation – on British sea slugs. ('Never did a man more closely resemble the objects of his study', wrote Richard Meinerzthagen, who had also just arrived in East Africa to join the King's African Rifles.) Eliot had moved his headquarters up from Mombasa to the new shanty town of Nairobi, which had sprung up around the railway marshalling yards, and was immediately converted to the view that the Highlands could and should be White Man's Country. It was the only way, in his view, that flesh could be put on East Africa's highly expensive backbone, the railway.

The land was practically empty and the Masai who roamed across it were economically useless, representing in Eliot's view only 'blank, uninteresting, brutal barbarism'. White farmers would provide freight for the railway, and of course they would civilise the natives in the process. Meinertzhagen, invited to dinner with the High Commissioner who admired his aunt, the formidable Beatrice Webb, was amazed when Eliot expounded his vision of East Africa as a thriving colony of thousands of English families, with the natives confined to reserves as cheap labour.

The Foreign Office also got cold feet after their initial enthusiasm for recouping their expenses. For in 1903 Eliot, having failed almost completely to attract anyone from England, sent a Commissioner to South Africa to recruit settlers there, and promised among other things a large block of Masai land near the railway to a South African syndicate. Two of his officials on leave in London complained of this wholesale appropriation of native lands and after a tremendous public row Eliot was forced to resign. He continued the recruiting drive unrepentantly, with a lavish book on the Protectorate. 'Here in British East Africa,' he wrote, 'is a *tabula rasa*, an almost untouched and sparsely inhabited country where we can do as we will' – superb 'English scenery' of rolling grasslands and lakes 'which I would feign see crowned with a few castles and temples'. The natives could also benefit from a decent covering, 'nakedness being one of those African customs,' Eliot frankly admitted, 'I would feign see done away with'.[5]

Meanwhile Lord Delamere, a cheerful philistine who liked Africans naked and himself preferred living in grass huts to castles, did his own recruiting via his land agent in Cheshire. Early in 1904 he had at last reached the farm Eliot had granted him: 100,000 acres of grassland slap on the Equator. He called it Equator Ranch. The land, he wrote home, was incredibly fertile, better than anything he had seen in New Zealand or Australia. 'If any Cheshire or Lincolnshire man brings me a letter from you,' he wrote, 'I will see that he gets a good 640 acres free.'

Between them, by 1904, Eliot's and Delamere's efforts had certainly set the ball rolling. The thin trickle of settlers suddenly became a flood, most of them footloose Englishmen from South Africa who had found the veldt after the Boer War a hard place to make a living. ('Settling Englishmen there,' Churchill had remarked wittily with a dig at Chamberlain, 'seemed more expensive than growing orchids.') Covered in red dust, the new arrivals emerged hopefully from the twice-weekly train to Nairobi and made straight for the Land Office. Nairobi's scanty hotels were soon packed out. A kindly clergyman offered his garden for a camp, which was soon known as Tentfontein. The Land Office proved quite unable to cope with the flood. Every new farm had to be surveyed and the surveyors collapsed under the pressure of work. One would-be settler, having at last got a surveyor to inspect his land, found the man lying twitching in his tent, begging him to keep off that impala with pink ears.

Half the settlers went bankrupt even before they reached their promised land. Most of the other half, after they got there. 'When I first saw this country,' a colonist told Churchill in 1907,

> I thought at last I had struck God's own country. I wrote letters to all my friends, urging them to come. I wrote a series of articles in the newspaper, praising the splendours of its scenery and the excellence of its climate. Before the last of the articles appeared my capital was nearly expended, my fences had been trampled down by troupes of zebra, my imported stock had perished, my title deeds were still blocked in the Land Office and I myself had nearly died of a malignant fever.[6]

Lord Delamere, as befitted a great pioneer, lost more stock and money than anyone else. The family estate in Cheshire was soon mortgaged to the hilt to support his ventures at Equator Ranch. First he tried stock; the imported sheep died like flies of lungworm and footrot, and the cattle developed pleuro-pneumonia, redwater and East Coast fever. Then he tried wheat, breaking in the oxen himself with a good deal of cursing. He would get up at four to supervise the ploughing, after snatching a breakfast of Thompson's gazelle chops to the sound of his favourite record, 'All Aboard for Margate'. The wheat crop did splendidly at first, then succumbed in turn to two kinds of rust. Equator Ranch, it turned out, at 7,000 feet above sea level, was exactly the altitude where they overlapped. Delamere had to set up his own plant-breeding station before he found a type of wheat which was immune to both.

Politically he was the colonists' natural leader – forceful, quick-witted and able, as one settler put it, to come at the officials 'from the top'. It was Delamere who led the stormy advance on Government House and sent the governor, Hayes Sadler (known disrespectfully as 'old Flannel Foot'), into a fluster with his 'intemperate' language. It was Delamere whom the new governor, Sir Percy Girouard, hastened

Lord Delamere (*left*) in outsize topee, consults with the acting Governor of Kenya, Frederick Jackson, 1909.

to invite to dinner. Girouard, fresh from Nigeria where white men stuck together, was taken aback when, on his first early morning run, he greeted a young official and got a snarl back, 'Go to hell, you bloody settler' – an indication of how far ill-feeling had gone. But he and Delamere got on immediately. Delamere's fiery temper, which did not improve with time, was balanced by enormous natural charm and courtesy. And from then on, a relatively halcyon period in settler–official relations set in.

Socially too, Delamere's eccentric style of life set the pattern for the rest of the richer English settlers, 'pigging it' in grass huts crammed incongruously with mahogany furniture from England. There were schoolboyish break-outs when they all foregathered. It was Delamere who, regardless of his neck (which he had dislocated from a fall out pig-sticking), led the scrum in the bar at the Norfolk Hotel, shot out the new gas lamps in Nairobi's main street, or encouraged everyone to hurl oranges through the windows of his own hotel in Nakuru. Visiting officials were often shocked, especially by his appearance. 'Met Lord Delamere at the races,' noted Hesketh Bell, Governor of Uganda, on a visit to Nairobi in 1908, 'an extraordinary-looking creature. Both he and Lord Cardross, another settler, seemed to glory in making themselves look like bushmen with long hair.' In fact, Delamere's long red hair had a practical function, like his topee, the largest in Africa. The leading pioneer of England's most equatorial colony was horridly susceptible to sun-stroke.

NJORO,
BRITISH EAST AFRICA,
VIA MOMBASA.
Lord Delamere
[by H.S.G.].

Delamere never suffered seriously, however, from one of the settlers' chief problems – how to persuade the natives to work. When he arrived at Equator Ranch, the Masai and he took to each other at once. The Masai offered to herd his cattle – and as a *quid pro quo* helped themselves with impunity to his young stock, much to his Scottish manager's disgust. English visitors to Delamere's hut would find his herdsmen, smeared with rancid butter and red ochre, squatting round the fire telling him Masai legends. 'I am bound to say,' wrote one aristocratic fellow settler, Lord Cranworth, 'that their presence detracted considerably from the pleasure of a visit. . . . Still, everyone has his weakness – mine is dogs.'[7]

Cranworth, like almost everyone else, had to make do with the Kikuyu – clever, he admitted, but born liars and worse still, born 'trade unionists'. Other settlers put the problem even more strongly. The native labour here, wrote one young Englishman, Arnold Paice, fresh from Natal, was absolutely rotten. The natives were not compelled to work and would only stay for a month at a time. 'The worst of it is if you thump them, they clear off before daybreak the next day.' 'Still,' he added more philosophically in his next letter home, 'why am I grumbling. All said and done, I would rather strive with wild beasts and wild men out here than with motor cars and "tame men" at home.' An awful lot of rot was written in the papers about the sons of the Empire's hard lot. People at home had just as hard a life, he wrote, and then there was that wretched social position to keep up as well.[8]

United by indignation at the Colonial Office's unhelpful attitudes, class distinctions among settlers really did seem to melt away, compared with those in the older Eastern colonies and in India. 'With the exception of the wastrel and the degenerate, all are welcome,' wrote Lord Cranworth expansively in his book *A Colony in the Making*, published in 1912. 'We want the capitalist, we want the skilled workman, most of all perhaps we want the man with a small capital who will bring out his wife and make a home.'[9]

Cranworth (family motto 'Virtue thrives on difficulties') later recorded in his memoirs, with Bertie Wooster-like candour, his own vicissitudes as a settler. Converted perhaps by Sir Charles Eliot's book, he and his wife had set off for the Highlands in 1905, after practising shooting wooden lions in the park at home. They started their life as pioneers in unusual comfort in a luxurious bungalow outside Nairobi rented to them by Ewart Grogan. (Grogan was one of the earliest and toughest of settlers and had made himself famous by walking from Cape to Cairo, aged twenty, to win the hand of the girl he loved.) 'After amply accommodating ourselves and family, there were two or three spare bedrooms, an excellent kitchen, servants' quarters and ample stables; while best of all, there were two baths in which one could count on the water being really hot.'[10]

Cranworth's first investment was a plantation over the border in Uganda, a thousand acres of coffee which grew like a weed until it caught die-back and did just that. His second investment, 14,000 acres of beautiful woodland at Londini, where he tried farming black wattle, cattle and pigs, represented as he put it 'my most strenuous personal effort'; but the enterprises proved expensive failures. Then he went into the timber business with Lord Delamere's brother-in-law, Berkeley

Opposite The Delameres' ranch, from Lord Cranworth's photograph album, 1906. *Above left* Lord Delamere. *Above right* Lady Delamere's hut. *Centre right* The guest annexe. *Below* The sitting room.

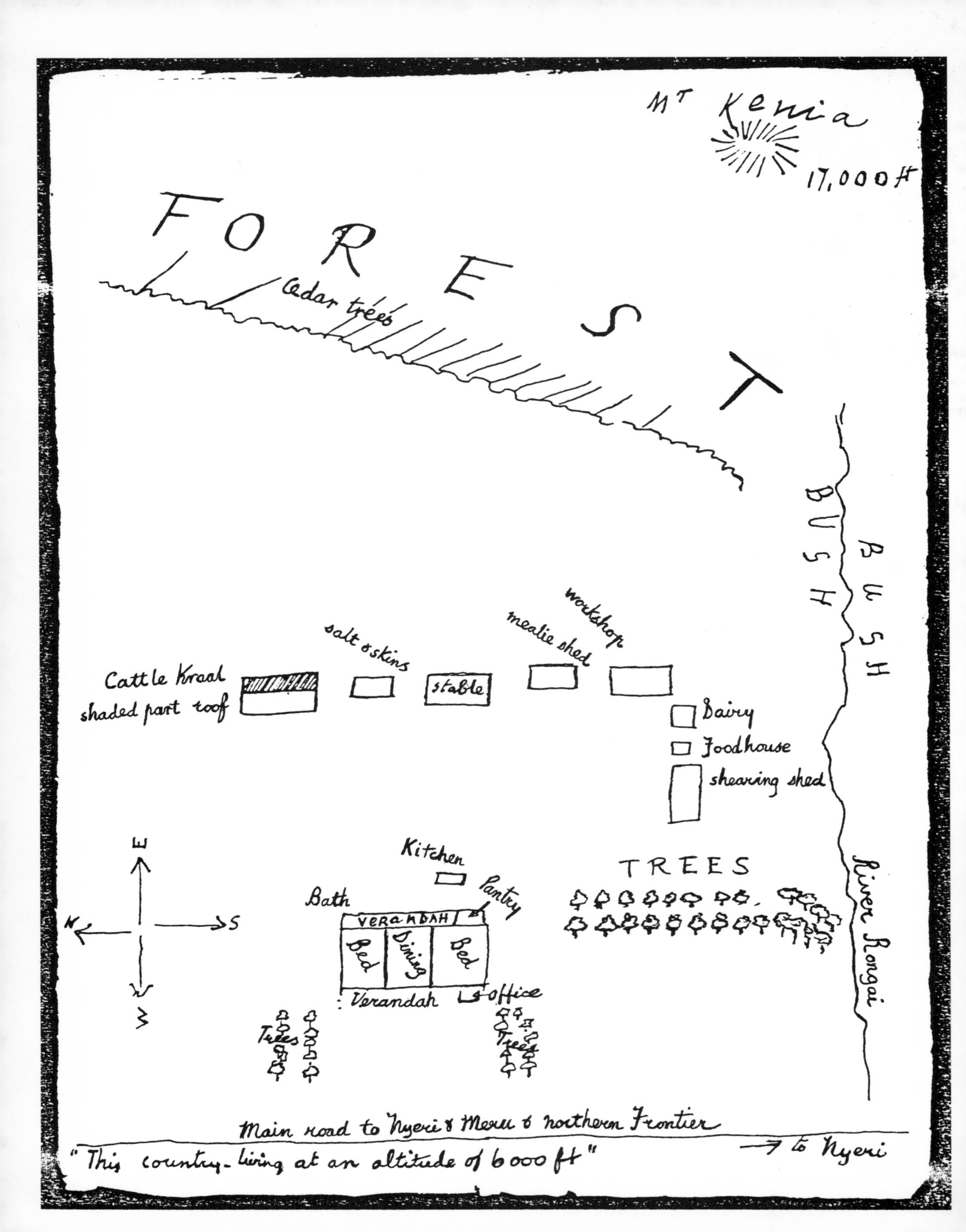
Mt Kenia
17,000 ft
FOREST
Cedar trees
BUSH
BUSH
workshop
mealie shed
salt & skins
Cattle Kraal
shaded part roof
stable
Dairy
Foodhouse
shearing shed
Kitchen
TREES
Pantry
Bath
VERANDAH
Bed
Dining
Bed
N
S
E
W
Verandah
office
Trees
Trees
River Rongai
Main road to Nyeri & Meru & northern Frontier
→ to Nyeri
"This country - living at an altitude of 6000 ft"

Cole, a project at which they both proved babes in the wood. Next he tried the hotel business, 'a tricky one'. His hotel at Nyeri, called The White Rhino, had plenty of customers but no cash, thanks to the chit system 'whereby no one ever dreams of paying for liquid refreshment on the spot'. His successor, a tougher-minded operator, put the hotel's name into practice by charging on sight. Next Cranworth joined Newland and Tarlton, the safari experts, who unfortunately chose that moment to expand into the import–export business and went down with all hands. The moral to be drawn from all these business ventures was, Lord Cranworth wrote sadly, that 'Profit comes before Pal'. After the war, he and his wife returned to the family estate in Suffolk. 'We were only dabblers,' he confessed, 'not true settlers like Delamere.'

Settlers at the other end of the economic scale were equally versatile in those early days. They had to be. Arnold Paice, the young Englishman from Natal quoted earlier, provides one of the most vivid examples. He arrived in Nairobi in 1907, his only possessions a few sheep and pigs, and his horse and dogs which he had brought up by sea from Durban. He trekked out to work on a friend's farm near Nyeri, literally throwing his sheep across the swollen streams on the way. After three years' hard work he had saved enough money to stake out his own farm and was allotted a block of land in Western Kenya on the far side of the Aberdare Mountains. He was the first white settler to arrive there. The land was well watered and fertile, he wrote home. Nairobi province would soon have to look to its laurels. But the early years were a hard struggle. He built a house of wattle and daub, 'small and not very swagger', he wrote home. Then he built one of brick, making and laying each brick himself with the help of a small native boy. He scratched a living by selling farm produce to the safari parties which passed through the area. He raised pigs, which had to be driven back over the Aberdare Mountains to market (a ten days' walk) and, like everyone else, he tried ostrich farming just at the moment when the market for ostrich feathers in Europe collapsed.

After the war Paice baked bricks in a home-made kiln and sold them to the new settlers in his district, and hired himself out to build their chimneys and fireplaces, at £1 a day. Henty would have been proud of him. He never went back to England and died on his farm in 1963.

When is a settler not a settler? When he is a planter. To men like Paice or Delamere, the distinction was quite clear. Settlers were people who made their home in a country and intended to stay for ever, building up their farm or business to leave to their children. Planters went out to the tropics to earn a living, to make a fortune as quickly as possible and then return to a well-heeled retirement in the Home Counties, to reminisce and nurse their livers. In practice, however, the distinction was much more blurred. Some of the sugar planters in the West Indies had been there for over a century, though their sugar estates were now half ruined. Planters in Assam and Ceylon had settled there for generations too and often preferred to spend their retirement on pleasant verandas swathed in bougainvillaea, rather than back in a chilly homeland, where they had heard that finding good servants was already a problem.

Opposite Plan of the first settler's farm north of the Aberdares in Kenya – from Arnold Paice's letter to his mother, 1910.

'The Second Generation': European children outside Nairobi. The East African settlers believed they were founding a permanent colony.

Many of the richer settlers in East Africa hedged their bets like Cranworth. Even Lord Delamere never sold his Cheshire estate. By 1914, East Africa had its share of absentee landlords. The most notorious example was Lord Kitchener, who had bullied his old protégé, Sir Percy Girouard, into granting him five thousand acres of land confiscated from the warlike Nandi tribe. To Edwardian grandees, a farm in East Africa where you might or might not spend the winter months was no different from owning a grouse moor in Scotland. The same process had already occurred further south. By 1912 only a tenth of the land owned by white settlers in Northern Rhodesia was farmed by the owners themselves.

Settlers or planters, Henty's hard-up public schoolboys were soon in glut even in the tropics. 'It is scarcely worthwhile to leave home, country and friends to live out here in an exhausting climate with heavy responsibilities on the salary of a clerk in a London office,' wrote the disillusioned mother in 1905 of a young 'creeper' or trainee planter in Ceylon.[11] But it was the old question of supply and demand. Here, as in England, there were numerous applicants for every respectable job. She urged anyone sending a son to Ceylon to study his disposition and count the cost. Life in the quietest of English villages was a vortex of gaiety compared to that here. To an English boy fresh from the cricket and football fields of a public school, the isolation was terrible and many were the stories of moral, mental and physical breakdown. The only drama was provided by the monthly visit of the dreaded V.A., or visiting agent, to inspect the books. Most of the new estates were owned by companies in Colombo instead of being run on the old planter–proprietor system.

Leonard Woolf, who predictably included all planters in his early diatribes against English colonial society, was surprised to find some congenial spirits among the younger managers. There were some really very good fellows, he told Lytton Strachey. While convalescing from typhoid above Kandy he stayed with one who had read theology at Cambridge. 'He is rather charming and strenuous and deals largely in philosophy. We had, before an admiring audience on whom he has completely impressed himself, a violent argument about the existence of time and he is now about to begin a study of *Principia Ethica* [Woolf's intellectual bible, written by his friend G. E. Moore]. One would hardly expect an evening like that in an isolated hill bungalow on a Ceylon tea estate.'[12] Woolf also got to know some of the older planter proprietors who still dominated the south of the island, living like patriarchal English squires. He was rather pleased to find himself, as a rising young A.G.A., considered a social catch by their wives and daughters, and almost succumbed to the charm of one girl, Rachel Robinson, whose father owned a beautiful tea estate in the mountains above Hambantota. Deterred from proposing perhaps by the thought of Strachey's disapproval, perhaps by a vision of Virginia Stephen in a white dress long ago at Cambridge, he set his bicycle firmly back down the hills towards Hambantota.

If life on a tea estate in Ceylon could be dull, necessitating frequent visits by wives and daughters to Kandy, Colombo or Nuwara Eliya, life on a rubber plantation in Malaya was duller still. Para rubber was the latest and most spectacular of tropical growths that drew Englishmen into the jungles. Like tea in Ceylon it was taken up by coffee planters, *faute de mieux*, after their crops had been destroyed by fungus. The story of rubber had a Jack-and-the-Beanstalk flavour. Seeds of *Hevea Brasilianus* had been smuggled out of Brazil in 1876 at the instigation of Sir Joseph Hooker at Kew. He packed some of them off to the Botanical Gardens in Ceylon and from there they were sent on to Singapore and Perak. In Perak, Hugh Low, earliest and greatest of the British Residents, nursed the seedlings devotedly in the Residency garden at Kuala Kangsar. Ten years later they were discovered there, flourishing and ready to tap, by the new head of the Botanical Gardens in Singapore, H. N. Ridley. He spent the next ten years 'ingerminating' *Hevea Brasilianus* into the Malay States. He stuffed the seeds into the pockets of every planter he met, promising they would make their fortune. To humour 'Mad' Ridley a few did plant them, though some of these chopped down the young trees when their leaves fell off, thinking them diseased. No one in Malaya was used to deciduous trees. Nor was Ridley helped by Hugh Low's successor as Resident, Frank Swettenham, who reprimanded him for growing 'exotics'.

It was the late '90s when the first plantations began at last to show a return – just at the moment when Europe got the bicycling craze. Next it was motor cars. Demand for rubber soared and the rush was on. An army of Malay and Chinese contractors fell on the Malay jungle with picks and axes, destroying 'that sea of vegetation' as Richard Winstedt wrote in one of the finest purple passages in his memoirs, 'wherein since the passing of the ice-age, tigers, elephants and rhinoceros, Australo-Magnon, Sakai and Negrito and Malay had glided as rapt and silent as fish in translucent ocean depths.'[13]

The jungle struck back – ferociously. Every ravine cleared was soon dancing with malarial mosquitoes, which reduced white overseers to shivering wrecks and killed off the work force in hundreds (on one Selangor estate nearly twenty-five per cent of the coolies died in one year). Government hand-outs and planters' handbooks buzzed with prophylactic advice, but despite all efforts the death rate remained shockingly high until the First World War.

Not surprisingly, the Malays showed no desire to work on the new plantations. Chinese and Tamils, imported from India, filled the gap. The Tamils were more tractable, advised *The Planter's Handbook* of 1904; the Chinese were best dealt with through their own headmen. Privately most planters, like the officials in the Malay Civil Service, continued to prefer the 'idle' Malay to both. Perhaps they envied his independence. By 1913 over a million acres of rubber had been planted and every drifter in Kuala Lumpur and Singapore had been drafted into a job. Meanwhile, district officers like Winstedt trembled for their favourite beauty spots. Would nothing escape the axe? Settlement officers who decided which areas could be felled were poorly paid and susceptible to bribes. 'Would one of them,' wrote Winstedt 'sitting in a rest house five miles from the land to be settled give away the Kinjong Falls, the pride of the district, in return for a case of Usher's Glenlivet.'[14]

If anyone needed the Usher's Glenlivet, it was the planters themselves. After the initial drama of felling the jungle, the only exciting thing about Para rubber took place in Wall Street or Mincing Lane where the price shot to a spectacular 12s.9d. per lb by 1910. Back in Malaya the rubber trees with their mottled grey bark, fleshy leaves and sweet heavy scent stood in relentless lines across the landscape, waiting to be inspected twice daily.

'Could any decent Englishman when he calls back to memory his home and surroundings in the old country,' wrote one exile despairingly from 'Up-Country, Pahang', 'ask any decent girl brought up under similar conditions to ... share the God-forsaken loneliness, the soul-shattering monotony and utter dreariness of a rubber estate?'[15]

'I knew a planter,' recorded Winstedt, 'who, having drunk a bottle of whisky and sung "Count your blessings one by one" far into the Sabbath, sat down in desperation and wrote proposals of marriage to three women at once.'[16] Up to the First World War there would have been few takers.

The solution, apart from more whisky, was, as Winstedt delicately phrased it, to choose as a companion 'one of the complaisant, amusing, good-tempered and

Opposite A rubber planter's house rises from cleared jungle, Selangor, early 1900s.

Part-grown rubber estate, early 1900s. 'Can any decent man ask any decent girl . . . to share the soul-shattering monotony and utter dreariness . . .'

good-mannered daughters of the east'. Ninety per cent of planters in the early days kept Asian mistresses: some Malay, some Chinese, some Japanese rescued from the establishments of Singapore. The only unwritten law was that no planter should take a mistress from his own estate. The liaisons survived long into the period when English wives were willing and eager to come out to Malaya, raising in the latter's minds the irritating suspicion that some Englishmen actually preferred them.

Occasionally a liaison breached other unwritten laws. The most famous case-history – dramatically documented by himself – is that of Robert Bruce Lockhart. Lockhart, an athletic young Scot whose family owned large estates in Malaya (his grandmother was known as the 'Rubber Queen' of Edinburgh), set off to make his fortune there in 1908. He spent his first year as a trainee outside Port Dickson, where he learnt to swear at Tamil coolies, dislike book-keeping, drink stengahs and gin pahits at the local club, and made a name for himself in the Negri Sembilan rugger team.

Then he persuaded an uncle to send him to open up a new estate in the foothills near Seremban. No European had ever lived there before, the place was notorious for malaria and there was a deposed Malay sultan in the village who was understandably hostile to the English. Lockhart's only links with civilisation were a pushbike and one Malay policeman. But he was soon as 'happy as a mahout with a new elephant' in his little kingdom, laying out new roads and drains and a football pitch, building a new house and dispensing justice to his work force. By a stroke of

luck he made his reputation by killing a cobra that had taken up residence in the local well with one shot from his revolver, and after that was able to bicycle past the toughest Chinese mining camp without a qualm. He learnt Malay and made friends with the local sultan – or rather his wife, a terrifying wizened old lady who was, Lockhart wrote, the Queen Victoria of her district.

It was this friendship which led to Lockhart's ill-starred romance. The sultan invited him to a *rong-geng*, a kind of dancing competition at which professional dancing girls dance and sing love quatrains and throw out challenges to the audience to compete. To return the hospitality, Lockhart invited the entire village to an even more splendid *rong-geng* on his estate. And there in the audience under the shadowy palm trees, he saw *her* (Lockhart's reading had been heavily laced with Loti) – 'a radiant vision of brown loveliness in a batik skirt and red silk coat', shining like a pearl in the torchlight. Dazzled, he summoned his Malay headman to ask who she was. The headman's answer was guaranteed to increase Lockhart's ardour. 'The crow does not mate with the bird of paradise. That is Amai, the Sultan's ward. She is married and about to divorce her husband. When the divorce is through, she will be married to the Sultan's cousin.'

For the next six weeks, Lockhart patiently stalked his bird of paradise. Every evening at five o'clock he stood on the corner of the road to watch her pass. He never spoke, she never unveiled ('It would have ruined everything'). Then one day, she paused, drew back her sarong until it showed the lotus-blossom in her hair, then disappeared like a startled hare. On fire, Lockhart pressed his headman to arrange a

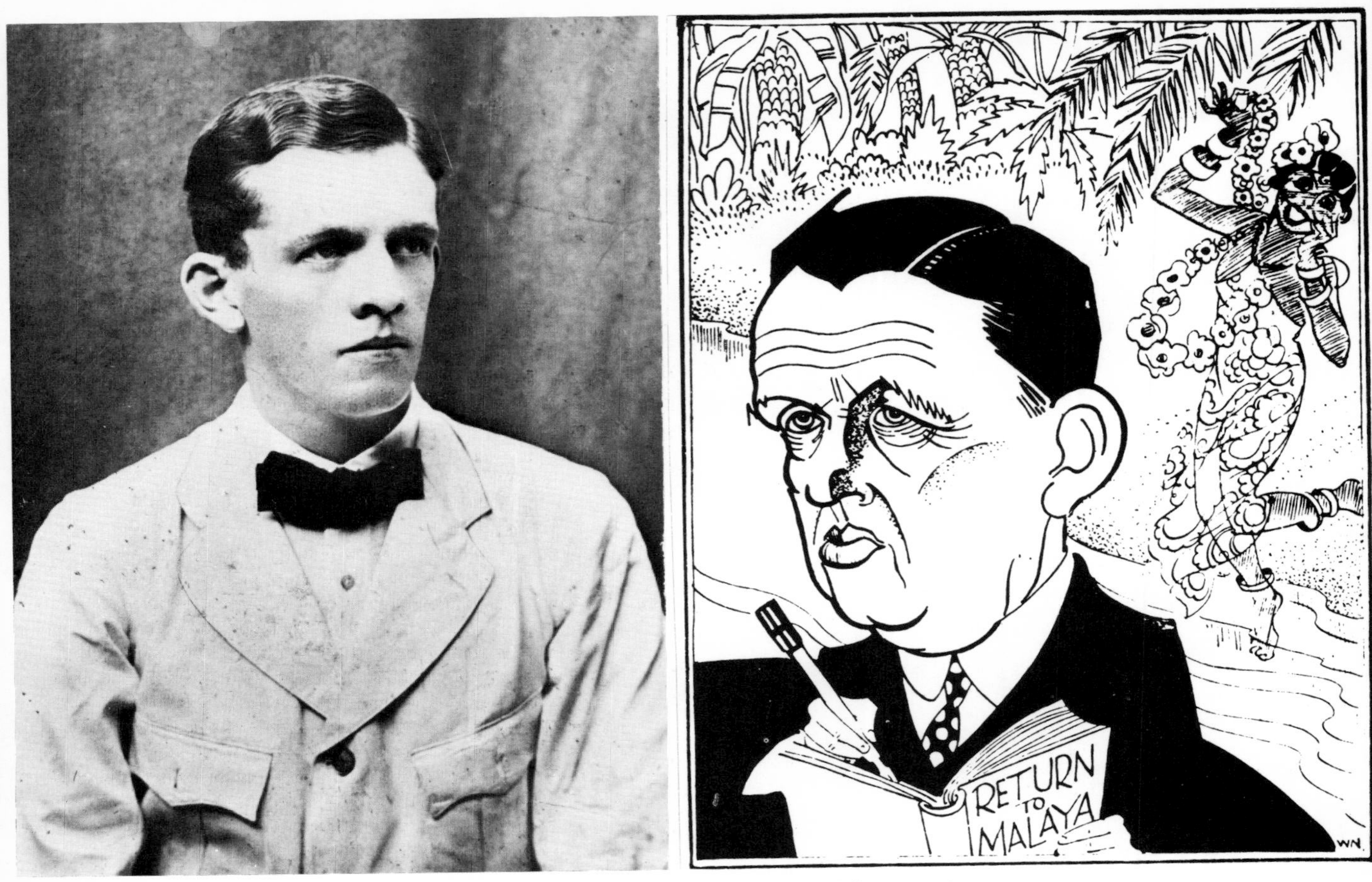

Robert Bruce Lockhart as a young rubber planter, 1908.

His return to Malaya, 1936.

real meeting. Two days later he was told to wait for Amai that night by the ninth milestone in the jungle. . . . He oiled his revolver, put on his rubber-soled gymshoes and set off, trembling with excitement, down a narrow jungle path and across a rickety bamboo bridge over the river. He reached the rendezvous a quarter of an hour early and crouched down to wait, gun in hand. Just as he started to despair, there was a footstep and Amai loomed up before him. 'For one fierce moment I held her in my arms trembling like the quivering of lalang grass at the first touch of morning sun.' Then he led her back across the bamboo bridge towards his bungalow.

After this fine Loti-esque beginning, the rest of the story was, Lockhart admitted, either tragic or comic. Amai stayed on at the bungalow, partly because it was too dangerous for her to leave. Lockhart was besieged by her royal relations demanding that she, a princess of the blood, should be surrendered at once and offering him the fairest 'houri' in exchange. The scandal even reached the ears of the British Resident.

Lockhart to buy time claimed he was preparing to become a Mohammedan. The ruling prince, Amai's cousin, was satisfied, but the old Sultan who ruled the village was not. Lockhart became a local pariah. His football team and his Chinese cook deserted him. Then he caught a particularly virulent form of malaria which no amount of quinine seemed able to cure. Wasted to skin and bone, he lay in his long-chair, cursing the headmen who came to ask him about the estate work; but determined to keep his bird of paradise. Amai, for her part, remained invincibly, maddeningly, cheerful. Unable to leave the compound, she played the gramophone from morning till night, driving Lockhart to such desperation with her favourite tune, 'When the trees are white with blossom, I'll return', that he would stagger with chattering teeth to the piano stool to play her the 'Blue Danube' instead.

It was Amai who brought the nightmare to an end by sending for the government doctor. The doctor took one look at his patient, grunted and went back to Seremban where he routed Lockhart's uncle out of the high poker game in the Sungei Ujong club. It was the height of the rubber boom and the uncle, flush with money, was just ante-ing up when the doctor told him he might need his stake to pay for his nephew's coffin. The next morning, the uncle arrived early at Lockhart's bungalow, had him wrapped in blankets and took him off in his car to hospital. Amai had vanished into the back room and did not appear to say goodbye. The sun glinted on her little silver slippers which lay neatly by the bottom step. 'They were the last I saw of her,' wrote Lockhart in his memoirs, 'the last I was ever to see of her.'[17]

Rather to Lockhart's discomfort there was a final sequence to this short-lived romance. Twenty-eight years later, Lockhart, by this time a well-fleshed Beaverbrook journalist who had been through one marriage and a great number of adventures, amorous and otherwise, decided to make a return trip to Malaya the subject of his next book. He was met at the quay by the news that Amai was alive and well and expecting to see him. His reaction was clammy nervousness, but clearly he could hardly refuse. Once again it was Amai who emerged best from their encounter. Still slender and well-preserved, she told Lockhart she was now married to the village muezzin, questioned him with interest about his own marital status and commented with devastating frankness, 'The Tuan has grown fat.'[18]

Lockhart's return to Malaya gave him the chance, like every old hand, to deplore the changes in planters' lives since his young days: the huge increase in the number of white women, who now directed all social life – 'I cannot think it is a change for the better'; the exaggerated concentration on alcohol (surely, not so different); the absence of intellectual interests; the lack of adventurous spirit – 'We had to carve our estates out of the primeval jungle.'[19] Nowadays, planters were nothing but managers. All the estates were owned by public companies who were finding it increasingly hard to compete with native-owned rubber. For the 'idle Malays', having shrewdly waited to judge the long-term prospects of the new crop, had taken to rubber-planting and tapping so successfully that they now produced two-thirds of the annual yield.

Lockhart noted also – a sad witness to the disastrous slump after the war when the price of rubber had plunged as low as $1\frac{3}{4}$d. a lb – the derelict bungalows of his old colleagues, their woodwork already half eaten by white ants. Planters had been reduced to begging in the streets of Kuala Lumpur and Singapore; and the British community had rallied round as best it could to pay their passages home. 'Poor whites' were the dread of every expatriate community in the tropics. There was soon a further reason to close ranks. In the '20s Somerset Maugham published a series of short stories set in Malaya. He unfolded tales of lust, incest, *crimes passionels*, against the setting of up-country plantations and clubs.

Of course, wrote Maugham, in reality these things happened no oftener in Malaya than elsewhere. The vast majority of the English there led ordinary decent humdrum lives. The world was not convinced.

> What men call gallantry and gods adultery
> Is much more common where the climate's sultry

as Lord Byron had written over a hundred years before.

If anything was needed to confirm that view, it was the stories which were to come out of that never-quite White Man's Country, British East Africa, now renamed Kenya. Unlike the English in most of the rest of the tropics, the East African settlers had had a war right on their doorstep, and those who had not enlisted in England had spent four frustrating years chasing the most brilliant of German generals, von Lettow-Vorbeck, round Tanganyika. They came back to half-ruined farms in an aggressive mood with renewed demands that idle young Africans should be compelled to work, and were reinforced by a new wave of soldier–settlers who believed it just as strongly. The old romantic pioneer spirit had gone, or at least so Karen Blixen, the most famous of Kenya's chroniclers believed. 'Before the First World War the Highlands were still in truth the Happy Hunting Grounds and the white pioneers lived in guileless harmony with the children of the land.'[20] It was not a view perhaps that the English Colonial Office had ever shared.

But among the richer settlers the role of pioneer did seem to have been replaced by something more raffish – breaking oxen by breaking marriages. George V, investing Sir Edward Grigg as Governor of Kenya in 1925, had no doubt where the trouble began. Men who should have known better, he had heard, had taken to dining in pyjamas. The governor should not allow it.[21] The King would have been shocked if he had known how far the rot had gone. Lady Francis Scott, a viceroy's daughter and a new settler described with amused horror a dinner with Berkeley Cole, Lord Delamere's brother-in-law, soon after she arrived. 'He slouched into the room in a very old pair of slippers and what looked like shrunken crêpe drawers and an old bedjacket which failed to hide his naked legs. During dinner a large cat wandered all over the table and a huge Russian Boer's hound ate off our plates as well.'[22]

At lunch with Lord Delamere (who was 'charming') she spotted an even worse portent. Most of the women wore shorts: 'very ugly and quite unnecessary.' The fashion had been started by Lady Idina Gordon, who, Lady Francis wrote cryptically, 'has done a lot of harm in this country.' Lady Idina, already married twice, was to marry and divorce five times in all, including the dashing Lord Erroll, victim of Kenya's most famous murder case. A new legend was on its way to replace that of the Happy Hunting Ground – the legend of Happy Valley.

Opposite George Grenfell, pioneer missionary to the Congo.

If I were a cassowary
On the plains of Timbuctoo,
I would eat a missionary,
Cassock, band and hymn-book too.
Bishop Samuel Wilberforce (1805–73)

5

PREACHERS

In 1901, the young Duke and Duchess of York, halfway through their royal tour of the Empire, attended a service in Brisbane Cathedral, where they listened to a rousing sermon from the Rev. Cosmo Gordon Lang on the Christian's duty to support missions to the heathen. The Duke of York, who did not agree,

The semi-jubilee of the Scottish missionaries at Blantyre, 1895.

challenged Lang after the service. 'You tell me with my views I can't be a Christian.' He could only state the premise, Lang replied; it was for the Duke to draw his own conclusions. 'Well, I call that damned cheek,' said the Duke of York, walking away angrily.[1]

This short exchange between the future temporal and spiritual heads of the Church of England illustrates neatly the widening fissure which had recently appeared between the English Church and State in their attitudes towards empire.

At the height of Queen Victoria's reign it had hardly been visible at all. Commerce, Christianity and civilisation were England's triple gifts to the world, the two former combining to bring about the latter. That was what almost everyone agreed; the greatest of missionaries and England's favourite national hero, David Livingstone, had said so when he returned from central Africa in 1858. And a host of intrepid Englishmen had gone to Africa since then in answer to his appeal, to carry on the task of bringing these blessings to the interior of the Dark Continent.

Wherever other Englishmen went in search of land or big game or trade or wars, they were almost sure to find a missionary had got there before them. When Lord Delamere reached the Tana River in 1897 after an exhausting trek across Somaliland, the first thing he saw was a missionary floating downstream under a pink

The extraordinary asymmetrical church at Blantyre, designed by the mission's leader, Dr Clement Scott.

umbrella in search of a site. Missionaries might be a bit of a bore, a bit of a joke, but Harry Johnston had declared that they were the greatest asset a thinly stretched empire could have. 'As their immediate object is not profit, they can afford to reside at places until they become profitable. They strengthen our hold over the country. They spread the use of the English language. They induct the natives into the best kind of civilisation. In fact each mission station is an essay in colonisation.'[2] Encourage them to breed – and missionaries were some of the few people who took their wives to Africa – and you would have the spores for future colonies. In fact it had been the sight of the missionary settlement at Blantyre in the Shiré Highlands which had convinced Harry Johnston that this part of Africa must be British, not Portuguese. Here was a little Arcadia, he wrote, 'sweet-looking English farm-houses, churches, cottages, roses, fat cattle, gobbling turkeys. A sight to rejoice poor Livingstone's ghost. . . .'[3]

Even Lord Salisbury had finally agreed, and had used the Scots missions as a lever to eject the Portuguese from that area. But all of that was in the heady days of Scramble. Now almost no one, least of all Lord Salisbury, wanted to add to the imperial burden. The missionary had ceased to be a useful unpaid ally and had now become a liability.

In the spring of 1900, just when the British had their hands full with the Boers in South Africa, a fearful convulsion had seized China, largely caused, it seemed, by a forcible injection of European religion and railways. The Boxers (self-styled 'Public-Spirited Harmonious Fists'), as the Chinese rebels were called, had killed over 32,000 Christian converts and 200 European missionaries. At the height of the crisis Lord Salisbury had addressed a rather belated warning to the Society for the Propagation of the Gospel at Exeter Hall, on the occasion of their 200th anniversary. There was an Eastern saying, he told his audience: 'First the missionary, then the consul, then the general.' It would be a terrible hindrance to missionary work in Asia should the notion get about that political expansion and missionary work went hand in hand.

In Africa too, and here perhaps the Prime Minister cocked an eye at the Church Missionary Society over to the north in Salisbury Square, precipitate attempts to convert the heathen had been the cause of many military expeditions. Bloodshed, he warned, would be a serious and permanent obstacle to that Christian religion of peace, 'which we desire above all things to preach'.[4]

The Church Missionary Society must have suspected that Lord Salisbury had one recent incident particularly in mind. In April that year a party of six missionaries, led by the fiery Bishop Tugwell of Western Equatorial Africa, had set off with Sir Frederick Lugard's permission to set up a pioneer mission in the new protectorate of Northern Nigeria. The great emirates of the north had been a lodestar for missionary ambitions ever since the ill-fated Niger expedition of 1841. And though the population was largely Muslim, the C.M.S. had convinced themselves that the Hausa, possibly 'the best race in Africa', would embrace a new religion which freed them from their Fulani overlords.

Tugwell's expedition had been scrupulously prepared. The party had spent a year in Tripoli, learning Hausa from pilgrims on their way to Mecca. When they arrived at Lugard's base at Jebba, their hopes seemed confirmed by the enthusiastic greeting they received from the villages round. They advanced to Zaria where the emir received them graciously, for political reasons as it happened, of his own. Jubilant, the little party then rode on to Kano, one of the most powerful trading cities of the interior, without waiting for Lugard's permission. And here, out of reach of military protection, things went badly wrong.

First they were kept waiting in a sweltering grass hut for several hours while the emir, Aliyu the Great, received other deputations. Then they were summoned to his presence, told to take off their shoes and stockings, and to advance on all fours, looking – as one missionary wrote back home later – 'like rats before a ferocious mastiff'.[5] After a brief exchange the emir ordered them peremptorily out of Kano and his territory. In fact they were lucky to have escaped with their lives. Aliyu had been inclined to kill them all as spies, and had only been dissuaded after a heated

Above The Church Missionary Society pioneer mission to the Hausa, 1899. (*Centre*) Bishop Tugwell and (*seated left*) Dr Walter Miller, the moving spirit behind the mission.
Opposite Anti-missionary propaganda produced during the Boxer rising: 'Killing the foreign devils and burning their books.'

discussion with his advisers, who feared retaliation by the white men at Jebba.

The little group of missionaries returned exhausted to Zaria, only to find the climate there now also distinctly unfriendly (they were lucky to find a military outpost nearby to fall back on). One of them, Claude Ryder, died almost immediately of dysentery and two others had to return by stretcher to the coast. The remaining three, including Bishop Tugwell, built a little mission hut on a hill above the Kaduna river, and managed to linger on precariously there till July without making any converts, until Lugard sent urgent instructions that they should return. He had been furious when he heard that the missionaries had gone to Kano without his permission. Their humiliation was a blow to white prestige, which he believed had endangered his entire administration and made almost impossible future negotiations by anything other than a Maxim gun. The military campaign against Kano that followed was to echo all too exactly Lord Salisbury's prediction.

Compared with most imperial administrators, Salisbury's and Lugard's strictures on mission proselytising were moderate. Salisbury was a devout Anglican, if a cautious statesman, and Lugard, though agnostic, was after all the son of missionary parents. By 1903 he had patched up relations with the C.M.S. and allowed one of Tugwell's original party, Walter Miller, to return to Zaria. He soon developed an odd dependence on this remarkable young man who spoke Hausa like a native, and used him as a sounding-board on all political questions. He even offered to give him official status as one of his Residents, which Miller on advice from the C.M.S. refused. Lugard's successor, Sir Percy Girouard, frankly avowed, however, his distrust of any 'missionary meddling' in the northern states. 'The best missionary for the present,' he wrote, 'would be the high-minded clean-living British Resident.'[6]

Miller's letters to the C.M.S. headquarters show him to be highly sceptical. Most of the officials, whom he knew well as they were sent to learn Hausa from him, were no doubt, he reported, 'brave English officers, genial, good-natured, but utterly ungodly, all living loose lives, *all* having women brought to them wherever they are.'[7] No wonder they did not want missionaries at close quarters.

An even more serious mark against them, he believed, was that they condoned oppression by the Fulani ruling class. The entire system of so-called Indirect Rule as practised by Lugard's successors was despotic and cruel. In Zaria itself he waged a long-drawn-out battle against the emir, only finally won in 1919 when Sir Hugh Clifford read a huge dossier of the emir's misdeeds, and had him dismissed. The truth was of course that in Nigeria as in most of the tropical Empire, missionaries and officials were now rivals on several levels. Many young officials (of whom a quite extraordinary number were clergymen's sons) brought an almost spiritual fervour to the administration. And in Nigeria, where so many of them were drawn, as Miller pointed out, from the most conservative class in Britain, they had no wish to spoil their romantic feudal protectorate by importing that well-known handbook for revolutionaries, the New Testament. There had been quite enough trouble in the south, where it was generally agreed that the mission boy was 'the curse of the coast'. At least one of Lugard's Residents in the north became a convert to Islam, a far more dangerous blow, Miller protested, to white prestige than anything the missionaries might do.

It was not only Islam which had made converts from the English by the early twentieth century. A few years before, both missionaries and officials had joined together to condemn a far more serious spiritual defection. In 1893 a short, plump, rather pretty grey-haired Englishwoman had arrived to an extraordinary reception in India. Annie Besant, whose name was already a household word in England, had arrived to preach her new faith, Theosophy, which she claimed distilled the ancient wisdom of both East and West.

For Annie Besant herself the role of religious leader presented an extraordinary volte-face from her previous career. Married at seventeen to a clergyman, she had progressed from doubts to atheism and finally left him to become a leading light of the Secular Society founded by Charles Bradlaugh. In 1885 she and Bradlaugh had stood trial together for publishing a pamphlet advocating birth control, and Annie had been hailed as the Devil's disciple, if not as the Devil herself. After Secularism

Two incarnations of Annie Besant: (*left*) as militant atheist, caricatured with her friend, Charles Bradlaugh, 1877, and (*right*) as the Theosophists' leader, 1897.

and Malthusianism, she had then taken up Fabian socialism under the influence of George Bernard Shaw, and had been the heroine of a dozen more radical *causes célèbres*.

Then, in 1889, W. T. Stead of the *Pall Mall Gazette* had sent her to review a book by Mme Blavatsky, founder of the Theosophical Society. She had been so gripped by the book, entitled *The Secret Doctrine*, that she had gone to visit the founder in person. There, mesmerised by Mme Blavatsky's throbbing voice and compelling eyes, she had become a convert to the doctrines which Mme Blavatsky claimed to have received from the Masters, her mysterious spiritual advisers in the Himalayas. Shaw, horrified at the news, rushed round to her office at the *Pall Mall Gazette* to denounce Theosophy in general and Mme Blavatsky in particular. Annie Besant listened to her ex-mentor with calm amusement, and pointed out slyly that perhaps it was her change to a vegetarian diet like Shaw's which had enfeebled her mind. Two years later Mme Blavatsky had passed over to the spirit world, entrusting her earthly mission to her famous disciple; and Annie had decided to go to India to replenish her spiritual stock at source.

Hardly had she touched Indian soil than she announced to an enthusiastic Hindu audience that she had been a Hindu Brahmin in several previous existences. From then on her progress was positively vice-regal. In four months she covered 6,000 miles, visiting the sacred places of India and addressing huge audiences everywhere she went on the subject of India's ancient wisdom. Clearly such enthusiasm must be channelled. By 1898, with the help of subscriptions from several prominent Hindus, Annie Besant was able to set up her first Hindu college at Benares, opened, as the *Theosophical News* pointed out, on the auspicious seventh day of the seventh month. It was an immediate success, and Annie Besant's own lectures were a star attraction. True to the principles of Theosophy, she illustrated them with stories of both Indian and Western heroes of history and legend, including Abraham Lincoln and her old friend Charles Bradlaugh, and handed out both the *Theosophical News* and G. A. Henty's adventure stories as reading matter.

So successful was the school that she and her helpers were soon hoping to found a chain of educational establishments all over India, and with a view to this she arrived in 1901 on, as it were, the very doorstep of the Masters' abode in the Himalayas, Srinagar, the capital of Kashmir. Here she was to do battle with one of the most redoubtable of Edwardian missionaries, Canon C. E. Tyndale-Biscoe.

Tyndale-Biscoe had arrived in Kashmir ten years before. Like Annie Besant he came from a professional English family with county connections and, like Annie Besant, he had experienced at first hand some of the trials of middle-class Victorian life. In Annie Besant's case it had been marriage at seventeen to a domineering, bigoted husband. In Tyndale-Biscoe's, five years (as he wrote in his autobiography) 'of HELL' at his public school, Bradfield, warding off bullies and buggers with his fists. At Cambridge, where he coxed the Cambridge boat, he had heard the great American evangelists Moody and Sankey speak, and had gone to offer himself to the Cambridge Mission. They sent him to work in the East End of London (darkest London being the traditional training ground for mission work), where he enthusiastically introduced his boys to cold baths and boating on the Thames. In 1890 he went to the C.M.S. to offer his services for darkest Africa, but was told his health would not stand it. Instead they sent him to Kashmir.

Tyndale-Biscoe arrived at Srinagar to find in the C.M.S. school where he was to teach everything he most disapproved of. First of all the school and the pupils were filthy. The pupils, high-class Brahmins, clearly did not believe that cleanliness was next to Godliness. Then he looked at his pupils' faces and received a worse shock. Vice was written all over them – the same vice he had seen at his hated public school. 'Now I knew at last why God allowed me to go to Hell.' Then he had been 'a weak helpless child', but now he was 'a Man and top dog, thank God'.[8]

Tyndale-Biscoe spent the next few years in an all-out attack on stench and sodomy. Clothes and boys were scrubbed, compulsory games and compulsory swimming introduced – part of what Tyndale-Biscoe liked to call 'the surgery of muscular action'. Special charts were set up to mark progress of mind, body and soul for each boy, and since Kashmiri schoolboys showed an unhealthy passion for lessons as opposed to games, higher marks were awarded for body than for mind. Soon Tyndale-Biscoe had them all prepared to jump, at a whistle, from the school windows into the river, and sculling like water beetles across the Kashmiri lakes.

BOY'S CHARACTER FORM SHEET

Name .... *Son of* .... *Entered Central School* .... *Class* .... *193* . *Entered* .... *Branch School*

Roll No. .... *Occpn. of* { *Guardian* / *Father* } .... *Left* ,, ,, ... *Class* .... *193* . ... *193* . *Left* .... *193* .

Age .... *Years* .... *Months* .... *Days* .... *Date of Marriage* .... *Father's Salary* / *Probable Loot*

Full Marks		
	Date	
	Class	
	Age	
	Average Age of Class	
	Position in Class	
	Ears and Throat	
	Eyesight	
	Teeth	
	Height	
	Weight	
	Chest Measurement	
	General Health	
	Tutor	
150	English	MIND
150	Urdu or Hindi	
150	Persian or Sanskrit	
300	Science and Drawing	
150	Mathematics	
150	History } or { Physiology	
150	Geography } or { Hygiene	
100	Caligraphy	
300	General Knowledge	
1,600	Total	
400	Gymnastics	BODY
200	Boating	
200	Swimming	
100	Headers	
200	Games: Cricket, Football, etc.	
100	Manual Labour	
1,200	Total	
200	Scripture	SOUL
400	Obedience, Respectfulness, Truthfulness, and Honesty | Masters	SOUL — CONDUCT TOWARDS
300	Pluck, Unselfishness and Good Temper | Boys	SOUL — CONDUCT TOWARDS
300	*Esprit de Corps* | School	SOUL — CONDUCT TOWARDS
300	Duty to Neighbours | City	SOUL — CONDUCT TOWARDS
	Colour of Heart	SOUL — CONDUCT TOWARDS
1,500	Total	
200	Deportment	SOUL — MANNERS
100	Absence of Dirty Tricks	SOUL — MANNERS
100	Self-control	SOUL — MANNERS
400	Total	SOUL — MANNERS
200	Cleanliness and Tidiness { Body / Clothes }	SOUL — DISCIPLINE
100	Attendance	SOUL — DISCIPLINE
100	Punctuality	SOUL — DISCIPLINE
400	Total	SOUL — DISCIPLINE
5,100	Grand Total	
	Signature of Principal	
	Remarks	

Canon C. E. Tyndale-Biscoe, a Maker of Men; and the character sheets from his school in Srinagar. Highest marks were awarded for progress of soul.

But it was Tyndale-Biscoe's attempt to bring progress in the third category, soul, which was to lead him to his clash with Annie Besant. Srinagar was notoriously one of the dirtiest cities in the Empire, the streets piled high with ordure. In 1901, after a particularly violent epidemic of cholera, Tyndale-Biscoe decided the time had come to show his boys the joys of community service. They would take spades and shovels and clean the streets themselves as an example to the rest of the citizens. Muscular Christianity in action. It was this daring step in Tyndale-Biscoe's avowed programme of Making Men of his Brahmin pupils which brought Annie Besant hot-foot to Srinagar from Benares. Tyndale-Biscoe, she had been told, was deliberately forcing Brahmin staff and boys to do sweeper's work against all of the rules of their caste.

Tyndale-Biscoe went round to explain his ideas to Annie Besant, at the Maharajah's palace where she was staying, but the interview was unsuccessful. Tyndale-Biscoe's memoirs do not breathe a spirit of tact, and Annie Besant was at the height of her enthusiasm for Brahmin wisdom. She refused to visit the mission school. Instead, with the Maharajah's blessing, she set up a rival Theosophical college just across the river. Tyndale-Biscoe's pupils and masters deserted to it in droves. Finally he was left with only about half a dozen boys and a handful of lower masters.

Tyndale-Biscoe seems to have had a kind of breakdown. Doctors ordered him to leave Kashmir and he spent three months travelling round India and Ceylon, where he slowly recovered his spirits. All the C.M.S. schools he visited confirmed his view that what was needed in India was not cramming but character-building. By the time he returned in good health to Kashmir he found that the school had recovered too. Annie Besant's rival college had lost its meteoric popularity, and many of the renegade students were begging to re-enlist as 'Biscoe boys'. Two years after the struggle, Tyndale-Biscoe was able to report with triumph that his school had doubled its previous peak to 1,600 pupils. 'Since Mrs Besant', he wrote, 'had promised her Brahmin friends to be reborn a Brahmin, we hope she might find herself in our school so we could teach her the joys of cleaning a filthy city.'[9]

Whether she ever did, Theosophical history does not relate, but she was to go through some startling incarnations in her remaining lifespan as Annie Besant. In 1909, she split the Theosophical Society by announcing the advent of a new Messiah, in the shape of a handsome fourteen year old Brahmin boy, called Krishnamurti. Many of her Hindu followers left and the English press had a field day over Annie's attempts to become a Holy Mother by adopting Krishnamurti legally as her ward. She was not helped by the fact that her fellow Theosophist leader and would-be guardian, the Rev. Charles Leadbetter, had already been in hot water for the kind of thing Tyndale-Biscoe most disliked – trouble with boys. Annie defended him loyally.

By 1911 she decided her role as Indian educator could not be divorced from politics, and became a passionate campaigner for Indian Home Rule. In 1918, after a brief period of internment by the British, she was elected the first President of the Indian National Congress.

Her final incarnation, however, was one which Tyndale-Biscoe might have approved. In 1916 she had called for the foundation of an Indian Boy Scout troop.

Biscoe boys jumping from the school thirty feet into the river below.

Baden-Powell, inventor of the Boy Scouts, rejected the plan on the grounds that there were not enough European Scouts to go round as leaders. Annie Besant indignantly set up her own Besant Scouts. By 1921 Baden-Powell had thought better of it, and Annie's Scouts were incorporated into the main Boy Scout movement. Annie herself was made Chief Scout Commissioner for India. She took up her new office with enthusiasm, wearing a special sari woven of khaki silk edged with green. In 1932 she received the supreme Scout honour from Baden-Powell, who made her a Silver Wolf. She died the following year at Adyar, the Theosophical Society's headquarters, free at last to rejoin the Masters and Mme Blavatsky in the Himalayas.

Meanwhile, in the Himalayan foothills, Tyndale-Biscoe doggedly continued the uphill work of turning Brahmin boys into Men. By 1930 his school was one of the most famous in the Indian sub-continent, the showpiece of the Church Missionary Society. Like Annie Besant, he earned Baden-Powell's highest accolade. 'Here,' Baden-Powell wrote, 'was a man who could put backbone into jellyfish.' He lived into a ripe old age, retiring in 1947 with the coming of Indian independence, and left Srinagar in style, drawn to the station in a carriage by thirty of his old boys,

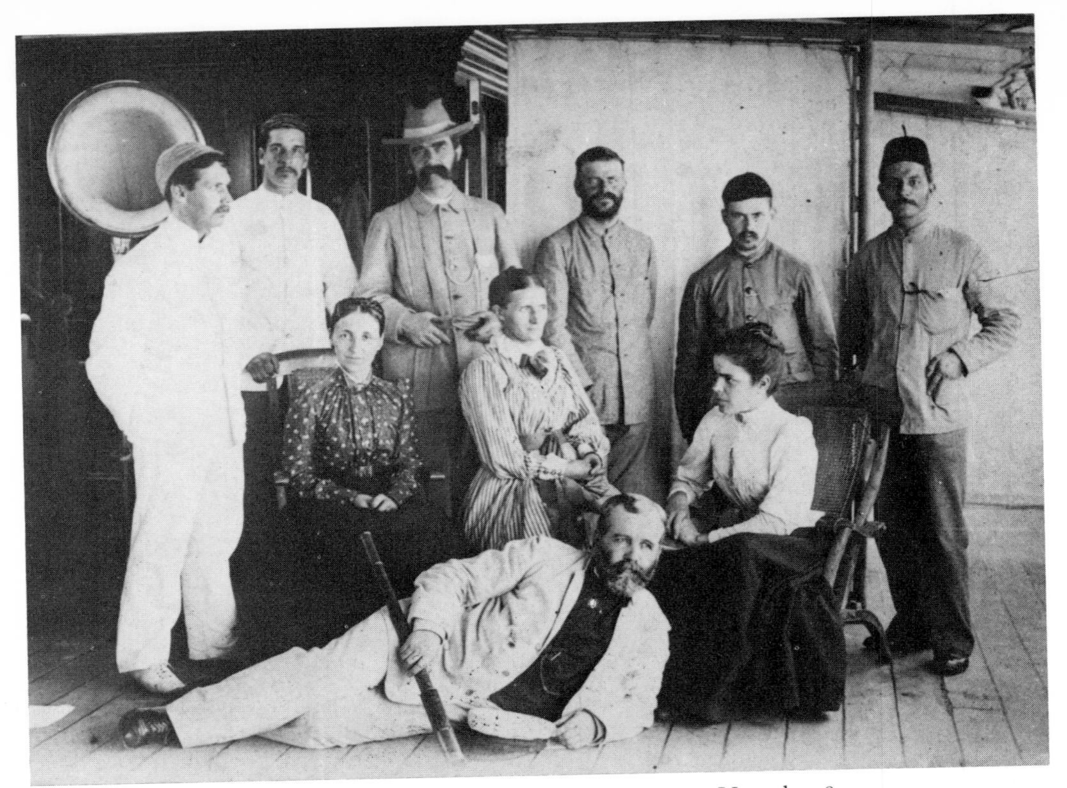

Bishop Tucker (*standing third left*) and fellow missionaries *en route* to Uganda, 1897.

preceded by the school band. From India he sailed to Africa, where he spent the last two years of his life in Rhodesia with his son, and was, his son recorded, 'much impressed by the vigour with which Africans rode their bicycles'.

Africa had been Tyndale-Biscoe's first choice – in one sense he might have done better there. Neither he nor Annie Besant had made much dent on India's old religious beliefs. Annie Besant had tried bridge-building on the astral plane; Tyndale-Biscoe, character-building. By 1900, most of the English missionary societies admitted they had made little headway wherever the great rival religions of the East – Buddhism, Hinduism, Islam – had already taken root. The most fruitful grounds for mission work had been the Pacific, and Africa south of the Sahara. In both of these the scramble by the European powers had been preceded or followed by a more or less amicable scramble between the Christian missions.

The most spectacular scramble had occurred in Uganda where, to everyone's horror in 1890, a full-scale religious war broke out between rival groups of Catholic and Protestant converts. Had the missions created another Belfast in Central Africa? Uganda was annexed to solve the problem, after an unusually heated debate in Parliament. 'It was no part', said the Radical, Labouchère, 'of England's duty to stop Protestant and Catholic missionaries cutting each other's throats.' The two main groups, the Catholic White Fathers, and the C.M.S., now maintained an uneasy truce from their rival hills outside Kampala, under a carefully neutral and increasingly godless *Pax Britannica*. 'Confound all these parsons,' wrote Sir Hesketh Bell after a few months as governor. Churchill, on his official visit in 1907,

The brick-and-thatch Anglican cathedral at Namirembe outside Kampala.

was told that if he visited one bishop he must visit all the others, and protested that he would not be dragged here, there and everywhere 'like a blasted starfish'. He was deeply impressed, however, by the mission schools and huge congregations he met everywhere he went, and especially by the burly and venerable figure of Bishop Alfred Tucker, head of the Anglican Mission.

Bishop Tucker, who looked and dressed like a Norfolk squire, had arrived in Uganda at the height of the civil war and had been a key figure in settling the dispute. His iron frame had survived seventeen years of tramping and camping across his vast diocese, wading through swamps and rivers, crossing mountain ranges and deserts, and carrying everywhere – as well as his Bible – his box of water colours. Before taking Holy Orders he had been a painter by profession. At fifty-nine, he boasted, he could still ride six hours in the saddle from one mission station to another, and then play three sets of tennis and win them all. Under his bracing leadership the Anglican Mission had gone from strength to strength. It now had nearly 100,000 converts, many of whom became in their turn lay teachers and preachers to the remotest tribes of Uganda and beyond. It would soon be possible, Tucker hoped, for the missionary element to die out altogether, leaving a self-propagating, self-sufficient Protestant church – on Anglican lines of course. He had already proposed putting the C.M.S. in Uganda under the control of the largely African Church Synod, much to some of his English colleagues' dismay.

Uganda was a phenomenon, everyone agreed. Nowhere else in Africa had missions found such fruitful soil – a centralised kingdom ripe for conversion. In Livingstone's old territory further south, progress among the fragmented tribes devastated by years of slave-trading, had been slow and difficult. The first group to respond to Livingstone's appeal had been the Universities Mission to Central Africa. This strange offshoot of the High Anglican Tractarian Movement of the mid-nineteenth century had sailed up the Zambezi with Livingstone in 1861. Their leader, Bishop Mackenzie, was soon faced with a classic missionary problem: how to avoid getting drawn into tribal warfare. A report of his daring attack on the Yao to rescue captured slaves brought down all the wrath of the great Dr Pusey. Christianity, the U.M.C.A. was told severely, was not spread by doing but by suffering. But within months the poor bishop and most of his band had died of fever anyway. His successor, Bishop Tozer, described by Livingstone scornfully as 'a vegetarian, non-resistance man', decided to recall the mission to the coast at Zanzibar until better times.

They returned to the interior in 1875 and established a shaky foothold on an island called Likoma, halfway down Lake Nyasa, hoping here to escape involvement in the tribal battles of the mainland. They did not, however, escape the mosquitos and died like flies in the '80s and '90s of malaria and blackwater fever. Their high death rate stemmed partly from the missionaries' belief that they could only make converts among the African villagers by living as simply as their flock. They were paid tiny stipends, lived in mud huts, ate native food and were all celibate. 'It was pathetic', wrote Harry Johnston, after a visit to Likoma, 'to see highly educated men from Oxford and Cambridge hollow-eyed and fever-stricken, crouching in little huts which no native chief would deign to occupy.'[10]

The Scots missionaries in the 'little Arcadia' at Blantyre (at the south end of the lake) were criticised for going to the other extreme. 'Riding around in machilas, with troops of native savages dangling behind them,' wrote one English visitor, 'they have the best houses, stores, workshops, gardens and anything else worth having, all paid for by their friends at home.'[11] They also interfered more in politics, as Harry Johnston had found when he was appointed Commissioner to British Central Africa in 1891. He had a prolonged tussle with the head of the Blantyre mission, Dr Clement Scott, who tended, he wrote, to ignore the existence of any other authority. The quarrel was patched up more or less after 'a great deal of tea-drinking, early dining and church-going' on Johnston's part, plus 'a timely subscription towards the mission hospital'.[12]

Just as formidable, though further removed from government, was Dr Robert Laws of the Free Church Scots mission on the western shore of Lake Nyasa. A bearded Aberdonian of few words and phenomenal energy, he had been in central Africa since 1875 and had never lost faith, unlike many early twentieth-century missionaries, that Christianity and Western civilisation must go hand-in-hand. His great industrial training school at Livingstonia was intended as a powerhouse of economic and moral reform, with the wonders of science enlisted to 'lead souls to Christ' – Livingstonia had the second hydro-electric scheme in Africa.[13] Nothing could have been in greater contrast to the High Anglicans across the lake. 'It is the root error of the day,' their bishop, Dr Hine, once confided, 'that missions exist to teach trades and make the natives "useful".'[14]

Bishop John Hine of the Universities Mission to Central Africa with his cats.

Though there is little doubt that it was the practical Scots missions who proved the most effective proselytisers, infusing the lake region with a stern Nonconformist ethic that lasted far beyond the Edwardian age, it is difficult not to admire that other extreme – the odd mixture of unworldliness, liturgical snobbery and 'hopeless altruism', as Harry Johnston saw it – of the U.M.C.A. And no one embodies it more likeably than John Hine, a frail gentle man who seems to have strayed into central Africa from Trollope's Barchester. Hine represents the opposite pole to Alfred Tucker's robust broad-church Anglicanism, though he knew him well and liked him. He got on remarkably well, too, with his Scottish colleagues, Laws and

Scott, preaching often in the church at Blantyre, a stunning asymmetrical Byzantine brick edifice designed by Scott himself. Like Laws, he had trained as a doctor before taking Holy Orders, and was the U.M.C.A's first medical missionary, a double role he often found overwhelming after he became bishop in 1897.

'Church bells ringing for evensong and so on and so on,' reads one hurried letter from Hine to the U.M.C.A. headquarters. 'Eyre seedy, W.P.J. [Johnson] very seedy, Glossop in bed 104°, W.Williams state of collapse with bilious colic – three boys ill. One lady shaky. Bustle, fuss, bother. Hoorah. Get away tomorrow to Unangu's peaceful hilltop – no more sick people for three weeks.'[15] (Unangu was the far from peaceful mission station which Hine had pioneered a few years before among the Yao, who were still given to burning witches and raiding for slaves.)

Yet no one ever caught better than Hine the 'romance of missions', the almost idyll-like quality of those early days at Likoma. Up at sunrise for matins and breakfast, then Bible instruction outdoors under the baobab trees with a tame stork listening in. (The Africans were introduced to the gospels in three stages: first as hearers, then as catechumens, then as baptised Christians – the High Anglicans prided themselves on the thoroughness of their preparation.) The rest of the morning would be spent in his dispensary, dealing with everything from surgery to drawing teeth, the latter operation usually attracting a delighted ring of spectators. In the afternoon he would play the harmonium for his friend Archdeacon Chauncy Maples, who was teaching his pupils canticles of his own composition ('rather a trial', Hine confessed). Then the two men would stride out together to visit the sick in the villages nearby. After evensong, the communal dinner. Maples, then head of the mission, would start to carve, then catch some remark and 'with his elbows on the table, a carving knife in one hand, fork in the other, his eyes fixed on the horizon looking out over the figure of the mad cook grovelling about in his kitchen, gazing into the far distant hills above the lake, he would talk for ten minutes, correcting an error or explaining a difficulty . . . till at last a murmur of protest recalled him to his task'.[16]

Even the most fascinating theological debate could not make Anglicans forget their stomachs and sometimes envy the fleshpots of Blantyre: butter, cheese, fresh vegetables. Hine vividly recalled one Likoma 'banquet' offered to an official government party proceeding down the lake – scrawny native chickens 'gaunt, untrussed, unadorned', preceded by the water in which they had been boiled as 'soup'. 'Like Nebuchadnezzar's meal of grass, it might have been wholesome but it was not nice.' From then on it was noticeable that official visits were always brief. Yet, Hine wrote:

> What more beautiful view on earth 'than to stand on one of the hills of Likoma and look over the mighty waters of Nyasa, to watch the sun going down forty miles across the lake, and hear the wild cry of the fish-eagles whirling round your head . . . or the thud-thud of the distant *ngoma* in some native village by the shore. And there all around you the great mystery of heathen life and the thought that in God's own time you had been sent to bring the light into the darkness.'[17]

Bishop Hine with U.M.C.A. mission staff at Zanzibar – he found his female staff very trying.

Chauncy Maples drowned in the lake in 1896 on his way home from ordination as bishop and for Hine, who succeeded him, things were never quite the same. He was not a natural leader, and would often have preferred the company of his cat Jorkins to some of his staff. The U.M.C.A. lady volunteers were a particular trial, always falling in love with the Scottish engineers who ran the African Lakes Company's boats. (The African Lakes Company also dated from Livingstone's time. It had been set up by philanthropic businessmen to supply the commerce side of Commerce and Christianity, and thirty years later the two were nearly always at odds.) But the troubles at Likoma were nothing to the troubles at the U.M.C.A.'s main mission at Zanzibar, where Hine was transferred as bishop in 1901. The place was full of Europeans who thought only of social pleasures, the influence of Islam was spreading among the natives and the U.M.C.A. itself was a hornet's nest of squabbles.

> Thirty women all wanting to pull in different directions [he groaned]. What a blessed thing it must be to live on Mount Athos, where no females have ever set foot for centuries, and all the hens are cocks and all the cats are toms. . . . I could hold my Likoma staff pretty well in hand, but one can't move here without giving offence or . . . causing someone to resign.[18]

Cleanliness next to Godliness: the U.M.C.A. mission compound in Zanzibar with the cathedral behind.

After six years he resigned himself, worn out by his fellow *mzungu* (white men) and malaria, and arranged for a brilliant young canon, Frank Weston, to succeed him. Weston had just produced what Hine thought a 'rather perilously speculative book' on Anglican doctrine and sometimes seemed unbearably convinced of his own rightness, but at least he had the energy and character to control the mission. Where in the world, Hine asked his old friend Canon Travers at the U.M.C.A. headquarters in London, was he to go himself? He could not bear to give up mission work. A medical post in Papua perhaps, where the Anglicans had one of their most promising missions. Or perhaps he could pioneer a new station in Mozambique by the Rovuma river – but that would be in Weston's diocese and might embarrass him. Ah, if only he could go back to Likoma. But there was a new bishop there called Trower, who had turned out a 'monstrous cuckoo'.

Hine spent the next year, miserably, among the bridge-playing Anglicans of Constantinople. Then in 1909, central Africa came once again to the rescue. The U.M.C.A. had decided to celebrate its fiftieth anniversary by opening a new mission field beyond the Zambezi into Northern Rhodesia. Rhodesia, north of the Zambezi, was already thinly colonised by other missions, notably the London Missionary Society (low-church Wesleyan), the Primitive Methodists (American) and of course the ubiquitous Catholic White Fathers. But there seemed plenty of room for the true Anglican Church to find converts too. The benefit would be

Bishop Hine picnicking in Northern Rhodesia, 1910. He walked nearly 3,000 miles in two years.

two-fold, as the Bishop of Glasgow told the U.M.C.A. meeting, for nothing would heal English civilisation, nothing restore efficiency to the Church 'but that compelling force which drives men out into the wilderness. . . .'[19]

Nothing bears sadder witness to the decline of that compelling force than the fact that the new crusade was to be headed by a frail 51-year-old retired bishop. But Hine, like an old war-horse scenting battle, was overjoyed. He deluged the mission headquarters with his plans – schools, hospitals, helpers and a cathedral at Livingstone (the capital of the colony). 'Just give me a few good men . . . sound, strong healthy Christians. I don't want any "mawkish ritualists", but people with clear heads and firm faith and good spirits and good appetites.' He would have a 'simple Gospel with no decorations'. Of course there was already 'the Protestant dissenter and the American schismatic rampant in the land'. He would have to deal faithfully with both. As for the white colonists, they would be a stimulant. His mission would be a mission for all – 'there must be neither Jew nor Greek, we must be ready to minister to white as well as black'. No doubt the white tribes were as heathen as the aborigines.[20]

So in 1910 Hine, accompanied by two helpers, set off to preach the Anglican version of the Christian message to a country of 290,587 square miles, two and a half times the size of England. In the next two years he was to walk nearly 3,000 miles across it, back in his 'native element', talking to village headmen, district commissioners and tribal chiefs, and visiting his fellow missions. The most widespread of the Protestant missions, the London Missionary Society, had fallen, Hine was sad to discover, into the usual errors of Protestant dissenters – worldliness and teaching 'trades'.

> They live in the most palatial houses and their expenses on themselves must be very great. They are all married and have families. They teach their boys to do good carpentry, but I cannot see what advantage that can be, as there's no market for skilled labour and the boys go drifting far away, seeking work and not finding it. . . . However, I don't doubt that they do their best.[21]

Far more serious, however, was the problem he was to encounter with the 'white tribe' at Livingstone, who were also his official parishioners. One of Hine's first official acts had been to lay the foundation stone of the new memorial church of St Andrew's. To his astonishment he discovered that the Livingstone Church Council wished to reserve the church for white worship only. Shared worship with whites would encourage Africans to think they were equal. The Council members viewed 'with dismay' the 'unhygienic' prospect of their children kneeling and sitting where all sorts and conditions of natives had knelt and sat. Deeply shocked, Hine refused to consecrate the church until the principle of racial equality before God was recognised by the parishioners. As to hygiene,

> I think the Church Council forget – forgive me for reminding them – that I myself am a doctor of medicine of London University and have had more experience (in the last twenty-two years) of native diseases than any of the medical Residents here. I should not therefore be likely or so foolish to admit anyone into the church whose health was such that I felt any risk attached to his presence there.[22]

What, he asked the settlers, would Livingstone think of his memorial church if he had known such restrictions were placed on it?

The settlers did not care what Livingstone might have thought. Only the intervention of Lord Selborne, the High Commissioner for South Africa, and the combined weight of the Archbishops of Canterbury and Capetown thrown behind Hine, compelled the Church Council to give in. Compared to such battles a twenty-mile trek through swamps and tsetse-infested bush was sheer relief for Hine. 'I am better among native races than pushing bigoted colonists,' he wrote. He set up his first mission stations in areas as remote as possible from white settlement, among the Tonga and Nsenga, after careful consultation with the other Northern Rhodesian missions. However misguided some of their views might appear to a High Anglican, at least they shared a common purpose. Whereas 'to the white colonists', wrote Hine sadly, 'any kind of heretical teaching is permissible, so long as the teaching is such as to keep the natives down, to prevent them from being anything but . . . drudge and servant. . . .'[23]

In autumn 1913, just as Hine was about to set off to confer with the Primitive Methodists on a joint translation of the New Testament into the Chila dialect, an extraordinary ecclesiastical thunderbolt rent the sky of Central Africa. It was thrown by Hine's chosen successor at Zanzibar, Bishop Frank Weston, and its target – ostensibly, that is – was a conference held at a little mission station at Kikuyu in the East African Highlands run by the Church of Scotland mission. The conference was attended by two Anglican bishops, Bishop Peel of Mombasa and Bishop Willis of Uganda (Tucker's successor), and representatives from most of British East Africa's dissenting missions. By 1910 the scramble for souls had brought East Africa no less than twenty different varieties of Christian mission. The aim of the conference was to work out as far as possible sound policy on a number of questions: native education, discipline, attitudes towards tribal customs, attitudes towards the white settlers who made incessant demands for more native labour, and religious instruction. The problem of the latter had become acute, partly because of the settlers' demands, for Africans now travelled willy-nilly across British East Africa to work on settlers' farms and would find themselves under the spiritual aegis of a different religious denomination from the one at home. Embarrassing evangelical differences were revealed.

At the end of the two-day conference, episcopal and dissenting missions agreed to work towards some common form of Protestant service and religious instruction. The conference was wound up with a service of Holy Communion, administered by Bishop Peel. A Scottish missionary, the Rev. Norman Maclean, wrote home jubilantly to report the conference's success in moving towards church unity in East Africa. How news of it reached Weston is not clear, but the report he received served as a match to a highly inflammable state of mind.

Ever since he had read theology at Cambridge, Weston had alarmed his colleagues by the intensity of his religious views. His first act on arriving at the mission at Zanzibar in 1898 had been to denounce his bishop for incompetence. The bishop was removed, which led in turn to Hine's removal from his beloved diocese of Likoma, back to Zanzibar. Unlike Hine, whose Anglo-Catholicism had become tinged with good-humoured tolerance and a keen sense of the priorities in Africa, Weston's fervour never abated. An inspiring speaker and a brilliant administrator, he terrified his colleagues by his habit of doing his thinking on paper and then publishing it. Hence the 'rather perilously speculative' book on doctrine of 1908. Like Hine, he tramped ceaselessly round his diocese, living largely on plum puddings which, as he pointed out, were easy to pack, very nutritious and could be eaten without cooking. But diocesan cares were not enough to keep him from concerning himself with the state of the Anglican Church in general.

Early in May 1913, laid up with fever, he wrote to Hine's old friend, Canon Travers of the U.M.C.A. headquarters, in deep concern about a most pestilent and dangerous book called *Foundations*, by W. G. Streeter, which he had just read. It raised the horrid spectre of Modernism (willingness to adjust church teaching in line with contemporary thought). Travers and Daryl Stone, principal of Pusey House, combined to soothe him: *Foundations* was the wrong battle-ground for an

Left Bishop Frank Weston of Zanzibar arrives in London, 1914, to denounce heresy.

Below Supplies for the British Army in Northern Rhodesia. Weston led his own troop of African carriers through the war without losing a man.

attack on Modernism. Then in August the news of the Kikuyu conference reached Zanzibar. 'Mombasa and Uganda have joined a new church,' wrote Weston to the surprised Travers, 'and (*D.V.*) we shall go out of communion with them unless they repent.'[24] In October he launched his bombshell, in the shape of an open letter to the Bishop of St Albans published in *The Times*, entitled '*Ecclesia Anglicana*: What Does She Stand For?'

'The Anglican Church', he announced, was 'entirely unfit to send missionaries to heathen or Mohammedan lands', owing to her 'chaotic system of Truth'. The Church at home was in mental chaos. The proof was, firstly, the iniquitous *Foundations* and, secondly the conference at Kikuyu, whose aim was to establish a new united Protestant church of East Africa and Uganda. For the two bishops, Peel and Willis, to collaborate in this non-episcopal Church was, Weston announced, to be guilty of 'heresy and schism'. He called on the Primate, Archbishop Randall Davidson, to indict them.[25]

'*Ecclesia Anglicana*' was followed by a letter to the Archbishop of Canterbury himself. 'It is quite intolerable, my lord, that you in England should send us out to the labour and suffering of isolated missionary work', while allowing heresy to flourish at home (a reference to Streeter's book). The Kikuyu conference had caused dismay and confusion to 'thousands of Africans', who must be 'publicly undeceived'. (Here Weston's imagination seems to have carried him away somewhat, since there was no evidence that any Africans in British East Africa or Zanzibar had heard of the Kikuyu conference, except for the printers of the U.M.C.A. press.) A private letter to Davidson added rather touchingly: 'Please do not think I am suffering from the climate.'

Hine in Northern Rhodesia certainly did. 'Weston must be mad. I hope he won't excommunicate me for collaborating with the Primitive Methodists,' he wrote to Travers, only half jokingly. He found the tone of Weston's letter to Davidson 'horrid . . . all that posing as a martyr. . . . disgusts me, but of course it appeals to women.'[26] Hine's mysogynist streak had not abated with age.

As a controversy, Weston's attack proved, unfortunately, to have an even wider appeal. Not since the days of Livingstone or the Uganda debate had the public taken

so much interest in missions. All through the autumn and spring of 1914 the battle raged in the columns of *The Times*, while Randall Davidson behind the scenes tried to calm the excitable Weston and soothe the insulted Willis and Peel. In December 1913 another attack from Weston in *The Times* drew the venerable Bishop Tucker, now retired to Durham, into the fray. If Bishop Willis was a heretic, he declared stoutly, 'So am I. If he is a schismatic, so am I. If he is to be sent to the stake, I am prepared to go with him.'[27]

In February 1914 Weston at last arrived in England to be met by a barrage of press at Charing Cross station. To Davidson's relief he was now 'open to wiser opinions than those he had in the isolation of Zanzibar given utterance to', and with careful diplomacy he managed to parry Weston's demands for a synod by promising a consultative committee at Lambeth in July. It opened on the 27th with a full complement of church dignitaries led by Cosmo Lang, now Archbishop of York, who had preached a powerful sermon – 'Blessed are the Peacemakers' – at the height of the controversy. But by now public interest had suddenly lapsed. A more serious threat to peace had materialised – Bishop Hine, finally on his way home after twenty-five years in central Africa, was travelling slowly across Spain visiting cathedrals. He crossed over into France to find the French army mobilising, and retreated in a hurry.

By the time the Lambeth conference had come to its decision – a compromise which predictably left both sides indignant – Weston had discovered a new enemy, as great a threat to the Church as Modernism: Prussia Incarnate. He hurried back to his mission in Zanzibar to find the German army from Tanganyika had interned most of his staff and had flogged and dispersed his African flock. Determined to fight Prussia Incarnate in person, he raised a corps of African carriers to take supplies up-country to the British defending the western border of Rhodesia – he was to lead them through the war without losing a man. Even this did not reconcile him to the other enemy; halfway through 1915 he learnt that the arch-Modernist Streeter had been given the post of Canon at Durham Cathedral. Weston at once publicly broke off communion with the Bishop of Durham.

After the war, there was to be another round against the two East African bishops. In 1920 they drew up the famous Bishops' Memorandum on the new order for compulsory native labour in Kenya. Though they deplored the recruiting methods used, they accepted the principle. Primed by J. H. Oldham, secretary of the International Missionary Conference, Weston launched a tremendous attack on the new legislation, entitled 'The Serfs of Great Britain'; a sequel to his wartime broadside against the Germans in East Africa: 'The Black Slaves of Prussia'. The order was cancelled by Churchill when he became Colonial Secretary in 1921.

In one sense it was another round also in that old evangelical debate: the relation of faith to work, of Christianity to 'usefulness'. To the majority of white colonists, as Hine had sadly noted, the question was academic. As one Kenyan settler had put it succinctly a few years before, 'A good system of compulsory labour would do more to raise the nigger in five years than twenty years of mission work.'[28]

Opposite John Samuel Swire, founding father of Butterfield and Swire.

In future, we must share the same bed, Celestials and terrestrials.
John Samuel Swire (1825–98)

Blessed commerce, the friend of the slave, the liberator of the oppressed.
John Holt, 1904

6

TRADERS

One of the things that struck Leonard Woolf during his journey out to Ceylon in 1904 was the odd malevolence shown to him and his fellow cadets by a stout English businessman from Colombo. Woolf and another cadet were having a pillow fight during one of the deck 'gymkhanas', each seated on a parallel bar, when Mr X, the businessman, who was the referee, suddenly whirled the bar violently round knocking them both to the ground, a joke which Woolf did not find funny.

The Singapore waterfront, early 1900s. *Opposite* Thomas Scott of Guthrie's, whose company built the main Singapore docks.

Once arrived in Colombo, however, Woolf thought he had discovered the reason behind the episode. Businessmen were socially outcasts, excluded by the three other English groups: planters, army officers and civil servants like himself. Only the grandest of tycoons would, it appeared, have been admitted as a member to the Colombo Club. 'In all of my seven years in Ceylon,' Woolf wrote, 'I never had a meal with a businessman.'[1] He does not seem to have had much regret.

Ceylon of course had long been governed from India and had inherited much of the imperial caste system at its most rigid (in Calcutta 'box-wallahs' rated only just above railway officials in social precedence). English officials, military and civil, preferred to ignore the commercial basis of England's oldest and most valuable slice of tropical Empire – the days of the nabobs were long past. Further east, however, Leonard Woolf would have found a very different social order indeed.

Singapore and Hong Kong, those two impressive monuments to English commercial enterprise, showed no embarrassment about their *raison d'être*. 'No one here talks anything but commerce,' lamented 'Mad' Ridley shortly after arriving in Singapore from Ceylon to run the Botanical Gardens.[2] And an Indian Army officer posted to Hong Kong to swell the garrison during the Boxer rising was puzzled to find that the merchant class was 'supreme', unlike India where 'almost every male is to be found either on the army or the civil list'. Not that this decreased social

demarcation lines. 'Why for instance should Mrs A. whose spouse exports tea be "haut ton", while Mrs B. whose husband imports cigars is not to be called on?' Even worse, he discovered that Indian army officers were not regarded as eligible dancing partners for merchants' daughters.[3]

Physically both cities were a triumph of enterprise over environment, 'touched with the magic wand of free trade', as English commentators liked to say. Hong Kong, once a barren rock, now crowded with tiers of warehouses, offices and banks rising above the packed harbour; Singapore, a swampy fishing village in Raffles' time, now the 'handiest city for business', as one American visitor wrote, that he'd ever been in – like a huge desk with each aspect of trade neatly pigeon-holed in its own street. The grid pattern of the streets still reflected Raffles' original plan for a town built like an Indian 'factory', though entrepreneurial exuberance had burst out in all the wrong places once his iron hand was removed.

Many of the leading merchant families had been there since Raffles' day. Like Guthrie's for instance, one of the most powerful. Alexander Guthrie had arrived in Singapore from the Cape in 1821, the year Raffles got his trading charter. The firm was now directed by his grandson-in-law, Thomas Scott.

In one respect, however, things had changed radically since Raffles' day. Trade not territory had been Raffles' declared aim. 'The extent of our possessions in India', he wrote, 'rendering further territory comparatively unimportant and perhaps objectionable.' But by 1860 the Singapore merchants were investing heavily in the Chinese tin-mining operations in the Malay States, and by 1870 they were calling on the English government to intervene to protect their investment from a series of civil wars largely precipitated by the Chinese miners. When Governor Ord remained obdurate, Thomas Scott and the other leading merchants resigned *en masse* from the Legislative Council. The next governor, Sir Andrew Clarke, proved highly sympathetic and by 1874 both Perak and Selangor had their British Residents in situ. The first British Resident in Selangor was James Guthrie Davidson, a great-nephew of Guthrie's founding father.[4]

By 1900 Guthrie's, like some of the other leading Singapore houses, had begun to extend their interests rapidly from tin to rubber, buying up half-grown plantations, investing in new ones and acting as agency houses for the rush of new companies that chased the boom. It was a case, as one commentator rather sourly remarked, of 'having made the cake, having it and eating it as well'. By 1910 one of Guthrie's plantations would be paying its directors 257 per cent.

Hong Kong's hinterland, by contrast, was tiny. The new territories of Kowloon were leased from China in 1898. Yet its taipans – literally, 'chief planks' – were richer and possibly grander still. Jardine Matheson – 'the Princely Hong' – could of

Henry Keswick (*centre*) and two future generations of Jardine's taipans – all descended from William Jardine – on the steps of his splendid baronial pile on the Peak, early 1900s.

course claim almost to have invented the place. It was William Jardine, a ship's surgeon, who in the 1830s had sent fast piratical craft carrying forbidden opium to prise open the China trade. Commercial enterprise, which soon brought indignant protests from the Chinese vice-consul to 'the Honourable Chieftainess of the Barbarians' (Queen Victoria) and finally to the impounding of the English merchants' goods. Palmerston's response had been a brisk naval action which forced the vice-consul to sign a trade treaty and to give up the rocky island opposite Kowloon as a safe refuge for British ships and men. The agreement having been successfully concluded, Palmerston thanked Mr Jardine for his help and advice.

By the Edwardian age the firm had long moved on from opium-trading to a vast medley of concerns, shipping, insurance, sugar-refining and banking; and Mr Jardine's grandson had now retired back to his estates in Perthshire, leaving management on the spot to their Scottish cousins, the Keswicks. The princely manners of the 'Princely Hong' still drove their trading competitors to distraction. John Samuel Swire, a tough Yorkshireman who had founded another famous combine, Butterfield and Swire, was spurred by rivalry with Jardine Matheson for most of his business life. 'We'll play the return match with J.M. & Co. and see who gets the best of the two innings,'[5] he wrote after a sharp tussle over the Yangtse river

Office of Swire's Taikoo Sugar Refinery, Hong Kong, founded partly to break a Jardine monopoly.

trade. His last competitive venture, the Taikoo sugar refinery set up expressly to break Jardine's control of the sugar market, nearly ran his own company on to the rocks in the '80s and '90s, In 1894 he defiantly declared a dividend after William Keswick had been reported to have said Swire's company could not afford one.

After John Samuel's death in 1898, some of the fire went out of the fight, though his business views were enshrined in a formidable series of memoranda for his successors. By 1910 John Samuel's son, Jack Swire, could report that Henry Keswick came up to him at the City Club and shook hands 'quite friendly like'. 'I think they know', he wrote, in explanation of previous brusqueness, 'that we have stronger men in the management at home and in the East than they have, and jealousy makes them feel green. . . .'[6]

Crowded on their rock like a colony of gulls, the business rivalries seemed fiercer than in Singapore, yet were usually conducted with at least a veneer of Oriental politeness. The new railway to the Peak, opened in 1888, had also helped to cool matters. Up there in the cool mists one could almost forget one was in the tropics. ('If you live on the Peak, your clothes rot; if you live in Victoria, *you* do', was a pithy Hong Kong comment.) And for business life down in the city, the Chinese themselves provided the perfect trading partners. All business with the mainland

Taipans take the train from the Peak, opened in 1888.

was still carried on through the traditional 'compradore' system. Many of the compradores came from dynasties as powerful and prosperous as the taipans themselves. Few taipans ever had to learn Chinese; all their dealings could be conducted in English, and the 'severe mental strain' involved in learning the language was, opined the director of the Hongkong and Shanghai Bank in 1904, 'too much to impose on a young man already struggling to learn his business'.[7]

Like the treaty ports further north, with their self-contained, self-sufficient English communities, Hong Kong remained curiously detached from internal rumblings in the Celestial Kingdom over the water. The Boxers, yes. There had been some unpleasantly close shaves and destruction of property, largely by the rescuing European troops. ('I am sorry to say English soldiers and sailors are as despicable a gang of thieves and villains as any', reported one of Swire's agents from Tientsin.)[8] Even when the Old Buddha, as the Chinese Empress was disrespectfully known, died in 1908 after a reign longer than Queen Victoria's, there seemed no serious cause for alarm. The 'Szechuan show' might develop into 'a pukka rebellion', reported Jack Swire. But when it did, Chinese business colleagues were able to reassure another English director that change would be effected quietly and without disturbance of trade.

A more constant irritant to the merchant colony in Hong Kong was interference from H.M.G. Hong Kong, like Singapore, had a Legislative Council, carefully weighted towards officials. In 1894 the unofficials, led by the masterful Henry Keswick, had tried to engineer a majority. Chamberlain had slapped them down sharply. Any step towards representative government would be wholly out of

Chun Koo Leang. Compradore to Swire's from 1884–1920.

place; especially since he noted that Mr Keswick's proposed unofficial new member was to be of English birth, an invidious exclusion of the Queen's Chinese subjects which he could not allow. A few years later there had been another clash when the governor, Sir Hercules Robinson, tried to increase the harbour dues – interference with the sacred status of Hong Kong as a great free port. This time the taipans won. 'The ideal governor', admitted an old Hong Kong resident, 'was the one who did least.' The merchants' *bête noire* had been the maverick Sir John Pope Hennessy, fresh from Africa, who had tried to involve the Chinese in governing the colony twenty years before. They still shuddered when they remembered him.

The appointment of Lugard as governor in 1906, another 'wild man' from Africa, was regarded with deep foreboding, reciprocated by Lugard himself. This mandarin world seemed horribly claustrophobic after his beloved open spaces in Nigeria. He was depressed to find all public opinion depended on the great merchant houses like Swire and Jardine Matheson. His most cherished improvement scheme, a university for Hong Kong, met with no support from the English business community until Swire's led the way with a generous £40,000. The reason, Lugard wrote rather bitterly, being Swire's wish to redeem themselves in Chinese opinion after an unfortunate incident on one of their boats. (He was wrong. Swire's Senior, J. S. Scott, though deploring English university education as a waste of time for English employees, was strongly in favour of it in Hong Kong, where it would allow wealthy Chinese to educate their sons in Western ideas and methods.)

Lugard's relations with the Hong Kong business community warmed a little when they both stood shoulder to shoulder to resist another piece of long-distance official interference. This time it was the Liberals, succumbing to one of their recurrent attacks of conscience. In 1908 the old bogey of the opium trade was raised again. It was still one of Hong Kong's main exports – 'For every soul our missionaries send to Heaven from China', declared a backbencher, 'the British government is now sending ten to Hell by this traffic.'[9] The new Liberal Colonial

Under Secretary, Colonel Seeley, hurriedly agreed that all opium dens in Hong Kong should immediately be closed down. Lugard, after personal investigation of the dens, inclined rather to William Jardine's often-quoted view that opium was not so much an evil as a comfort for the Chinese worker. He managed to negotiate a stay of execution by a long, well-reasoned dispatch to the Colonial Office.

In Singapore the Opium Commission set up to study the question was chaired by the forceful director of Guthrie's and took a tougher, more businesslike line. The Chinese, who 'were not children' should be allowed to take opium if they wished. Any official ban would only drive the traffic into more dangerous channels. To control the trade it should now be made a government monopoly. The profits resulting could be used towards the ultimate extinction of the opium traffic and would also provide a useful contribution towards government costs.

If opium cast an occasional disreputable shadow over the glittering progress of free trade in the East, no one, or almost no one, doubted it had all been worthwhile in the end. With or without territory, trade continued to show a healthy growth.

In much of newly acquired Africa, however, the situation seemed the reverse of Raffles' original dictum. Territory, yes, but where was the trade? What were the commercial benefits to be had from dealing with the Sudan, for instance, which largely consisted of thousands of miles of waterless desert; or east or central Africa, with their scattered tribes living at subsistence level? No wonder the Arabs had stuck to slave-trading and ivory – the only two commodities which repaid the transport costs. The brave talk in the '90s of untapped tropical wealth sounded remarkably hollow ten years later. Even Salisbury publicly voiced his doubts. 'The more our Empire expands and the more our imperial spirit grows, the more we must urge on all those who have to judge that these things are matters of *business*', he reminded a Tory audience, a note the Liberal press heartily approved. But of course it all depended on your view of business. Chamberlain had always argued that Africa was a long-term investment which would need government finance to prime the pump. If tropical trade did not exist it must be invented by planting new crops. Look what rubber was starting to do for Malaya, or tea for Ceylon, or bananas for the Canaries (instigated by his friend, the Liverpool shipping magnate Sir Alfred Jones).

The trouble was that many of Chamberlain's new colonial governors and officials in Africa had the traditional aristocrat's distaste for trade and traders. 'They are a class I much distrust,' Lugard wrote to Flora during his first tour in Nigeria.

> Their aim is purely dollars but they talk with an excess of unctuous righteousness ... I could never have the patience to sit at the same council table. They would loathe me and I them and I should forget and become sarcastic, which irritates a commercial magnate more than cayenne pepper does a dog.[10]

(Poor Lugard, he had at that point no inkling that in less than eighteen months he would find himself having to sit in council with the far more weighty commercial magnates of Hong Kong.)

Mary Kingsley (*centre*) in West Africa with friends, 1894.

In fact, the Niger Delta was one of the few places in tropical Africa which had proved its commercial value. In the early nineteenth century Liverpool had discovered a respectable alternative to the slave trade in West Africa – palm oil, expressed from the fruit of the wild palm trees which grew in limitless forests along the coast. Vegetable oil was vital for many of the new industrial processes, and for making soap. The drive for cleanliness at home in England and for godliness abroad (i.e. an end to the slave trade) neatly coincided, and after initial surprise the African chiefs and middle-men quickly adapted to dealing in the new commodity.

Part of the 'unctuous righteousness' Lugard so disliked among the traders stemmed from their genuine conviction that legitimate trade had helped drive out slavery. Though the old alliance between commerce and Christianity had broken down (partly because the English traders disliked the competition provided by the 'mission boys'), more than one trader had come to attribute a mystical significance to his work.

> Trade . . . the beneficent daughter of liberty and industry. The giver of human happiness! The creator of wealth. The supporter of social existence! Blessed commerce, the friend of the slave, the liberator of the oppressed. . . .[11]

wrote one Liverpool merchant, John Holt, in the same year as Lugard's complaint to Flora.

And in the late '90s the West African traders had received a welcome boost to self-esteem from that most remarkable of Victorian travellers, Mary Kingsley. This

A lonely trader looks out from his store in the Niger Delta.

intrepid spinster had set off, aged thirty, for the White Man's Grave for want, she wrote, of anything better to do with her life. She paddled her way single-handed down rapids and crocodile-infested rivers and fell in love in the process with the whole tribe of West African traders or 'palm oil ruffians', as they were traditionally known. Her best-selling book, *Travels in West Africa*, painted a humorous and likeable picture of the English trader, living his lonely hazardous life on hulks in the rivers of the Niger Delta. Never, she wrote, had she encountered such a chivalrous, humane, kindly class of men. And unlike the missionaries, whose effect on the natives was so disastrous, removing the old moral tribal restraints and failing to substitute new ones, the traders' contact with African natives did nothing but good. Even the English trade in liquor, so often attacked by the Nonconformist lobby in England, did no harm. The West African native knew how to hold his drink better than many a white man and the native palm oil wine was far more dangerous than trade gin.

In her second book, *West African Studies*, she went further. Encouraged by great Liverpool merchants like Sir Alfred Jones, she entered a brilliant if illogical plea that since trading interests were what was primarily at stake for England in West Africa, the traders themselves should be allowed to govern the country through a kind of council based in Liverpool. Government by officials would, she pleaded, be as harmful as the missionary influence and a great deal more expensive. The white man's burden was a burden on everyone, England and Africans alike. Chamberlain, who had longer experience of commerce than Mary Kingsley, rejected her plea as impracticable and Mary sadly departed in 1900 to do her bit for another embattled group of traders, the *uitlanders* of the Rand.

The cause of West Africa was still uppermost in her mind, however, judging from a letter to her friend John Holt. 'I do not think I am going back on W[est] A[frica] by going to S[outh] A[frica],' she wrote. 'Still, it is the grave of reputations, but if mine survives it will be stronger, and every ounce of popularity I get is thrown in to the side of the trader and the manufacturer of England and thus the official will not be able to say I am provincial in my views.' The letter's next paragraph gives a witty *aperçu* of a Colonial Institute dinner. 'An official not knowing who I was – a pretty thing . . . said: "Do you know Miss Mary Kingsley?" "I never met her," said I. "Oh," he said after a few words, "you know *we* say she smells of the Palm Oil Tub." Of course I never let on; but I'll palm oil tub them when I have done with them.'[12]

Mary Kingsley was to die before she could return to that particular battle. She caught typhoid from the Boer prisoners she was nursing in Pretoria a few months later. But her influence provides one leitmotif behind the battles over trade in West Africa during the next decade. The most violent was between two of her personal friends and heroes among the great trade lords of Liverpool, John Holt and Sir Alfred Jones. In fact only her tact and charm could have restored temporary good will between the two men. Holt was a Gladstonian Liberal who disliked Chamberlain intensely, along with 'stock exchange sharks' and all the other aspects of 'constructive imperialism'. Sir Alfred Jones was on excellent terms with the Colonial Secretary and had just received a knighthood in the Honours list for the new reign.

In the '90s they had been briefly allied against the third great trade lord in West Africa, Sir George Goldie of the Royal Niger Company. But the alliance had broken down when Holt, as head of a group of merchants called the African Association, had sold some of his boats to Jones on terms which Holt believed Jones later reneged on. From then on he had a deep distrust of Jones's commercial ethics, as well as his politics.

Both in fact had started life in the same shipping office as boys. But whereas Holt had gone from there to Africa to make his fortune, Jones had risen inside the firm to become manager and from there to make a bid for the famous shipping line of Elder Dempster. His declared aim was to monopolise the whole shipping trade of the West African ports, and by the 1890s he had absorbed all his competitors. Like many of the great Far Eastern shipping lines, he then set in operation a tough rebate system which effectively discouraged new competition, much to the anger of many of his fellow traders including Holt. (It is ironic that it was Jones whose help Chamberlain had enlisted to break another shipping company's monopoly in the West Indian trade.)

By 1900 he was known as the 'uncrowned king of West Africa', with a string of other interests as well – a banana company in the Canaries, hotels in the West Indies and oil mills in Liverpool. The year before he had helped found the Liverpool School of Tropical Medicine (a complement to Chamberlain's in London). He was President of the Liverpool Chamber of Commerce and consul for King Leopold's Congo Free State, whose trade he carried on a Belgian subsidiary of the Elder Dempster line.

Holt's business was built up more on land than sea. Starting in a trading post in Fernando Po, by the 1870s he had built up a chain of stores far up and down the West African coast and into the interior, directing his agents in person with a stern Nonconformist hand. ('Sir,' reads one of his earliest surviving letters, 'I am informed that you have been in a constant state of drunkenness ever since you arrived at Balla.... From a knowledge of your past habits I presume this to be a fact. Consider yourself dismissed without further ceremony.') He conceived a deep respect and liking for his African suppliers and trading partners, to whose muscle and enterprise he claimed he owed everything, and developed an almost fanatical belief in the benefits of free trade. He had fought several battles in its cause in the '80s and '90s: one against the famous King Ja-Ja of Opobo, who had tried to enforce a trading

Opposite top Sir Alfred Jones, the 'uncrowned king of West Africa'.

Left John Holt, pioneer West African trader.

Opposite below The Liverpool office where they both began work.

Below King Ja-Ja of Opobo, the European traders' most formidable rival in West Africa, in African and European dress.

monopoly over all the surrounding tribes (Ja-Ja was eventually deposed by Harry Johnston); another against Sir George Goldie's Royal Niger Company, whose monopoly and 'oppressive regime' were, Holt wrote to Salisbury, 'a scandal viewed from the enlightened standpoint of the nineteenth century'.[13]

The nineteenth century had closed with an ominous setback for 'enlightenment'. In 1899 one of Holt's agents in the French Congo had a consignment of rubber they had bought from some of the local natives seized by the local French Concessionaire

Company. Holt claimed the French action infringed the free trade guarantees of the Berlin Act of 1885. The French authorities dismissed his case. Both the land and the natural produce on it, they ruled, belonged to the Concessionaire Company. The legal battle brought Holt into touch with a freelance journalist called E. D. Morel, who was soon to involve him in his greatest battle yet.

Morel, like Jones and Holt, had started work as a Liverpool shipping clerk. He had joined Elder Dempster aged eighteen in 1891. Quick-witted and bilingual in French, he was soon put in charge of the department which dealt with trade from Leopold's Congo Free State. As he read the company confidential reports he gradually became convinced that there was something radically wrong with the way the colony was run. There were persistent reports of atrocities and the trade statistics were very odd indeed. Almost none of the normal trading goods were going into the Congo, except 'prodigious quantities of guns and ammunition', and

Left E. D. Morel, the moving spirit of the fierce battle for Congo reform.

Right The Royal Python (King Leopold) strangles the Congo native: *Punch*, 1906.

enormous amounts of wild rubber and ivory were coming out. How were the latter being paid for? Further investigation confirmed what he feared. A series of acts had transferred the land of the Congo from the natives to King Leopold's private ownership. All pretence at normal trade had ceased. Instead, vast profits were being produced by forced labour of a 'terrible and continuous kind'.

Morel went to Jones, told him of his conclusions and received a cold response. Holt's case, coming a few months later, seemed providential. Here was the same evil process at work, alienation of the natives' rights to their own land and the breakdown of bona fide free trade. If Holt could be enlisted, his case against the French Congo concessionaire system could serve as a lever to topple Leopold's far more sinister regime next door. Holt, fiercely self-reliant and wary of publicity, was at first unwilling to be involved in a general political crusade. 'So far as I am able to discern,' he replied to Morel, 'my destiny arranged by Providence is to be a distributor of merchandise.'[14] More practically, involvement with Morel would hardly help his private negotiations with the French. By the next letter, however, Morel had persuaded him where duty lay. He would do what little he could.

As vice-chairman of the West African section of the Liverpool Chamber of Commerce and a highly respected figure, Holt's little was in fact considerable, and was soon allied to Morel's brilliant pen. Morel had resigned his job with Elder Dempster and was now devoting himself full time to journalism, with the financial backing of Holt and, surprisingly, Jones, his old employer. In March 1903, the associated Chambers of Commerce adopted Holt's resolution that the government should investigate the Congo monopoly system which was in direct opposition to the Berlin Act, which guaranteed freedom of trade, and contrary to interests of traders in general. In May there was a fiery Commons debate on the Congo issue, which Balfour's shaky government found it impossible or impolitic to oppose. 'We had an overwhelming majority', wrote Sir Charles Dilke to Holt triumphantly. Leopold's government's reaction to English requests for an inquiry was, however, an angry dismissal. Even the liberal Belgian press denounced the English agitation as a Liverpool merchants' plot to seize the fat Congo profits for themselves, *'l'esprit de lucre de Liverpool'*.

In fact the campaign was now proving a serious embarrassment to the most powerful of the Liverpool traders, Sir Alfred Jones. Jones had endorsed Morel's campaign for Holt's fight against the French concessionaires with enthusiasm, but the shift of the attack to the Congo Free State, for which he was Leopold's consul, brought a flurry of agitated letters. Things were nothing like as bad as painted, he told Morel. Any cases of cruelty reported to Leopold would immediately be put right. Surely the matter could be left to the English consul's official report.

In December 1903 the English consul, Roger Casement, at last returned the results of his official inquiry which confirmed almost everything the Congo reformers had claimed: wholesale intimidation of the population, and appalling brutality committed by native troops and Belgian officials to force the natives to collect rubber as taxes. Jones, now under intense pressure from Leopold to head off the reformers, desperately dispatched his own investigators up the Congo, including the American explorer Mrs French Sheldon, who he hoped might prove as influential as Mary Kingsley. The style of her report, however, bore no resemblance to Mary Kingsley's sparkling prose. 'Time has been exhausted in my efforts to find the Truth', she wrote. 'I have marched by tedious marches into the forest; voyaged all weathers by canoe; have lost no time or opportunity in seeing *everything*'. Everywhere she had found 'progress, work, happy natives as a rule for they *hate* work', and 'magnificent fidelity and abnegation' from the Belgian officials, who strove to accomplish King Leopold's ideal.[15]

Mrs French Sheldon's counter-report, however, proved a damp squib compared with Casement's. So too did Jones's plea to the Foreign Office that Leopold would cancel his contract with the English shipping line if Casement's report was published, thus losing valuable trade to the Germans. Pure bluff, in Morel's opinion.

By 1905 the Congo Reform Association had an impressive backing of bishops, peers, M.P.s and proconsuls, including Lord Cromer and Sir Harry Johnston. 'Sir

Alfred Jones is on his knees', reported a jubilant English missionary to Holt. 'He does not know where to turn.'[16] In fact, Jones's last serious attempt to head off the reform movement was through an appeal to the English missions. In the autumn of 1905, he wrote to the leading Protestant mission in the Congo to tell them that Leopold was prepared to hand over the most notorious concession area, the A.B.I.R. concession, to a new company to be chaired by Jones. It would be run by an ex-English governor from Southern Nigeria, Sir Ralph Moor, on the best English liberal lines, with of course absolute liberty for the natives to trade with it when they wished. A *British* monopoly, sharing what could be achieved by humane methods, would set such an example that the Belgian concession company in the Congo could soon be expected to follow. 'Sir Alfred Jones,' wrote his assistant, 'realises that if you treat the natives with perfect fairness, there is no difficulty in getting out of them what you desire.'[17]

The English mission reported with agitation back to Holt. Should they accept? Holt thundered back by return of post. On no account should they be associated with Jones's scheme, which was entirely a device by him and Leopold designed to stop their mouths. 'It might be interesting to shareholders but not for the rights, liberties and lives of millions of the human race.'[18] The missions in turn sent a snubbing reply to Jones. As a spiritual movement they could not be associated with a commercial company, but they were delighted of course to hear that 'Sir Alfred Jones's personal views now differed so strongly from those of His Majesty King Leopold'.

In 1907, finally goaded into a public apology for defending Leopold's regime, Jones gave an aggrieved interview to the *Daily Star.* He had felt his position acutely and ventured to hope that nobody who knew him would believe him 'to be callous and cruel'.[19] He died two years later, by coincidence only a few days before his dangerous patron, King Leopold. As an old colleague, Holt sent his condolences to Elder Dempster on the death of their Senior, but he could not bring himself, he told Morel, to subscribe to Jones's memorial. 'I told [his successors] that Jones's figure in a top hat and frock coat on St George's pierhead did not appeal to my sense of what should be done to a man who had made his money out of Africa and who had thought about Africa all his life.'[20] As for Elder Dempster itself, 'like the Congo regime, it shows signs of improvement; another set of men and another set of ideas are in command now'.[21]

Moral victories are seldom conclusive. Holt's long duel with Jones had ended in a personal victory, but the battle for free trade was less satisfactory. In 1908, Belgium had reluctantly annexed Leopold's *domaine privée*, but the free trade which Morel and Holt had hoped for failed to materialise. The Belgian government's agent, Max Horn, made a personal appeal to the Liverpool Chamber of Commerce to set up trading posts, but there were no takers. No one wished to be associated with the Congo, partly because Morel's propaganda had done its work too well, and partly for practical reasons; compared with the coastal trade, the Congo presented great difficulties and doubtful returns. And as the new British consul pointed out, the areas offered had already been half ruined.

Right Sunlight soap, Lever's most famous product. *Opposite* Its chief constituent, the oil palm.

Max Horn next approached the former consul, Jones himself, who put him on to an old colleague of his who might be interested, William Hesketh Lever. It was the beginning of the biggest trading enterprise in tropical Africa yet.

Lever's interest in West Africa dated back at least ten years and was a natural corollary of his soap business. In his early experiments with soap boiling in the 1880s he had discovered a strong customer preference for a blend of soap which contained nearly fifty per cent vegetable oil, derived from either palm kernels or copra, the dried flesh of the coconut. In a moment of inspiration he had called his patent brand of soap 'Sunlight', and by the late '80s had so increased his sales that to extend production he had taken over fifty acres of swampy wasteland up-river

from the Liverpool docks, just far enough to be out of reach of Custom dues, and built Port Sunlight. Not the first industrial village, it was one of the most all-embracing both in its architectural range – every street had cottages in a different style – and in Lever's benevolent control over all aspects of his workers' lives. Production and sales rose spectacularly. By the late '90s Port Sunlight was producing over 50,000 tons of soap a year. The late '90s also saw Lever's growing obsession with the fear of being 'squeezed' for his supply of tropical vegetable oils and his desire to extend his control to this area too.

In 1896 he bought a partnership with a West African trader called Charles Napoleon de Cardi (another of Mary Kingsley's friends) who had trading posts in the Niger Delta. But by 1900 it had been absorbed into Goldie's Royal Niger Company, one of the companies Lever was hoping to bypass, and soon afterwards he sold out his shares. His next venture into tropical oil trading was on the other side of the world, in the Pacific.

In 1902 he bought out a copra trading company which owned a number of coconut plantations. The following year, however, the price of copra slumped owing partly, wrote Lever, to 'the opening up of the West Coast of Africa by railways, which have brought enormous quantities of palm oil and palm kernels to the coast'. Further investments in the Solomon Isles proved equally disappointing, largely because of the natives' reluctance to work for regular hours and wages, unlike Lever's employees in Port Sunlight. Lever's solution, to import Hindu labourers 'to these beautiful islands from the teeming millions of India', was blocked by the government of India.[22]

It was the first of a long series of confrontations with the official mind which left Lever genuinely perplexed. His own record as a benevolent employer was impeccable and he believed as firmly as Chamberlain in England's duty to develop her tropical estates. 'To leave the production of copra in the hands of natives, who stop producing as soon as they have supplied their own limited wants, will not give the world the copra it wants.'[23] The labour shortage in Lever's Pacific Plantations Company remained acute (and eventually forced its closure). By 1905 Lever had decided anyway that the Pacific islands offered him too small a field of operations and he was making a second attempt to break into West Africa, where his agents reported an almost unlimited hinterland of natural palm oil forest.

But once again he ran up against Colonial Office opposition. Lever's plan was to establish plantations of oil palms of moderate size and to install a large crushing mill at each plantation, which would not only process the palm oil fruit grown in the plantation, but also that brought in by Africans from the forests all round. It would be a factory 'in the modern sense', which Lever was convinced would make production of palm-kernel oil more economic. The Colonial Office, partly as a result of the Congo agitation, was now deeply opposed to the alienation of native land in West Africa, and saw no reason to make concessions to 'the soap boilers of the world'.

Lever, obsessed with his vision of happy communities of Africans bringing in their produce to Lever Brothers' mills and promoting progress, next tried a shrewdly oblique approach. He wrote to Morel, whom he rightly believed to have great influence in the Colonial Office. He was now not interested in plantations, he wrote, simply in putting up his mills in areas of natural palm forest, with a guarantee from the Colonial Office that no one else would be allowed to operate crushing machinery within twenty miles of him. Without this, Lever Brothers could not risk the capital involved. Of course the natives would still be free to crack their palm kernels themselves and sell the oil elsewhere.

Impressed, Morel tackled his friend Charles Strachey in the Colonial Office. 'On the face of it Mr Lever's ideas appear to me to be worthy of every attention,' he wrote. 'The advent of a crushing industry into Southern Nigeria could surely be an excellent thing for the country.' The Africa trade was face to face with the biggest thing yet seen. 'Here is a man, a commercial genius with unlimited capital at his disposal', and decent and honest as well.

'The real difficulty,' he wrote to Lever, 'would come not from the Colonial Office but from the merchants', who had after all 'made our position imperially in West Africa by their enterprise.' Lever should read *West African Studies* by Mary Kingsley, 'the finest woman who ever lived, who understood the traders better than anyone.'[24]

At this point, November 1910, Morel left for a long-delayed visit to West Africa on one of Holt's steamers, to see colonial government and commerce *in situ*. He was confident he had smoothed Lever's relations with the Colonial Office and was therefore deeply surprised and shocked to hear, two months later, that Lever had negotiated a huge concession area in the Congo with the Belgian government.

Given Lever's temperament and his extraordinary energy (he was once described by a business rival as more ruthless, more dogmatic and more autocratic than Napoleon), the deal offered by the Belgian government was irresistible. It also provided a salve to his feelings as a wounded suitor to the Colonial Office. They had offered him, finally, only a five-mile radius for his mills which, he later wrote to Morel, was simply ludicrous. By contrast the Belgians were prepared to offer him a lease for over a million acres of land which, after thirty-five years, given proper development, would become the company's property. Inside this area Lever's company, specially created, called La Société Anonyme des Huileries du Congo Belge, would have the status and duties of a sub-government. It could build roads and railways, organise river steamers and telegraphs, and it would be obliged to set up schools and medical services – a paternalist conception of business which immediately appealed to Lever. It was after all Port Sunlight again on a gigantic scale. From swamp and jungle Lever would create model industrial and agricultural communities in the Heart of Darkness.

As a capital undertaking, the risks were gigantic, but Lever, who still had absolute control of all his companies, was a born risk-taker. Indeed this was the problem which faced Morel and Holt when they contemplated the deal. No one else would have been prepared to take such a risk. After a further correspondence with Lever which Morel passed on to Holt, even Holt himself admitted, half convinced, that Lever's scheme was the best they could hope for. 'Mine are old-fashioned ideas,' he wrote.

> I see this man prepared to go out to the Congo with his wife and a number of people, all well equipped with modern ideas of economic progress and how to develop industries.... In the case of Lever I think much of the man himself and his great ideals of life and duty. I hope that in the Congo his advent will tend to heal the great open sore produced by the terrible economic regime inaugurated by Leopold and his followers.[25]

Lever lost no time in starting the development of his new project. In 1911 thousands of tons of machinery were dispatched to the first of the five sites he had

Left Lord Leverhulme, and (*opposite*) snapshots from his expedition by stern-wheeler up the Congo.

marked down as potential trading and milling centres, to be called, naturally enough, Leverville. Their transit, by boat, railway, river steamer and overland, hundreds of miles into the interior, required a miracle of organisation and effort in itself. The site of the new town had been carved out of a steep hillside, which meant that thousands of tons of earth had to be shifted. Native labour, though plentiful, was, reported his agent, 'poor, underfed and entirely cannibal'.[26] The food provided from Liverpool for European employees was so monotonous that three Belgians deserted during the building works in a stolen canoe. Yet despite everything, three months after the landing of the first loads at Leverville the first consignment of palm kernel oil milled there had reached Lever's factory in Brussels. In April 1912, Lever was able to present the first tablet of soap in person to King Albert of the Belgians.

Five months later Lever, his wife and staff, set out to see the Congo project for themselves. They steamed up the mighty river on one of the company's wood-burning stern-wheelers, Lever keeping firmly to his usual routine at home. 'Rise at 5 a.m. Shave, cup of tea at 5.15. Cold bath at 5.20. Breakfast 6.30. . . . Oil and Fats Committee 8.30 a.m.' He noted in his diary the points of interest along the river: a bunch of elephants 'bigger than Jumbo' (the famous denizen of London Zoo);

women cannibals with teeth filed like a saw; a lunatic chained to a log. When the boat moored at night by a village, the party would let off fireworks and give a magic lantern show (slides of Port Sunlight, Lever noticed, caused particular interest).

Serious problems, however, were waiting for them when they arrived. The mills could not operate without a steady supply of oil-palm fruit gathered by the natives in the forests round about. The Congo natives, like those of the Pacific, Lever found totally lacking in the Protestant work ethic. The local chief, Womba, 'after twelve months or less of selling fruit, is rich and lazy, has ten wives and . . . has gathered little or no fruit.' The oil palm, he noted, was regarded by the natives as a bank account and 'he no more thinks of going to the bank for fruit for money when his wants and ambitions are supplied than a civilised man'. Once again the labour problem loomed over his enterprise like 'an ominous dark cloud'.

At least the town planning of Leverville itself could be improved. Lever devoted the last day of his visit to issuing instructions to the company surveyor to alter the layout of the streets, with all the dynamism of a twentieth-century Raffles. But, he noted in his diary, 'the Congo is a land to teach one patience'.[27]

It was twelve years before Lever returned in person to the Congo and twenty years before it returned any real profit on the capital invested. But his enthusiasm for the project never abated. It fulfilled, more than any other of his ventures, his passion for social engineering. 'There', he once wrote, 'one has room to breathe, to grow, to expand, and the possibilities are boundless. One can . . . organise, organise, organise – well, very big things indeed.'[28] But it failed to blunt his insatiable appetite for Africa.

Even before the Congo deal was finalised, Lever had bid for a huge concession of land in French West Africa, described optimistically by his agent as 'beautiful, well wooded country, almost like English parkland'. It proved to be a total financial loss. Out of six million acres only ten thousand were suitable for planting. Then, despite his complaints of the 'ludicrous' terms offered by the Colonial Office, he had gone ahead with his plans for crushing mills in British West Africa. In fact they ran consistently at a loss, justifying to some extent his arguments to Morel. The natives on whom the factory depended for supply quickly realised the strength of their negotiating position and would only sell at a price which made the processed kernel oil uncompetitive in the open market. The basic error, however, was Lever's. As several of the Liverpool traders had warned, there was almost no economy in processing palm kernels on the spot. The oil was harder to transport than the palm kernels, and there was no local market for the residual oil cake.

Lever's third move to secure his sources of supply was at first more successful. Like an octopus he slowly absorbed all the old trading companies on the coast which Mary Kingsley had so admired. First MacIvers of Liverpool, then the Cavalla River Company (which traded in Liberia), then the Bathurst Trading Company, John Walkdens, Kings of Bristol (the oldest of all West African trading firms) and finally, in 1920, the great Niger Company itself. This last mouthful nearly proved fatal. The directors of the Niger Company, knowing that the fat

Defiant trademarks of two West African trading companies which banded together to resist Lever in the twenties. They later merged with him as part of the United Africa Company.

wartime profits from palm oil and groundnuts were about to collapse, staged a brilliant piece of window-dressing for Lever's benefit. They bought plots of land at stations along the new railway line from Port Harcourt in order to make their trading interests seem even wider, and then offered the company for £8 million to Lever on a take-it-or-leave-it basis. Lever was in America when news of the offer arrived. Without insisting on a look at the company's books, he cabled to his agents to accept. 'Price high but suicidal if we had let opportunity lapse.'[29] Only after the deal was completed did the directors discover the Niger Company's assets were less than they seemed and that the Company owed £2 million to its bankers.

At the same time the price of palm-kernel oil collapsed by fifty per cent, leaving Lever with a £9 million loss on existing stocks. He was saved only by a brilliant accountant, but at the price of at last relinquishing his own total control over the company. Hitherto he had raised money on non-voting preference shares. Now the banks forced him to issue debenture stock. He expressed his feelings in a biting public attack on the Niger Company directors for their deception. (It is perhaps a measure of the directors' secretive tactics that the company's founder, the venerable Sir George Goldie, quite misunderstanding the situation, had offered £20,000 of his personal fortune to stave off Lever's bid.)

Meanwhile, the remaining West African firms – Miller's, Swanzy's, Thomas Harrison – whose quarrels had almost made Mary Kingsley despair of them twenty years before, had hurriedly banded together in a rival conglomerate, the African and Eastern Trading Company, to resist Lever. In the autumn of 1920, however, he offered them terms so breathtakingly attractive that they accepted. Much to the shareholders' disappointment, the offer was withdrawn when the truth about the financial straits of the Niger Company were discovered. Ten years later, after a long trading war, the two companies were finally merged, to become the United Africa Company.

By 1925 Lever himself was dead. He had taken his last voyage up the Congo in 1924 at the age of seventy-three, much against his doctor's advice. Though he found plenty to criticise, as usual – bad town planning, squandering of resources, too many managers – on the whole he had been much elated by what he found. Seven mills were now processing 60,000 tons of palm nut kernels, 17,000 natives and 200 Europeans were employed and a thousand kilometres of road had been laid. There were ten hospitals, three large schools and hundreds of sound brick houses for the natives. 'What a change in twelve years,' he wrote in his diary, '... we have really only begun to scratch the soil ... we are all full of enthusiasm and confidence in the future of our Belgian Concessions.'[30] His mood sombred noticeably on the next stage of his journey, to British West Africa. Apart from the trading companies none of his ventures had been a success, due entirely in his mind to the Colonial Office's misguided policy on land tenure and the obstruction of officials on the spot. Even the river Niger itself he pronounced inferior to the Congo.

Lever's visit to Nigeria ended with an historic and much publicised quarrel. By this time the Governor of Nigeria was Sir Hugh Clifford, an old opponent of Lever's. He had clashed with him before the war when trying to get concessions in the Gold Coast. In 1923 Lever, at the annual general meeting of the Niger Company, had declared amongst other things his belief that the encouragement of trade and commerce was the first duty of colonial administration. Clifford had announced this in Lagos as a most monstrous and mischievous heresy and a public insult to himself. African interests in Nigeria were paramount.

The Liverpool Chamber of Commerce had tried to heal the breach by inviting both Lever and Clifford to one of their dinners, during which Lever had publicly complimented Clifford as a man with the highest ideals in the British Empire. And when Lever's yacht cast anchor at Lagos a few months later, Clifford invited him to dinner at Government House. The evening appeared to go well and next day Lever dispatched a reciprocal invitation to Clifford to dine on his yacht, *Albion*. Clifford abruptly refused, claiming that Lever still owed him a public apology for his reckless and damaging charges against the administration, an extraordinary volte-face which can best be explained by Clifford's incipient manic-depression.[31] Underlying it, though, was the traditional chasm which existed between administrators and commerce. To Lever, commerce under his direction meant progress and was, by definition, beneficial. To Clifford, any European intervention for motives of profit led, if not carefully watched, to exploitation and a breach of England's sacred trust to protect native peoples.

Oddly enough, both could have quoted Mary Kingsley in their own defence, but the debate, in Lever's case, ended there. Six weeks later, back in England from his voyage in the tropics, he caught a severe chill and died of pneumonia.

Opposite Lord Curzon and his wife Mary pose with vice-regal tiger.

The hills are beautiful and useful. Where there are hills there are forests, and where there are forests there are tigers. Where there are tigers, great personages like Viceroys come to shoot them and this is very good for a State.

Indian schoolboy's essay, 1906

7

HUNTERS

'Come and stay with us in India,' Lord Curzon wrote expansively to a friend in the first days of vice-regal glory, 'and we will arrange for you to shoot tigers from the back of elephants or elephants from the back of tigers, whichever you prefer.'[1] Big game shooting was the natural corollary of administering England's tropical estates, and a stream of influential visitors flowed out from England to enjoy it too. It was all part of the service, part of

The governor's game-bag: Sir Hesketh Bell poses with his trophies in Uganda, 1908.

the propaganda of empire, a chance to show off 'improvements' to the right people or talk over imperial burdens after a congenial day's sport in jungle or veldt. It gave a sense of the vastness of England's domains – that 'sense of space in the blood' which, as a character in one of John Buchan's novels put it, was 'the beginning of learning to think imperially'.[2] To those who disliked imperial thinking it was of course yet further proof of the general beastliness on which the Empire was built. Big game shooting, like fox-hunting, was an expression of 'savage instincts' and upper-class self-indulgence. To which all the usual fox-hunters' arguments were returned. There was nothing wrong with 'savage instincts', they were a healthy antidote to too much modern civilisation.

> Yet if once we efface the joys of the chase
> From the land and outroot the stud,
> Goodbye to the Anglo-Saxon race!
> Farewell to the Norman blood![3]

Besides, what other activity could provide such natural social cement? How better could the English bridge the gap between themselves and the native races? Every Anglo-Indian had a warm spot for his old shikari – 'Pukka white men,' as one remarked, 'except for their colour.'[4]

But it is impossible not to feel what a very bloodthirsty Empire it had become by 1900. *Homo sapiens* on the whole may have now enjoyed *Pax Britannica*, other species as yet did not. Official photograph albums bulged with groups clustered round slaughtered game: His Royal Highness's tiger, the Viceroy's bear, the High Commissioner's lion. Government houses and vice-regal lodges were thick with trophy heads, beautifully mounted by Rowland Ward. And they were only the tip

Frederick Jackson in his early hunting days in East Africa.

of the iceberg – there were thousands more back in Edwardian England. To shoot well was one key to professional and social success. After all, the Prince of Wales did little else and the King had the largest game larder in Europe at Sandringham.

At least two distinguished Edwardian governors, Sir Alfred Sharpe and Sir Frederick Jackson, started their careers as big game hunters. Sharpe had met Harry Johnston by the Shiré river in 1889 while stalking a waterbuck; and had been quickly enrolled as a deputy commissioner. (When Johnston departed, Sharpe succeeded him.) Frederick Jackson had come out to East Africa in the 1880s to shoot game at the suggestion of Rider Haggard (who later made him the model for the immaculate Goode in *King Solomon's Mines*) and rose likewise to be a highly popular governor of British East Africa and Uganda. Both men always retained a slight hankering for their old profession. Even the soberest of administrators, like Cromer, enjoyed an occasional venture into the bush. 'How long', implored Lady Cromer's maid pathetically when she accompanied her master and mistress on a safari into the Lado Enclave, 'how long must we tarry in this shrubbery?'[5]

One of the odder proconsular rivalries blew up in 1908 when Elinor Glyn was making her famous début on stage on a tiger skin. Both Curzon and Milner sent round one they had shot themselves, the next morning. Sadly for Milner, Elinor Glyn had eyes only for Curzon's.

Of all the sporting rituals of empire the vice-regal tiger shoot was the grandest. Its sheer size was often self-defeating. The noise and bustle made it surprising, as Mary Curzon pointed out, that there was any game left at all within miles. Only in the magnificent game preserves of the native states like Gwalior and Hyderabad could a satisfactory bag be assured. (The Maharajah of Gwalior was so keen a shot himself

The vice-regal tiger shoot: Lord Curzon (*standing second right*) disports himself at Dacca.

that he even imported African lions for variety.) Swaying lines of elephants and vast armies of beaters headed the tiger towards the Viceroy, and the tension was enormous until a ritual kill had been accomplished. One Indian shikari fainted with horror when a teasing A.D.C. pretended to raise his gun and pre-empt the Viceroy's shot. Often more serious accidents occurred – Curzon's loader, who had got down to flush out a tigress from some rocks, was killed before his eyes in Hyderabad. Curzon was shaken, but not enough to put him off negotiating a large transfer of territory from the Nizam during the banquet which followed. Sport and politics were combined as smoothly in India as on the Scottish grouse moors.

For lesser ranks the pleasures were simpler but no less keen. A passion for *shikar* – field sports – permeated the whole of Anglo-India from top to bottom. For one thing it was gloriously cheap. Many a subaltern who had never owned a hunter or shot a pheasant at home for lack of funds found a whole range of sporting opportunities within his means east of Suez. There were famous jackal hunts like Ooty (Ootamacand) or the Peshawar, with fields and breakfasts to rival the Quorn and hunting country that looked delightfully, deceptively English. There were snipe and duck in the *jheels* and paddy-fields to be found behind almost every cantonment and, in the drier areas, sand grouse, partridge and quail. And despite the incursions of a century of Anglo-Indian sportsmen there were still huge tracts of jungle teeming with larger game – panther, tiger, samba, swamp deer, cheetah and bear.

If you were stationed in central India, at Cawnpore, Jubbulpore or Belgaum, the jungle was almost at your doorstep. With an indulgent colonel you might disappear after a panther or tiger over a weekend. Elsewhere, big game shooting was usually a matter for the Christmas camp or the two months' annual long leave. You booked your forest block, ordered your large-scale survey map to pore over for weeks or months beforehand till you knew every path or stream, and then 'away from the heat and dust of the plains to the cool and peace of the jungle where you could not walk a hundred yards without seeing a track or hearing a sound that tested your jungle lore'.[6]

The highland jungles of the central provinces were the most sought-after – wild, tumbled hills and streams that ran in all directions, with wild aboriginal forest-dwellers who made the most skilful of native trackers. Or there was the Terai – a huge 600-mile stretch of thicket and forest along the Nepal frontier interspersed with park-like glades where the villagers had burnt the elephant grass. Or the hill tracts of Chittagong and Assam where you could still hire for a song an elephant that doubled as transport and tracker. A well-trained elephant could point for tiger or bear as well as any gun-dog.

By 1900 most of India's jungles had their own guardians: the Indian Forest Service, who carefully regulated the shooting to preserve the game and warded off the depredations of tree-fellers. These were the true jungli-wallahs, scornful of 'brass hats' and self-important officials, mines of experience who would as likely as not find their way into print (*Tiger Days*; *Shikar Notes for Novices*; *Leaves from an Indian Jungle*; *Through Sunlight and Shadow*). They could advise the visiting sportsman on where to site a *machan* (shooting platform) and post his stops and beaters, though the best sport of all was, in the view of most old shikaris, to stalk the tiger on foot. Any fool could sit up in a tree and murder a tiger as it walked underneath him.

For an officer fresh from England, however, where the fiercest opponent available had been a stag, his first encounter with a tiger was as momentous as his first day's fighting on the North-West Frontier. Richard Meinertzhagen, whom we have already met in East Africa, described it like this in classic subaltern style:

> 'Aha, my pretty puss,' I muttered and taking very careful aim, pulled the trigger. With a roar he bounded back into the wood and all was stilled.

Meinertzhagen followed him into the bush and finished him off with his Mannlicher. Then 'we dragged him into the open and I danced with delight'.

His second encounter with a tiger gave him an object lesson in caution. This time it had been shot by a fellow subaltern up a tree. They were 'dancing a sword dance round the body . . . Hatter was pulling its tail and making a noise like a barrel organ, little Graham was dancing a reel on the body and I was talking nonsense just in front of his nose', when there was a roar. 'Graham was sent sprawling and the Hatter and I collided round the other side of the tree.'

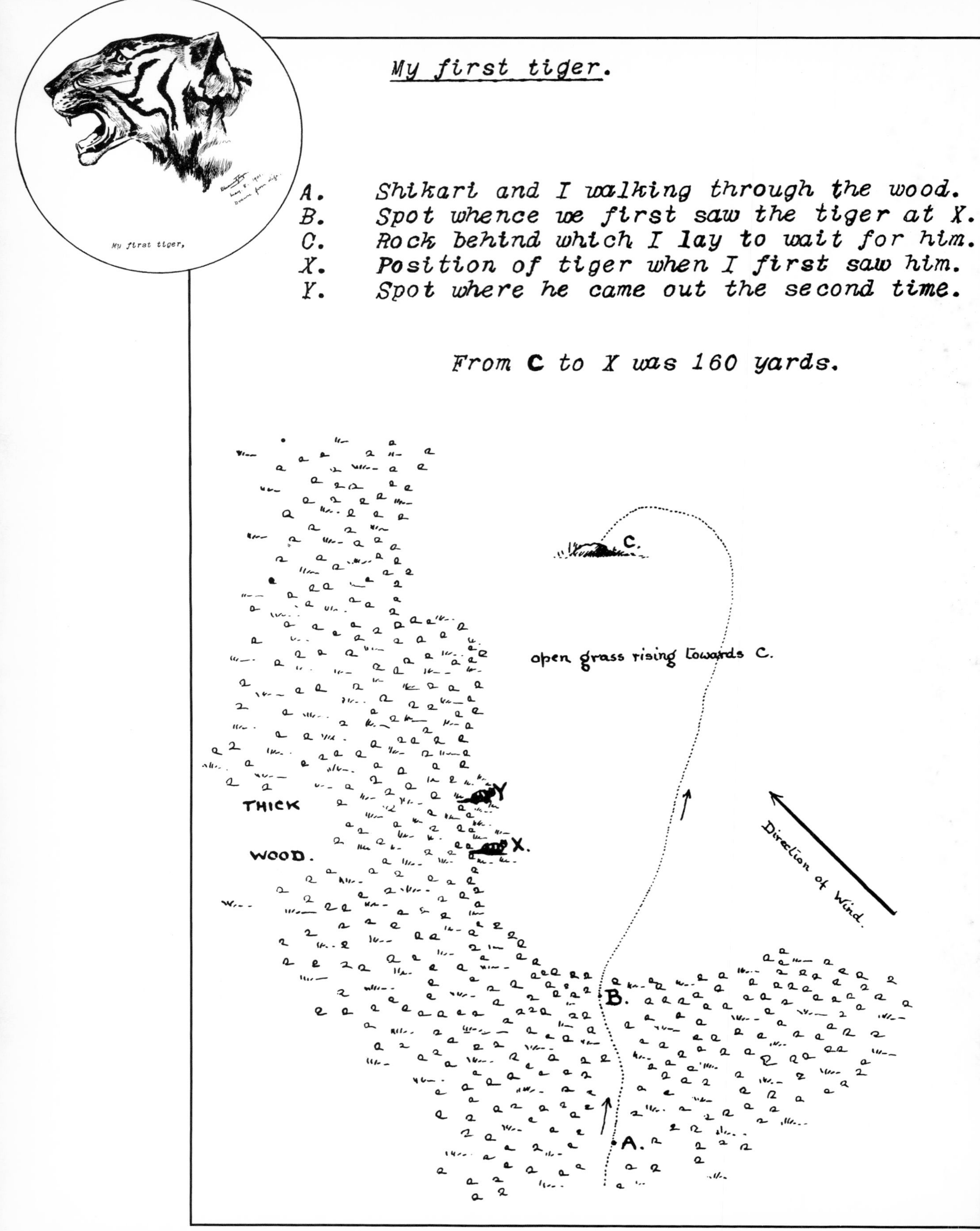
My first tiger.
A. Shikari and I walking through the wood.
B. Spot whence we first saw the tiger at X.
C. Rock behind which I lay to wait for him.
X. Position of tiger when I first saw him.
Y. Spot where he came out the second time.
From C to X was 160 yards.
C.
open grass rising towards C.
Y
X.
THICK
WOOD.
Direction of Wind.
B.
A.
My first tiger,

There was one animal which, in the Anglo-Indian sporting pantheon, rated as high if not higher than the tiger. If tales of tiger days filled many a handsome gold-blocked volume, the thrills of sticking 'pig', as he was affectionally known, could drive strong men to verse. Countless ecstatic pages celebrate pigs' bravery and cunning: the headlong dash on horseback through long grass and over hidden rocks and nullahs, the pig's wild jinks or swerves, his gallant last charge against his pursuers' spears. For aficionados, fox-hunting paled in comparison – 'a mob of pretty dogs yow-yowing after a poor little beast that is only too happy to escape', wrote one scornful Anglo-Indian colonel, whereas the Indian wild boar was a worthy opponent. Two hundred pounds of solid muscle and bone with eight-inch tushes which could rip open a horse or its rider, sometimes fatally. In almost every cantonment in India social life revolved round the Tent Club of ardent pig-stickers. One indulgent commanding officer whittled official barrack duties down to three days a week, which left four days clear for 'pig'. To many subalterns, pig-sticking was the real business of the Indian Army and even generals were apt to claim that pig-sticking was the finest possible military training.

Subalterns' sports. *Above* Baden-Powell's sketches from *Pig-sticking and Hog-hunting*, 1888 – 'The charger charged' and 'The race for first spear'.
Opposite Richard Meinertzhagen's meticulous sketch of his first tiger and where he found it. Nilgiri hills, 1901.

'South Africa: the sportsman's ideal.'

No officer put the case for pig-sticking with more panache than Robert Baden-Powell. Pig-sticking made his reputation. As a young subaltern in 1883, he won the Kadir Cup, the Grand National of pig-sticking and *the* sporting event of the Anglo-Indian year. Five years later he wrote the standard book on the subject, enlivened by the pen-and-ink drawings at which he was a dab hand (as indeed he was at everything else). Pig-sticking, he pointed out, taught horsemanship, endurance, quick-thinking and an eye for country. It gave a 'mental tonic and a jollier outlook on life in a land and climate where such revitalising was sorely needed'. And it was sociable, engendering *esprit de corps*, unlike big game hunting which was a solitary occupation, encouraging the Englishman's natural misanthropy.

The spread of Tent Clubs had transformed the hot weather spent in barracks from one long nightmare 'into the healthiest and happiest part of the year'. There was no need now for anyone but family men to go off to the usual 'poodle-faking' at hill stations. Finally of course it improved relations with the natives no end. Baden-Powell thoroughly recommended it to political officers as well as the military. If anything would stave off disloyalty in India it would be pig-sticking, which brought English officials into touch with village headmen in a way which could never be achieved 'through official correspondence and chipprassies'.[8]

'South Africa as many have found it.' (Both from J. G. Millais's book, *A Breath from the Veldt*, 1899.)

This last piece of political wisdom was given special emphasis in the revised and enlarged edition of Baden-Powell's book, which appeared in 1924, by which time 'disloyalty' had probably gone beyond anything pig-sticking – or vice-regal tiger shoots – could have solved. But Baden-Powell's own military career at least had been a shining endorsement of his early training on 'pig'. His fame reached its apogee at the start of the new century, which found him literally holding the fort at Mafeking. He emerged from the siege in May 1900 a national hero: the plucky little commander who had never been without a cheery jest to keep up the defenders' spirits and an ingenious riposte for the enemy. His views on military training were quoted endlessly in the great debate which followed the war's early disasters, summarised by one writer as 'hunters versus sportsmen'. Most of the Boers clearly fell into the former category, having, as he pointed out, 'few sports not connected with warfare; I mean, the war against wild beasts.'[9]

Strictly in terms of game-shooting rather than warfare, however, the Boers were judged by the opposite canon and found wanting; for the war brought a chorus of disappointment from the British officers on the veldt. South Africa, once a legendary paradise for game hunters, was now, they reported, almost a desert. Even in

India officers engaged in routine campaigns against wild Afridis or Pathans on the frontier could be sure of better sport than out here. There was not an elephant left south of the Limpopo river; precious few south of the Zambezi. Eland, rhino, giraffe and buffalo had all virtually disappeared. Their extinction was chalked up as a black mark against the Boers who hardly understood, lamented one Englishman, the 'elementary significance of our British term "sport". No sense of respect for game, no admiration of its grace and beauty ever penetrated minds debased by decades of slaughter.'[10] The Boers thought only in terms of biltong, dried meat or leather for harness – little better in fact than the natives, who used the same word for meat and game.

In blaming the Boers the English were as usual indulging in their habit of historical self-deception. For a good many English 'sportsmen' had cheerfully contributed to the rout. Unlike India, where *shikar* had been and was in general a sideshow, albeit an all-absorbing one, for the military and officials, Africa had attracted from the beginning the full-time professional European hunter. The difference of course was ivory. In India the elephant was usually too valuable alive to shoot, the hunter's ally rather than his quarry. To many Anglo-Indians the idea of shooting something so huge and intelligent was almost a sacrilege. 'I would as soon blow up the Tower of London,' declared Baden-Powell. But all attempts to domesticate *Loxodonta Africana*, the African wild elephant, had failed. Economically he remained useless till dead, when he became very valuable indeed. A good pair of tusks weighing 50 lbs each could fetch up to £150 for the hunter in 1900. A whole succession of Englishmen (even those with impeccable social credentials) had grasped that here was the ideal way to combine sport and profit.

One of the first to make the veldt famous was Rouleyn Gordon-Cumming, a Scottish baronet's son who had transferred for health reasons from the Madras Cavalry to the Cape Mounted Rifles. He had then thrown up his commission entirely, deciding that 'the life of a wild hunter was far preferable to that of a mere sportsman', and he spent the next five years ruthlessly shooting everything he met. His trophies, including a live Hottentot and Bushman, were put on show in the Great Exhibition and, together with his racy accounts of his adventures, did much to encourage successors. Another unlikely propagandist for professional elephant hunting was David Livingstone. In Livingstone's view, anything that drew Englishmen into the African interior, be it land, souls or ivory, could only improve the place. One of his closest friends was the great hunter William Cotton Oswell, to whom he wrote glowing descriptions of the herds of fine tuskers he passed on his exploration up the Zambezi and Shiré rivers. It was Livingstone's *Travels* which laid the germ of what can best be described as a missionary fervour to hunt game in the most famous hunter of the next generation, Frederick Courtenay Selous.

Selous's hunting career spans the whole late Victorian and Edwardian age and shows again how difficult it is to draw a boundary between amateur sportsman and professional hunter. In Selous's case the progression was almost the opposite to Gordon-Cumming's. Son of the chairman of the London Stock Exchange and educated at Rugby (where he devoted most of his time to poaching and birds'-nesting), he announced to his family at the age of nineteen that he wished to try to make his living by shooting elephants. He arrived at Algoa Bay (the future Port Elizabeth) with £400 in his pocket as capital, only to find to his chagrin that the palmy days of hunting elephants on the veldt were already over. To find any game at all he had to trek far north-east to Bulawayo, King Lobengula's capital. Lobengula roared with laughter at this stripling's request to hunt anything so large and dangerous as elephants, and Selous's first encounter with them was nearly a disaster. His over-enthusiastic loader stuffed a double charge of powder into the heavy four-bore gun he had bought from a Dutch hunter, and the recoil knocked him backwards and nearly broke his arm. He afterwards wrote that his shooting never fully recovered; the advent of high-velocity rifles in the next two decades shortened the odds against elephants enormously.

In fact much of Selous's early hunting was a physical ordeal which only the most dedicated of hunters would have followed through. Most of the elephants had retreated into the 'fly' – the tsetse-infested bush where they could only be pursued on foot, a highly dangerous and exhausting procedure compounded by malaria and hostile natives. At one point Selous lost everything except his shirt and wandered for three days and nights without food or water. It was the hope of finding a hunter's paradise where horses and oxen could be used (plus a good deal of the explorer's itch) which drove him further and further north into central Africa and eventually across the Zambezi.

The quest was unsuccessful in terms of hunting. He never found enough ivory to do more than cover the cost of his safaris. Even north of the Zambezi, most of the elephants had been cleared by native hunters working for white traders. But his account of his explorations fired Rhodes' interest in the area, with historic consequences. Rhodes later used Selous's immense prestige to obtain financial and political backing for his new colony north of the Zambezi, and enlisted him to lead the pioneer colony into the Promised Land.

In the meantime, what brought Selous the living he urgently needed was not so much his gun but his pen. By 1880 he had decided that the days of elephant-hunting were finished and was talking despairingly of trying ostrich-farming in South Africa instead. But his first book, *A Hunter's Wanderings in Africa*, published the following year, was an immediate best-seller and from then on he was in constant demand to write and talk on all matters African – human or animal. Unlike many hunters, who tended to have a misanthropic streak, Selous was the ideal subject for 'lionisation'. Despite his charming natural diffidence he was a born story-teller who combined a *Boy's Own* directness and simplicity with a naturalist's eye for detail. No one else could give his listeners such a whiff of the African jungle, of what it felt like to be charged at close quarters by a wounded buffalo, or to be knelt on by an elephant. When describing his adventures he would almost act out the scenes in question, becoming in turn an antelope or a lion. And then there were those extraordinary blue eyes: 'clear and blue', wrote his friend and biographer J. G.

Right 'Big game' – Frederick Selous by 'Spy', 1894.

Opposite Illustration from Selous's *A Hunter's Wanderings in Africa*, engraved by his sister.

Millais, 'as the summer sea ... the eyes of a man who looks into the beyond over vast spaces'.[11] Rider Haggard based the hero of *King Solomon's Mines*, Allan Quartermain, almost entirely on Fred Selous.

The success of Selous's book also brought him his most important commissions: to shoot specimens for the Natural History Museum in Kensington, and for rich private clients like the Rothschilds at Tring. The late '80s saw a great boom in trophy-hunting and interest in game, largely owing to the talents of Rowland Ward, Selous's friend. Ward was a trained sculptor who could literally put life into death. His *tableaux vivants* were as much in demand by millionaires as French furniture and Italian pictures. And his famous game lists, published from 1892 on, inspired every amateur to imitate Selous.

Selous's own African hunting was seriously curtailed after 1895 when, as his biographer rather coyly put it, the great hunter at the age of forty-three was 'finally winged by a little fellow with a bow and arrow'. He married a clergyman's daughter who, after a brief spell in Rhodesia as a settler – just as the second Matabele war broke out – made it clear that she preferred the Home Counties where the natives were friendly and the lions stuffed. From then on Selous limited his big game hunting forays to two or three trips a year, largely to Europe and America. During his visits to the Rockies he made friends with another veteran hunter, Theodore Roosevelt, who had always admired him. Selous, in one letter to

Roosevelt, rather touchingly confided the conflict he felt between the demands of family life and the call of the wild. Roosevelt was highly sympathetic; he felt the same himself and in his case the problem was compounded by the demands of politics, which were 'always acute in the Fall when the hunting was at its best'.

Selous, no politician, found himself unexpectedly in political hot water the following year, 1899, when he bravely deplored the Boer War in a letter to *The Times*. Although a firm believer in England's expansion, which after all he had promoted in central Africa, he was no jingo and had always defended old Boer hunting comrades against the denunciations of his fellow English sportsmen.

By the time the dust had settled back on the veldt in 1902, Selous's prestige was fully re-established and the waves of sportsmen, keen to emulate his prowess, were larger than ever. Access to the far interior was after all so much easier now that railways and *Pax Britannica* had pushed north as far as King Leopold's Congo. One district officer in Selous's old hunting-ground north of the Zambezi complained gloomily to his chief that his entire time was now spent organising carriers for visiting sportsmen and most of his salary on rounds of whisky and soda. The full brunt of the invasion, however, fell elsewhere. Zambezia had too many natural disincentives: a ferociously hot climate during most of the shooting season and twenty-foot high elephant grass, which made it almost impossible to track game,

An elephant-hunter in Uganda, early 1900s, combining sport and profit.

except for the two months after it had been burned off. Then there were Selous's old enemies, malarial mosquitoes and tsetse fly. Hunting in British Central Africa, admitted one veteran, still required a good deal of 'persevering push'. The same problems arose at the other end of Africa. Railways and Nile steamers could carry the sportsman comfortably as far as Khartoum, where the governor, Sir Reginald Wingate, and his lady provided delightful hospitality. He could then take a private steamer (for £20 to £30 a day) on up to the rich shooting grounds of the Sudd. But heat and mosquitoes made life pretty near intolerable as soon as he set foot on shore. Even Selous, who made the trip in 1909 in search of a giant eland for his collection, was quite overcome by the ferocity of their attack.

In the first years of the century, however, word had spread rapidly of a new El Dorado to the East, as rich in game as the veldts of Gordon-Cumming's day, and with a climate to match. What opened up this particular playground was of course Lord Salisbury's lunatic line, the Uganda Railway. The railhead had hardly reached the East African Highlands before one district officer, Francis Hall, was reporting that a new social phenomenon had hit his *boma*: 'Three lords for lunch, and Delamere is due next week – we shall soon qualify for the aristocracy.'[12] Delamere of course had originally reached the Highlands the hard way, starting up the Horn of Africa, a traditional jumping-off point for safaris, and trekking across the semi-deserts of western Somaliland. He had been shooting in Somalia every year since 1891, mostly lion which he rode down on horseback. In one year alone he sent back a consignment of thirty lion skins to Rowland Ward.

The western Highlands along the Uganda border, however, offered that irresistible combination, sport *and* profit. Sir Harry Johnston, Uganda's High Commissioner, wrote to Lord Salisbury in 1900:

In regard to persons supposed to be sportsmen pure and simple who come out to this part of the world, I would point out to Your Lordship that there is often a very practical purpose attached. Lord Delamere for instance left this part of the country last year with £14,000 worth of ivory; his medical officer, Dr Atkinson, who remained behind, has been steadily shooting elephants ever since'.[13]

East Africa's game was saved from the fate of South Africa's just in time, by strict licensing laws introduced in the same year. Though visiting sportsmen from India found the £50 licence fee monstrously high, there was a general wave of approval. *Punch* celebrated the event with a cartoon showing lions, elephants and hippos advancing in a menacing throng on the cowering passengers of the Uganda Railway. The caption read: 'The result of carefully preserving the big game.' The Uganda Railway, delighted, reprinted it as an advertisement for its Cook's Tours. British East Africa, it announced, was now *the* winter paradise for British aristocrats.

An impressive assembly of connoisseurs came to investigate Paradise in its first few years. Selous came out in 1900 and pronounced the hunting and climate the best he had ever known, though very expensive. All the other well-known sporting pundits wrote accounts of their safaris: Abel Chapman, the famous hunter–naturalist, Captain Chauncy Stigand from British Central Africa and Baden-Powell back from South Africa. Then there were the professional white hunters, ready to cater for the British aristocrat's every need.

Foremost in the business were two tough Australians, Newland and Tarlton. They had extended their operations up from Mombasa to Nairobi when the latter was hardly more than a marshalling yard. Their porters were the smartest in Africa, wearing white knickerbockers and dark blue jerseys with 'N & T' across the chest, and some of the most famous shots worked for them: Will Judd, an immaculate dandy with shiny brown boots and gaiters; R. J. Cunninghame, a spare blue-eyed giant with a huge curling black beard; and Leslie Tarlton himself, who was reputedly the best rifle shot in British East. A Newland and Tarlton safari was not cheap, a four-month tour costing at least $2,500. But the service was comprehensive: the porters carried everything from bathtubs and drawing-room-sized tents to silver and vintage wine. The white hunter planned the trip to suit his clients' taste in game and was constantly on hand to stop the charge of any wounded animal, shoot extra game if the bag was not impressive enough, or smooth over the problems of animals shot in excess of licence. On mixed safaris, increasingly common, he might have to act as ladies' maid and it was rumoured, wrote one settler, that 'even more intimate tasks have been required'.[14]

Then there were the freelances: the American Paul Rainey, with his bearhounds; Tarpon Dick, who hunted with a lasso; and cheerful bounders like John Boyes – 'king of the Wa-Kikuyu' – who had run away to sea on a tramp steamer aged fifteen, arriving in East Africa while the railway was still being built, and set himself up as trader and warlord among the tribesmen south of Mount Kenya. In the early days of the Protectorate he had been *persona non grata*, but now he was part of the scenery, with a fund of hair-raising anecdotes to dazzle tourists. 'What did you do then?'

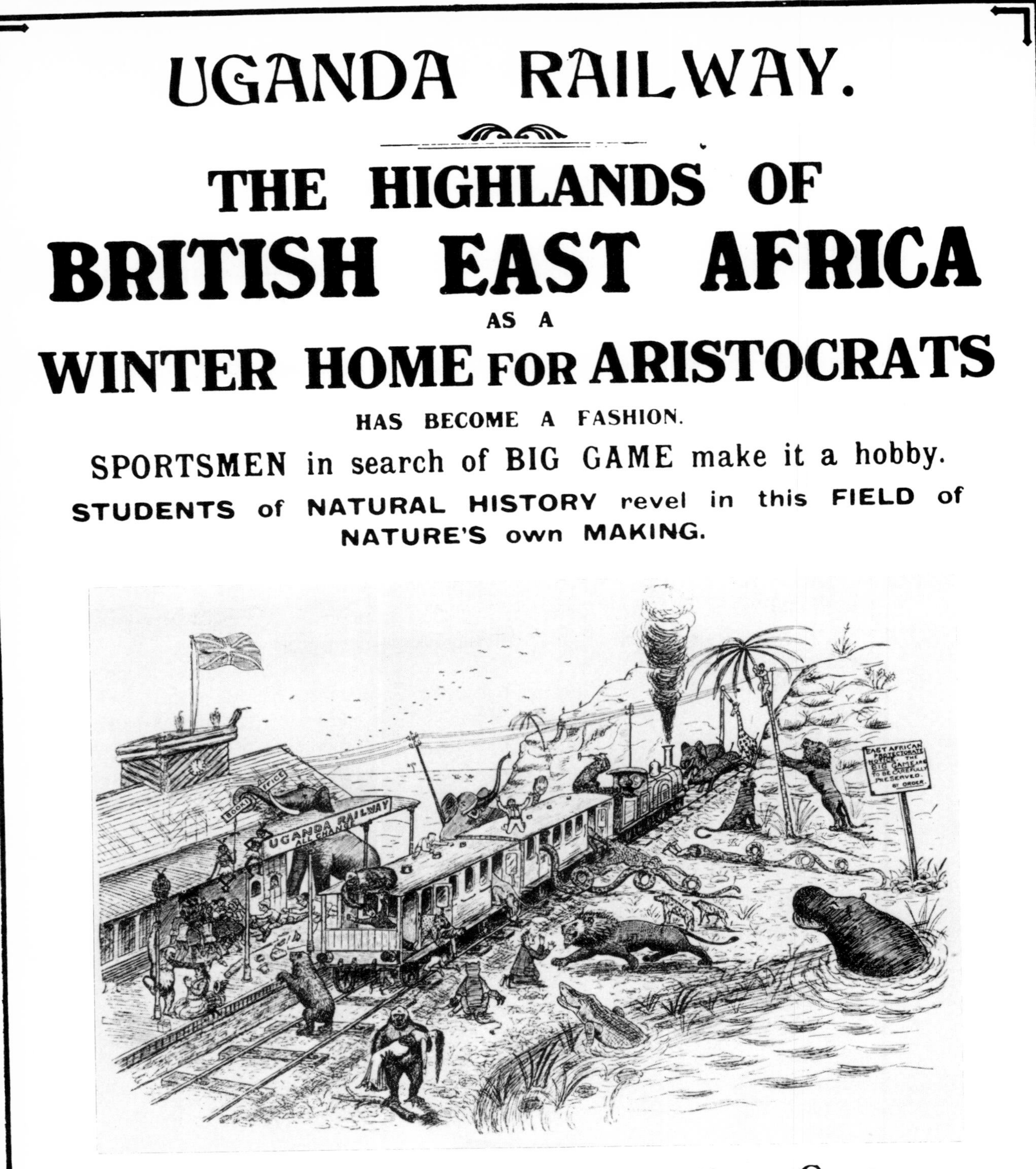

UGANDA RAILWAY Observation Cars pass through the Greatest Natural GAME PRESERVE in the WORLD.

For reliable information, etc., address:
PUBLICITY DEPT., UGANDA RAILWAY,
DEWAR HOUSE, HAYMARKET, S.W.

they asked, about to set out for 'savagedom'. 'I blotted them out,' was Boyes' standard reply.

As the settler population increased after 1903, almost every settler made something on the side out of the safari trade, providing fresh butter and vegetables for Newland and Tarlton's luxurious caravans, or hospitality and advice. Lord Delamere's Blue Posts Hotel was a favourite watering place for safaris, and 'Pop' Binks, one of the earliest settlers, gave up farming in favour of game photography, providing a stuffed lion for any sportsman who had failed to bag his own. Most of the settlers were hunters at heart anyway, for whom farming was second-best. 'When we make our fortune out of sisal', says Elspeth Huxley's neighbour in one of her novels about her East African childhood, 'I shall go home every winter to hunt the fox in County Meath and in the summer I shall come back here to hunt the elephant. Ah, what a grand life that will be!'[15]

The *annus mirabilis* of East African hunting was 1909. The previous spring Selous had received a letter from his old friend, Theodore Roosevelt, asking him to plan a prolonged safari. His presidency would soon be at an end and he had arranged to shoot specimens for the Smithsonian Institute. Selous threw himself into arranging the trip with characteristic thoroughness. He persuaded Roosevelt, who had hoped to 'trust to the native', to hire Newland and Tarlton's best white hunter who would take all the burden of camp arrangement off Roosevelt's shoulders. He himself would accompany Roosevelt on the voyage out, then peel off to do some quiet shooting of his own with another old friend, Northrup Macmillan. Privately he confessed that it was the worst time of year for hunting. After the rains the whole country would be smothered in long grass, and he doubted if he would get the black-maned lion he particularly wanted.

But apart from the lion, which eluded Selous, it was one of those imperial set-pieces when everything went perfectly. Roosevelt and Selous embarked together from Naples on a boat packed with the flotsam of Empire. Foresters, officers, planters, district officers, subalterns *en route* for India – a fine set, Roosevelt noted, these young Englishmen 'who might have come straight from the pages of Kipling'.[16] By day they would foregather on the deck round Selous who, like some great tribal hero, would recount his adventures. Besides Selous, Roosevelt had brought another valuable asset from the English sporting world: a Holland & Holland gun which had been delivered specially to the White House before he left. Everyone who mattered had contributed to the cost: Curzon, Wingate, Lugard, Sir Harry Johnston, Sir Edward Grey (listed by Roosevelt as Foreign Secretary and author of *Dry Fly Fishing*), Sidney Buxton (Postmaster-General and author of *Fishing and Shooting*), the Earl of Lonsdale, Lord Rothschild, Lord Desborough and Selous himself.

At Mombasa there was another old hunter to greet him, Sir Frederick Jackson, acting governor-general. On the train up to Nairobi, the three men were able to discuss such fascinating topics as protective colouring in game, and were delighted to find themselves in agreement.

Opposite 'The result of carefully preserving the big game' – publicity poster for the Uganda Railway.

Roosevelt spent the next few months in East Africa, staying on settlers' farms, including that of that 'mighty hunter', Lord Delamere, and pronounced himself a total convert to the East African way of life. Not only were the Highlands white man's country, but they were the ideal playground for sportsmen. Delamere's only failure was to procure for Roosevelt one of the rarest of game animals, the forest-dwelling bongo, which had only recently been discovered; the problem being, as Lord Cranworth put it, that 'Colonel Roosevelt's bulk and conversational powers somewhat precluded him from tracking'. The porters had christened him Bwana Tumbo, tactfully translated by the East African press as the 'portly master'.

Then the giant cortège filed westwards to Uganda in pursuit of elephant and white rhino, and from there northwards to the Upper Nile – more or less the same route as Churchill had followed on his safari two years before.

Roosevelt's account of his shooting trip, *African Game Trails*, was published the following year and became an immediate best-seller on both sides of the Atlantic, further fuelling the fame of B.E.A. But despite its praise for the British in Africa, it was not entirely successful with his ex-hosts. Roosevelt carefully listed the game totals shot by himself and his son Kermit: 512 animals, excluding game for the pot. Of the big four which were seen as the sportsman's real challenge, they had shot 17 lions, 12 elephants, 11 buffalo and 20 rhino, including 9 of the rare square-mouthed white rhino which had become extinct over most of central Africa. It was this last figure which shocked the English.

Opposite Theodore Roosevelt on safari *en route* to Uganda, 1909.

Right Roosevelt with victim, from the title page of his *African Game Trails*, 1910.

'Do those nine white rhinoceros ever cause ex-president Roosevelt a pang of conscience or a restless night? I for one venture to hope so,' wrote Lord Cranworth.[17] Even the impeccably courteous Frederick Jackson found it a matter of regret to learn from Colonel Roosevelt's own showing that 'he had been so utterly reckless in expenditure of ammunition'.[18] Selous of course would have passed no judgment on his old friend – he was anyway engaged in a European conference on game conservation. But *African Game Trails* administered one more jolt to the British sporting ethos. From game-killers to insatiable trophy-hunters, they were now emerging as ardent conservationists. It was of course only enlightened self-interest – if there were no animals left, there would be nothing to shoot.

Two years before Roosevelt's trip, one ex-hunter had already proclaimed the sportsmanship of the future: shooting your big game by Kodak and flashlight. Surely, wrote Sir Harry Johnston in the introduction, the time has passed when every young or middle-aged Englishman 'who had been crossed in love . . . must go out to Africa to kill big game.'[19]

Not entirely, it seemed. There was no noticeable slackening in the numbers of sportsmen who made their way to Africa and India equipped with Rigbys and Holland & Hollands. No doubt, as one settler put it, the trophies of camera-shooting had many advantages – they were 'beautiful, less bulky and didn't smell' – but there was nothing to beat the thud of a bullet. It took another twenty years before the sportsmanship of the future made any serious impact on the English upper crust and before titles like *With a Camera in Tiger-Land* edged their way onto country-house bookshelves alongside the Badminton and Lonsdale sporting libraries. And, as if to prove how thin was the veneer of sportsmanship, 1909 provided East Africa with its biggest temptation yet.

In December, just as Roosevelt's stately caravan was embarking for Entebbe, a wave of excitement ran through the hunting world. King Leopold of the Belgians was dead, and the Lado Enclave, a huge wedge-shaped piece of savannah and swamp between the Nile and the Congo forest, was open. This was reported crammed with magnificent tuskers, the largest reservoir of elephants left in Africa.

What had happened was that a break had occurred in the thin web of European administration in central Africa. The Lado Enclave had been claimed by the British after the collapse of the Mahdist state in the 1890s, but leased by them to King Leopold for convenience, the lease to run until six months after his death. When that unpleasant king died (removing in most Englishmen's view the darkest blot on the colonial powers' escutcheon) most of the Belgian officials, instead of waiting to hand over the white man's burden to the English, retreated westwards to the more agreeable posts along the Congo itself, leaving the Lado natives and elephants to fend for themselves. The results confirmed, if anything ever did, the British imperial thesis that Africa could no longer be left to look after herself. Every hunter, sportsman, remittance man, or anyone who had ever dreamt of making their fortune, dropped whatever they were doing and headed for the Lado. 'Into the Enclave then came this horde,' wrote one of them, Walter 'Karamoja' Bell.

> At first they were for the most part orderly law-abiding citizens but this restraint was soon thrown off, finding themselves in a country where even murder went unpunished. Every man became a law unto himself. The Sudan had no jurisdiction for six months, and the Belgians had gone. . . . Some of the men went utterly bad and behaved atrociously to the natives. The natives became disturbed, suspicious, sly and treacherous and the game was shot, wounded or killed by all sorts of people who had not the rudiments of huntercraft or shooting.[20]

Bell himself was a cool professional who had been shooting elephants since he was seventeen and had perfected the 'brain shot' with the small-bore high-velocity rifle, so that he could drop an elephant on its knees without its companions even noticing. (In old age he was to be almost as legendary a figure as Selous.) He himself had managed to arrive in the Lado ahead of the horde, and after narrowly escaping being shot by a jumpy group of Belgian askaris on the border, had made his way eventually to the uplands on the edge of the great Congo forest, and found the kind of paradise every elephant-hunter dreamed of.

> High, cool and rolling hills: running streams of pure water in every hollow. The sole bush, a few forest trees lining their banks. In the wet season covered with high strong grass, it was now burned off and the fresh green stuff was coming

Elephants browsing in the Lado Enclave, sketched by 'Karamoja' Bell, 1909.

up. In the far distance could be seen, from one of the highest places, a dark line. It was the edge of 'darkest Africa', the great primeval forest spreading for thousands of square miles. Out of that forest and elsewhere have come hundreds upon hundreds of elephants to feed upon the young green stuff. They stood around that landscape as if made of wood and stuck there. Hunting there was too easy. . . .[21]

In nine months in the Lado Bell bagged 210 elephant (almost a quarter of the total he was to shoot in a long lifetime) and took out over five tons of ivory. John Boyes, the 'king of the Wa-Kikuyu', was another professional who struck it rich. He made three forays into the Lado, taking out half a ton of tusks the first two times. On the third trip, which was only weeks before the British were due to take over, he grabbed so much ivory he could hardly find enough porters to transport his hoard. The same problem faced 'Karamoja' Bell. He decided to bury his hoard of ivory until he could return in a few months, and he marked it with a wooden cross which proved most effective – none of it had been disturbed when he came back.

On his way through the Lado, Roosevelt was entertained by a boisterous group of ivory poachers, including John Boyes, and gallantly toasted them as the 'gentlemen adventurers of central Africa'. Boyes claimed that the ex-President was seriously tempted by their invitation to him 'to chuck all his political work and come out like the great white man he was and join us'.[22] Perhaps he was, briefly.

Opposite John Boyes surrounded by his loot in the Lado Enclave, 1909.

Right African porters bringing home the ivory.

'They are a hard-bitten set, these elephant poachers,' Roosevelt wrote with undisguised approval in *African Game Trails*.

> There are few careers more adventurous or fraught with more peril or which make heavier demands upon the daring, the endurance and physical hardihood of those who follow them. Elephant-hunters face death at every turn, from fever, from assaults of warlike native tribes, from their conflicts with their giant quarry.[23]

As far as the Foreign Office in London were concerned, the sooner the breed became extinct the better. A nasty parliamentary row blew up over the Lado poachers. 'Was it true', Mr Baker asked Sir Edward Grey, 'that the destruction of big game was proceeding practically unchecked?'[24] One rumour claimed that over a thousand elephants in the Lado had been rounded up and were being slaughtered *en masse*. Selous, consulted on the subject, pooh-poohed the rumour. No amount of men, however numerous, could round up such a large body of elephants – the elephants would be more than a match for them. Although he had taken part in many dangerous adventures, he would certainly have drawn the line at such a scheme.

By 1911 the party was over. The hard-core professionals melted off over the borders into the Congo itself or French Equatoria. Bell went to Liberia, where he was assured the bush was full of elephant. It was, but they turned out – to his disgust – to be a dwarf breed who carried only pint-sized tusks.

By a nice irony it was in the midst of another debate on game, this time duck-shooting on Lake Naivasha, that the East African legislative assembly heard the news, four years later, that they were now at war. Hunters, settlers and visiting sportsmen alike hurried off to enlist for the most serious shooting-match yet. The oldest and most famous recruit for the East African Army was Frederick Selous. Having pulled every string he could, including a personal appeal to Kitchener, he finally got himself gazetted to the 25th Royal Fusiliers, which contained most of his East African friends. The first inspection parade brought a temporary lapse on the part of the 64-year-old lieutenant. One of the officers inspecting was Richard Meinertzhagen, by now a naturalist and hunter of some fame himself. 'Selous was there in front of his platoon,' Meinertzhagen recorded, 'looking very serious and standing strictly to attention. We recognised each other at once and were soon deep in the question of the validity of the Nakuru hartebeest and the breeding of the Harlequin duck in Iceland. We both forgot we were on parade, much to the amusement of Selous's platoon who stood rigidly to attention throughout the discussion.'[25]

When the campaign began, Selous was much cheered to find he could still outmarch men a third of his age. 'The men say when I fall out no one will be left standing in the battalion,' he wrote home. 'This is of course nonsense, but as far as standing fatigue, sun, thirst, etc. I really think I am better than most of them.' He marched bare-legged, as in his old elephant-hunting days, carrying a large native stick and wearing the familiar grey double terai on the back of his head, refusing all transport and insisting on sharing all hardships with his platoon. To his men and the rest of the army, struggling with fever, dysentery, jiggers and all the other attendant horrors of jungle warfare, he soon became not so much a hero as a kind of patron saint. 'Anything mean or sordid literally shrivelled up in his presence,' wrote one young officer. It was an odd apotheosis for an old elephant-hunter. He was killed by a sniper's bullet during a skirmish in 1917, and was buried with a simple wooden cross under a tamarind tree in the forest.

The whole East African Army mourned him. General von Lettow-Vorbeck, Commander-in-Chief of the German Army, sent his deepest regrets. Baden-Powell added Selous's name to his roll call of scouting heroes, which already included Charlemagne, Richard Coeur-de-Lion, General Gordon, Speke, Baker and Mary Kingsley. *The Times* in London devoted nearly two columns to his

Opposite F. C. Selous's private collection of trophies at Worplesden. He left them after his death to the Natural History Museum.

Captain F. C. Selous, D.S.O. – the last photo before his death.

obituary, listing his early exploits as hunter, explorer and naturalist and recalling his modesty, his superb physique, his charm. The next day a letter added the authentic voice of sporting England. It reminded readers that,

> Before making the supreme sacrifice for his country, Selous had already made another almost as great. Throughout his career as a sportsman and big game hunter, he invariably offered his finest trophies as a gift to the nation, keeping only the second best for his private collection. All big game sportsmen will appreciate what it meant to part with his best specimens.[26]

Opposite Cricket bridges the Edwardian divide between East and West: Prince Ranjitsinhji and his lifelong friend, C. B. Fry.

How is this reason (which is their reason) to judge a scholar's worth,
By casting a ball at three straight sticks and defending the same with a fourth?
Rudyard Kipling, 'Kitchener's School', 1898

8

PLAYERS

When Frederick Selous ceased to be a full-time hunter after his marriage, he became among other things an enthusiastic cricketer, playing regularly for his local club in Surrey, where he staged a famous annual match, 'Big Game Hunters versus Worplesden'. To a large extent the English addiction to games and game shooting were complementary: both vital ingredients in what made up a sportsman and gentleman. Country-house cricket succeeded country-house shooting and hunting as agreeably as the seasons themselves. In the tropics, where the seasons were often odd or even non-existent the pace was more frenetic.

An idealised view of life for non-commissioned ranks in India. But few men below the rank of sergeant were allowed to bring out wives, and venereal disease was rampant.

A young subaltern in the Indian Army could expect to cram a whole gamut of sporting activities into his day. A jackal hunt before breakfast; polo or fives or hockey in the evening. Then perhaps an uproarious rag after dinner in the mess, especially on guest nights, a moonlit steeplechase ending with the winner jumping the mess table, or a rugger scrum in which one party would try to break up the other by launching their heaviest men in a succession of flying leaps onto their backs.

Baden-Powell recalled nostalgically the favourite game of his day, known as the 'Bounding Brothers of the Bosphorus'. It had been invented by the colonel's brother, 'a quiet harmless planter from Bihar'. They would pile all the mess furniture into a pyramid in the middle of the room with the writing-desk in front. Then each member of the mess clapped his hands three times, rushed forward shouting 'I am a Bounding Brother of the Bosphorus' and turned head over heels on to the pile of furniture. 'Quite simple but . . . it hurt if you landed on the upturned legs of a chair.'[1] Even the rock-like Kitchener could unbend at times. Lady Minto described in her journal the farewell dinner in 1909 given for him as Commander-in-Chief by the staff. 'They had a most rowdy evening. They all sang choruses, did acrobatic feats which ended in bruised bodies and broken heads. The attempt to make Colonel Dunlop and Colonel Birdwood cockfight was unsuccessful.'[2]

Since Baden-Powell's day as a subaltern the cult of organised sports had even shown signs of increasing in India and in the rest of the tropics. For one thing there was now a widespread conviction that violent exercise was the key to good health. Men who played polo, in Lugard's opinion, rarely fell ill and his friend, General Willcocks, Commander-in-Chief of the West African Frontier Force, attributed his good health to running a mile before dinner every day, although he had only one good leg. Yet only a few years before, Sir Patrick Manson, the founding father of tropical medicine, had included *violent* exercise among the dissipations especially to be avoided in hot climates.

In the army there were also sound military reasons for the increasing cult of sport. Since the 1890s the number of cases of venereal disease in India had shot up to horrifying proportions: over fifty per cent of the army in 1897 were admitted during the year for treatment. This was mainly due to one of the English conscience's periodic spasms. After tremendous agitation in the press, led by the then Commander-in-Chief's wife, Lady Roberts, the official military brothels in India had been declared closed. Since no officer was supposed to marry before he reached the rank of captain (perhaps in his mid-thirties) and non-commissioned ranks until they had served at least five years, the problem of providing legitimate sexual outlets was acute. Kitchener, who became Commander-in-Chief in 1902, tackled the problem with a battery of moral exhortations and threats, recommending those two traditional public school remedies: good example and more and more organised games. 'Drink and idleness' were the causes, he told his officers, of the disease problem. It was the officers' duty to keep the men busy by inculcating a love of games and outdoor sports. No officer who succumbed himself could expect to see active service, and 'no soldier who is unable to exercise due restraint in these matters can be expected to be entrusted with command over his comrades. Every man can, by self control, restrain the imprudent and reckless impulses which so often lead men astray. What would your mothers, your sisters and your friends at home think of you?'[3] He had never, by all accounts, found much difficulty in controlling these reckless and imprudent impulses himself.

By 1909, when Kitchener left his command of the British Army in India, the venereal statistics had dropped to a militarily acceptable two and a half per cent per annum. But the improvement was undoubtedly due more to the discreet re-opening of properly supervised military brothels than anything else. Frank Richards, whose memoir *Old Soldier Sahib* gives a brilliantly vivid picture of life for 'other ranks' around this period, wrote that nearly everyone used the Rag, as it was called. This was open every day from twelve noon until eleven at night, and had twice-weekly inspections by army doctors and strict provisions for hygiene. To go with the half-caste prostitutes or native girls who lurked outside every cantonment

Army gymnastics display at the Delhi Durbar, 1903. Kitchener as Commander-in-Chief stressed athletics as a cure for 'reckless and imprudent impulses'.

was considered a 'horrible form of suicide'; but Richards records that to abstain altogether from sex was considered to be unhealthy in a hot climate like India. So much for official propaganda attempts to purify the troops by sport alone.

At officer level, however, the exhortations, combined with violent exercise, do appear to have been partly successful. Richard Meinertzhagen, by no means the most biddable of subalterns, recorded wistfully the temptations of being offered a beautiful Toda girl by a local chief, after he had killed a man-eating tiger in the Nilgiri hills which had been pestering the village. 'She was fifteen or so with a fair skin and lovely features, but I am glad to say that my self respect won a short sharp fight with animal instinct and I firmly said she must go back to her father.'[4] The temptation continued for several days as she kept coming back to his tent at night, bringing honey and begging to be allowed to come back to his barracks as a servant. Meinertzhagen had to tell his shikari not to let her into the camp again. He felt rather a brute 'for she was so pretty and simple in her ways and so unlike an ordinary native', but undoubtedly he would have been in serious trouble if he had brought her back. Subalterns' morals were supervised fairly strictly by their commanding officers. A trip to Kashmir to shoot sheep would be approved, but a subaltern asking for two months' leave in Mussoorie, notorious for its population of pretty Eurasian girls, would almost certainly be turned down.

The most convincing proof of the Indian Army's high moral tone is the sense of shock experienced by its officers when transferred to more far-flung posts of Empire. In 1902 Richard Meinertzhagen was posted to the King's African Rifles in Nairobi, after he had had a row with his senior officer in India. He described his fellow officers there with deep disgust. One drank like a fish, one preferred boys to women and was not ashamed, and all the rest brought their native women into mess. He threatened a formal complaint if they did not reform at once. 'They were furious', he wrote, 'but complied.'[5]

A year later a similar whirlwind swept through the Southern Nigerian regiment of the West African Frontier Force. Hugh Montagu Trenchard (the future Air Marshal Lord Trenchard) was at this stage a lanky young major who had made a name for himself organising and playing regimental polo in India, and then as a daring patrol leader of irregulars in the Boer War. After a casual encounter with a recruiting officer at a country house weekend, he volunteered for the Nigerian service where there was some 'real work' to be done.

The drinking, gambling and womanising in Calabar and Lagos, he was warned, were past belief. His first morning in the regimental mess confirmed this view. The officers filtered in unshaven in pyjamas while the colonel sat apart in rigid silence, properly attired, and turned a deaf ear to the boasts of sexual exploits around him. Trenchard first proved his mettle to his fellow officers by leading a successful 'pacifying' expedition into Ibo territory, then forced the unfortunate colonel's resignation and set about reforming the mess. He prohibited gambling, forbade *any* consorting with native women, and packed off the worst offenders to England. Then he rebuilt the ramshackle barracks at Lagos and laid out playing fields and provided trophies for soccer, golf, tennis and polo. The regimental morale was soon reported to have shown a vast improvement. Trenchard, however, contracted an abscess on the liver, perhaps from all his exertions, and had to be shipped home.[6]

How long the improvements survived after his departure is not recorded. The West Coast climate and the 'Old Coasters' ' traditional aversion to exercise sapped all but the most iron resolves. Decima Moore Guggisberg, wife of the Gold Coast's director of survey, recorded at the same period the sad decline of one English cantonment at Sekondi. In the space of one year the tennis court had become a ruin, its net hanging 'in rotten strips; the cricket ground was a foot deep in grass and the golf links buried beneath a ten-foot scrub'. And the Europeans, instead of having an hour of healthy amusement, now spent their time 'strolling slackly from bungalow to bungalow with no aim in life but to get to the dinner hour'. It was all, she thought, for want of one good example.[7]

Such edifying or depressing tales would of course have been no surprise to the England Trenchard and Guggisberg had left behind. Few educated Edwardians doubted that games-playing and moral and physical health were inextricably intertwined. The extraordinary transformation of the great English public schools in the last half century seemed to have proved it conclusively again and again.

Thanks to Thomas Hughes's famous best-seller *Tom Brown's Schooldays* (reprinted almost every year since its publication in 1864), the innovator of the system was popularly and erroneously seen as Dr Arnold at Rugby. In fact, Arnold had shown little or no interest in games and deplored what he saw as the brutality of soul reflected in 'cultivated athleticism'. Arnold's disciples, however, were less confident of achieving reform by Christian example and quiet walks through the countryside. The English schoolboy's traditional leisure pursuits were unsociably savage – poaching, birds'-nesting, snaring rabbits, throwing stones, ratting and setting ferrets – and none of them were likely to endear him to the local landlords or

Left The result of playing – and not playing – games, sketched by Baden-Powell.

Opposite Kipling attacks the British games-playing ethos in 'The Islanders', 1903.

townsfolk. (Selous's account of his schoolboy escapades in the Lincolnshire woods as a poacher is a perfect example of the kind of thing squires disliked.)

By the 1870s most public school historians could report that a *civilised* out-of-doors life – cricket, football and wholesome sports – had replaced the old games. The lessons engendered at the same time: team spirit, plucky unselfishness, obedience, grit, learning to take a beating gallantly in the same spirit as a victory were obviously, it was noted, also ideal qualities for young empire-builders, successfully blending aggression with self-abnegation, and the Darwinist principle of the survival of the fittest with Christian morals. Tom Brown and his friend Harry East, who went out to command a platoon in India, were the very stuff the Empire was made of. Real life school magazines and *Boy's Own* annuals regularly celebrated cricket and football heroes alongside the deeds of Empire – 'An Old Boy in the Bush', 'On the Warpath in Manipur', 'With the Frontier Light Horse in Zululand', etc.

By the turn of the century, games were rated higher in moral value than lessons themselves. 'There is more learning in the playing field than in the classroom', wrote Andrew Lang in a glowing preface to a book called *Kings of Cricket.*[8]

Oddly enough, one of the dissentient voices was Kipling's, a natural Stalky among the ever-swelling crowds of Easts and Browns. Kipling combined a curiously romantic vision of public school and Empire with a savage sense of their mutual absurdities.

> Thank God who made the British Isles
> And taught me how to play.
> I do not worship crocodiles
> Or bow the knee to clay.
>
> Give me a willow wand and I
> With hide and cork and twine
> From century to century will
> Gamble round my shrine.

One of Kipling's bitterest poems, 'The Islanders', was written in 1902 at the end of the Boer War, comparing the efficiency of colonial troops with England's bumbling amateurs:

. . . ye fawned on the Younger Nations for the men who could shoot and ride!
Then ye returned to your trinkets; then ye contented your souls
With the flannelled fools at the wicket or the muddied oafs at the goals.

The solution, Kipling believed passionately, lay in compulsory military service. He made his point deliberately in traditional cricketing terms:

But each man born in the Island entered at youth to the game –
As it were almost cricket, not to be mastered in haste,
But after trial and labour, by temperance, living chaste.
As it were almost cricket – as it were even your play,
Weighed and pondered and worshipped, and practised day and day.[10]

In parodying or pillorying cricket especially, Kipling had attacked the Empire's most sacred cow, for cricket was the imperial sportsman's game *par excellence*, the one whose moral value was seen as especially valuable. Football was always slightly suspect, partly because it had already split into two camps, the professionals and the amateurs, and partly because the huge football crowds from the '90s reminded too many imperial pundits of gladiatorial spectacles and their corollary, the decline and fall of the Roman Empire. (Anti-imperialists like Wilfrid Blunt dourly condemned football for a different reason, as another sign of militarism and brutality, 'the rehabilitation of Napoleon and other war-making scoundrels'.)[11] But cricket, which had miraculously fused the amateur and the professional tradition, seemed to represent the best of England. It had achieved, it seemed, in sporting terms what Tories (and Liberals) devoutly hoped for in politics – an alliance of classes, yet with each recognising its proper place (coming out of its own door in the pavilion, so to speak).

And the same of course went for relations between administrators of England's great dependent Empire and those they ruled. Imperial literature, especially its verse, becomes so thick with cricketing metaphors towards the end of the century that it is hard to know which to choose: straight clean bats, sticky wickets, stealing a run, keeping your end up, playing the game. (P. G. Wodehouse once wrote that he was the only writer of his generation who had never rhymed 'leather' with 'weather'.) The most famous incentive to play the game was Henry Newbolt's poem, 'Vitae Lampada', with its dramatic transition from close and cricket field to the blood-sodden sands of an imperial frontier war. Baden-Powell so admired it that he adapted it as a pageant for his Boy Scouts when he founded the movement in 1908. Newbolt's other best-known poem was his 'Ode to Clifton Chapel', with its exhortation:

To set the cause beyond renown
To love the game beyond the prize
To honour as you strike him down
The foe that comes with fearless eyes.

But after 1901, of course, it was not so often a question of a glorious last innings against overwhelming odds, but of how to provide stonewalling, slow steady bats to hold the Empire together.

Ralph Furse: cricketing values in the Colonial Office.

By historic coincidence it was to be Newbolt's son, Francis, and his son-in-law Ralph Furse, who were to do just that in the Colonial Office for the next forty years. Furse, an old Etonian brought up from earliest childhood on deeds that won the Empire, cricket and cold baths, joined the Colonial Office as a recruiting officer in 1910 and stayed there (with the exception of the war years) until 1948, marking the Colonial Service indelibly with his values. Francis Newbolt joined him there in 1919. In his memoirs Furse recorded that cricket permeated the Colonial Office from top to bottom, literally as well as metaphorically, when he arrived. When the Colonial Secretary (Lewis Harcourt) had gone home, the junior officials would set up their stumps in the State Office, which was 'quite long enough for a decent pitch';[12] they bowled from the great door and used the marble fireplace as wicket.

One of Harcourt's predecessors, Alfred Lyttleton, had been one of the great cricketing heroes of all time. Captain of cricket at Eton and at Oxford, he played for Middlesex in the 1880s and his batting and bowling had once been described by no less than W. G. Grace as 'the champagne of cricket'. A charming, essentially modest man, Lyttleton, according to his sister, saw himself as captain of the eleven during his time in the Colonial Office and he was to die, sadly but suitably, in 1913 from peritonitis caused by a blow in the stomach from a cricket ball. Even Joe Chamberlain, a non-public school man, had been infected by the passion for cricket. Hesketh Bell, who visited Highbury in 1899, recorded that the great man had installed an ingenious mechanical device for playing cricket *indoors* after dinner, perhaps to make his visiting colonial officials feel at home.[13]

Just how successful public school cricket and football swells proved when they actually arrived in the colonies as administrators was another matter. Kipling was by no means the only critic of flannelled fools. In 1913 Herbert Branston Gray launched a violent attack on the games-playing ethos in *The Public Schools and the Empire*, listing semi-facetiously the ten commandments of a public schoolboy:

1 There is only one God, and the Captain of football is his Prophet.
2 My school is the best in the world.

The Straits Team, 1897. Inter-port cricket was a regular fixture in the Far East.

3 Without big muscles, strong will, and proper collars there is no salvation.
4 I must wash much and in accordance with tradition.
5 I must speak the truth even to a master, if he believes everything I tell him.
6 I must play games with all my heart, with all my soul and with all my strength.
7 To work outside class hours is indecent.
8 Enthusiasm, except for games, is in bad taste.
9 I must look up to the older fellows and pour contempt on newcomers.
10 I must show no emotion and not kiss my mother in public.

He accused the public schools of turning out 'a useless drone trained only to wield a willow or kick a bladder', whom no decent white colony would accept as a citizen. 'The public schoolboy is a more conspicuous failure in Australia and Canada than a conspicuous success in the wilds of Africa or plains of India.'

But in general opinion remained optimistic that for the non-white Empire the public school games-playing ethos worked well enough, although it was a pity it could not be allied with a better all-round education.

> Many a lad, ignorant of the rudiments of useful knowledge, who can speak no language but his own and writes that imperfectly, to whom the noble language

of his country and stirring history of his fathers are almost a sealed book, and who has devoted a greater part of his time and nearly all his thoughts to athletic sports, yet brings away with him something beyond all price, a manly straightforward character, a scorn of lying and meanness, habits of obedience and command and fearless courage. Thus equipped he goes out into the world and bears a man's part in subduing the earth, ruling its wild folk and building up the Empire.[14]

In terms of prestige it was notable that none of the new colonial services rated more highly than the Sudan Political Service, with its preponderance of cricketing and rowing Blues.

In the older colonial services of the eastern Empire the days when a Resident like Sir Frank Swettenham could recruit a staff primarily for their batting and bowling skills were nearly over. 'The era of work has succeeded the era of play,' wrote one old hand regretfully in 1904. 'Planters' and miners' associations take the place of cricket and sports and the bankers turning out for rugger now is a matter of comment.'[15] But some interest in games was still an important common denominator of social life, a proof of clubbability. If hunting often provided a welcome escape route for Englishmen from social rituals and the ties of 'civilisation', English games – croquet, tennis, cricket – provided the easiest and most natural way of meeting your fellow Europeans at the club. Though there was intense admiration for great hunters like Selous or 'Karamoja' Bell, who were loners and who could live among wild men and beasts and return apparently unscathed, most colonials preferred their jungles to be kept at bay or visited in small doses. Isolation among alien or savage cultures was seen as dangerous. The first step on the downward path to 'going native' could begin when you stayed at home drinking in your bungalow instead of joining the others at cricket or tennis and drinking in the club.

Even Leonard Woolf, who was far removed from the habitual games-playing stereotype, made a point of turning up regularly every evening at the Jaffna Tennis Club. At one point during his time in Jaffna he shared a bungalow with a pathetic character called Dutton, a nervous recluse who spent his time writing poems about fairies and playing sickly German *Lieder* and Gilbert and Sullivan on a badly strung piano. Woolf decided Dutton must be helped and encouraged him to come down with him to the tennis courts in the evening. Dutton finally screwed up courage to do so and from then on came down every evening to play 'a hopelessly incompetent game' with two female missionaries. Soon afterwards, he married one of them, much to Woolf's surprise. The attempt to straighten out Dutton by tennis, however, proved ultimately unsuccessful. A year or two later Woolf called on them in Matura, only to be told by a sobbing Mrs Dutton that the marriage was a complete failure and Dutton was hopelessly queer.[16]

Most of the great colonial clubs of the eastern tropics were founded originally to promote games. There were cricket clubs, polo clubs, rifle clubs, golf clubs. . . . In a tightly packed port like Singapore, shortage of playing fields could lead to trouble.

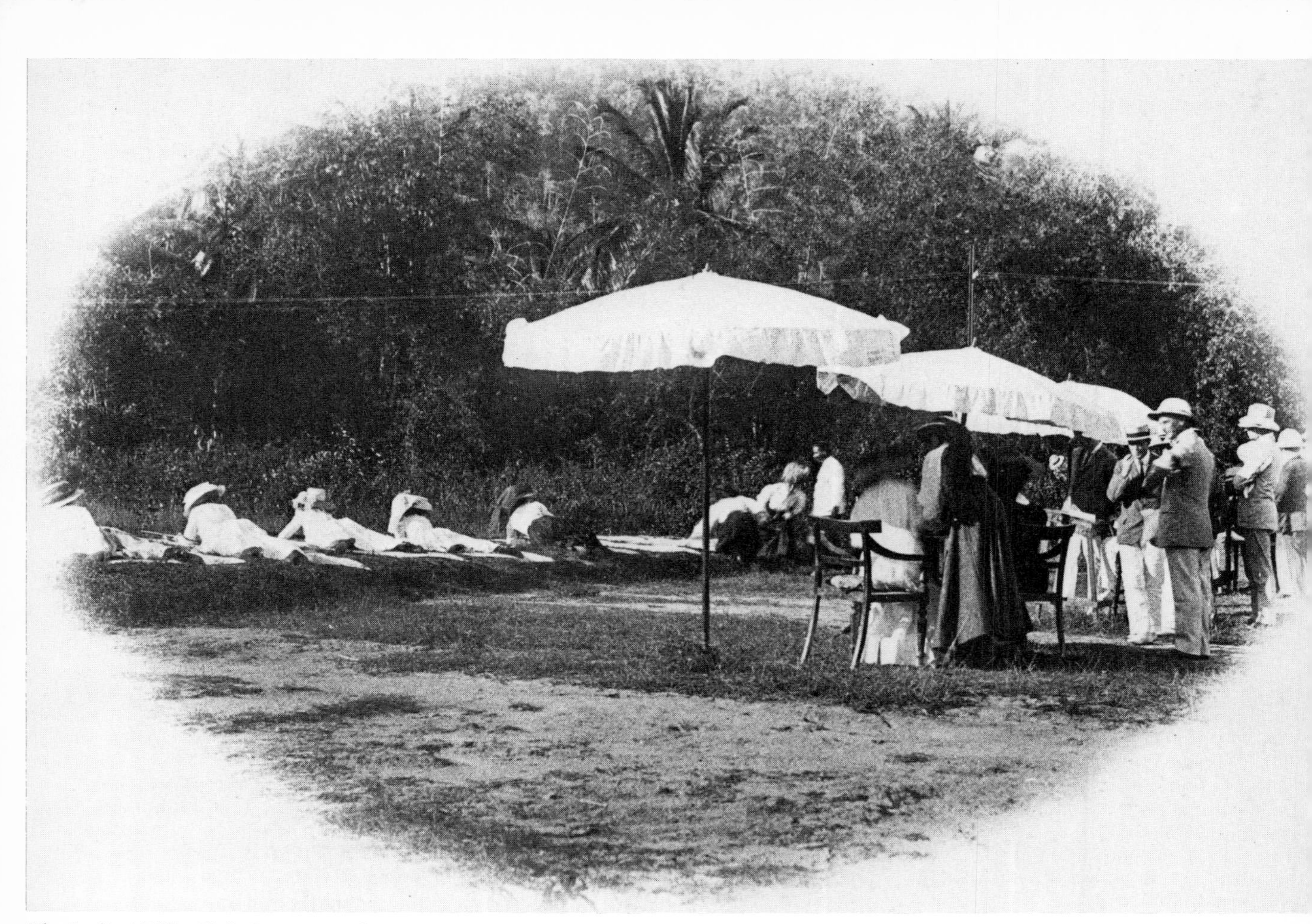

The Ladies' Rifle Club, Penang, early 1900s.

In 1898 a tremendous row broke out in the Sporting Club when it was discovered that the committee had given permission for polo to be played on the links two days a week. But the most ubiquitous club of all was the Race Club. Racecourses were a recognised form of territorial marking throughout the tropics. 'From my experience,' wrote Cromer, quoting Curzon, 'I would say the first thing an Englishman does in the outlying portions of the Empire is to make a racecourse. The second is to make a golf course.' He himself recalled arriving in Cairo shortly after the battle of Tel-el-Kebir to find the administration in 'a state of the utmost confusion but a racecourse already laid out and a grandstand erected'.[17] Racing mania had spread like wildfire up and down the treaty ports of China in the '60s and '70s and by 1900 there were courses all over the Malay States too; at Taiping, Kuala Lumpur, Seremban and Ipoh, even in North Borneo and Sarawak, despite the steaming hot climate and the tiny British community. In 1900 at Kuching race week all the races were won by the same horse, or rather pony, whose rider, a tall officer called Lewis, rode with his feet almost touching the ground.

Once the grandstand had been put up, every effort was usually made to keep things sportingly amateur and minimise distinctions of wealth. Ponies in the treaty

The race-course at Happy Valley, Hong Kong, 1897.

ports were brought in unbroken as 'griffins' and sold off by lot at fixed prices to ensure everyone a sporting chance. The fact that promising-looking ones were resold almost immediately to the highest bidder and that great companies like Jardine's regularly won most of the races was neither here nor there.

Ensuring a sporting chance could of course be used when necessary to keep out the wrong sort without openly doing so on racial grounds. The Nairobi Jockey Club was to refuse the Aga Khan's application for membership in the '20s on the grounds that his horses and those of other rich Indians would provide unfair competition. The racing in Kenya must be kept 'cheap, clean and simple'.

Indeed, reconciling 'fair play' and 'team spirit' could often prove an impossible business. Though most colonial officers genuinely believed and hoped that sport and the games ethos could and should transcend racial and social barriers, in practice it was all more difficult than in village or English county cricket. In England Prince Ranjitsinhji was as famous and honoured a cricketing hero as W. G. Grace or 'Plum' Warner or his friend C. B. Fry. East of Suez things got more difficult. Could a club, even a sporting club, be a successful club without being exclusive, a cave for Europeans only? George V, who toured India as Prince of Wales in 1905, was astonished to learn that no Indian, whatever his education or birth, could join a European club, and remained unconvinced when told that this was vital to give the official classes relief from their duties.

In the Malay States, where English administrators had remained tactfully conscious of their status as 'advisers' only to native rulers, most of the early clubs were multi-racial. J. H. M. Robson, an old Malay hand, wistfully recalled the early days in the Selangor Club when racial distinctions were unknown, and everyone would gather for a curry tiffin at the house of the leading Indian in the community, K. Thanboosany Pillay. The Selangor Club was popularly known as the 'Spotted Dog' in honour of the alleged mixture of colour among its members. But the very fact of its spots brought its social downfall in the next decade.

In 1890 the Lake Club was founded, which rapidly became the haven for Kuala Lumpur's white élite. By 1894 the secretary of the Selangor Club noted sadly that whereas it had once been an honour for the Resident to be president of the club, it was now much more of an honour to the club that he consented to serve as president. The same process happened in Perak. The Perak Club, founded in 1880, was upstaged by the New Club, opened in 1894, which only admitted whites and then only of a certain class.

The larger the pool of Europeans the greater the disposition to internal snobberies, India providing the supreme example. 'Clod-hopping collectors' would not have attempted to take themselves or their families to Simla, where the fast 'Simla set' could be so unfriendly – the same Simla set whose company Curzon had compared cruelly to dining with the housekeeper every day. Tyndale-Biscoe recorded disapprovingly a garden party in Kashmir at which he asked a visiting Anglo-Indian officer to arrange a tennis four. The officer looked round the other guests and announced superciliously: 'I do not know anybody here.' 'It is so distressing,' wrote Tyndale-Biscoe, 'that in India, where there are so many castes, Britishers should be such fools as to copy this evil custom by bringing class distinctions into sport.'[18]

In the smaller out-stations of Empire, groups of exiles clung perforce to the same small rock. The Jaffna Tennis Club in Woolf's time included five civil servants, three wives, two female missionaries and one choleric retired captain from the Ceylon Rifles.

In West Africa there was often not even a clubhouse. After perhaps an erratic game of polo played among the ant-hills on half-wild native ponies, the tiny community would gather, each man with his own deck chair and whisky bottle and supply of soda, probably on the D.C.'s veranda, and drink and talk until it was time to turn in. 'Scotch clubs' they were appropriately named. Yet the invisible walls were still there. One of Cary's novels – set in the '20s – describes the appalling humiliation of an Oxford-educated Nigerian princeling who tries to draw up a chair among the Europeans.[19]

To Woolf's jaundiced eye everything about the English in Ceylon was like a scene out of a bad novel – larger than life, thoroughly stagey. Even the sunsets seemed unreal. 'We were always consciously or subconsciously playing a part, acting on stage,' the backdrop, he decided later, being imperialism. No doubt it would be easy to detect subconscious imperial motives in the other traditional pastime for English colonial society in the tropics – dressing themselves up. Except of course that it was what they also did at home.

Where dressing up differed from most of the other outdoor sports of Empire was of course that it was gloriously heterosexual. The craze for amateur theatricals represents above all the rise of the 'Mem' – that sickly enfeebled creature so often described in early Victorian Indian memoirs, lying in her darkened bungalow while her husband rides round his district or plays polo. By the end of the century she had emerged triumphantly into the limelight. Or rather the footlights of Simla or Poona or Singapore. Theatricals were the mixed sport *par excellence* and rumoured to have precisely the opposite moral effect to cricket. The two most dangerous things for a woman in India, Maud Diver had warned in a book largely designed to refute Kipling's scandalous picture of Simla society in *Plain Tales from the Hills*, were military men without wives and amateur theatricals. Certainly a success on the Simla stage could be a head-turning experience. Take its effect on Lady Eileen Elliot, the eldest of Lord Minto's three beautiful daughters, who received rave notices for her annual appearances.

In 1909 she played the heroine in Clive Fitch's melodrama called *Truth*. 'The play was a *great* success,' Lady Minto wrote in her diary.

> Scindia was so deeply moved by a scene between Eileen and her husband that he rushed away, sank on a sofa, tossed off his head-gear and brushed away his tears with its embroidered fringe. One of the Indian clerks covered his face with his

Lady Eileen Elliot, the Viceroy's daughter, stars in *Truth* at Simla, 1909, opposite Lord Francis Scott.

hands, muttering 'My God, my God, but this is good acting.' Rumour has it that Lord Kitchener was seen surreptitiously wiping away a tear.[20]

'What a pity,' wrote a Simla paper, 'that this noble young lady should not take her place on the stage for which she seems born. A more charming actress could not be found in all India.'[21] In 1910 she starred again, this time as the heroine of *The Thief* which, it was reported, gave full scope to her histrionic powers. The following year, after the Viceroy's return to England, Lady Eileen caused a flutter in the social press by announcing her plan to go on the professional stage back in London. 'Many society people will experience a severe shock,' reported *Vanity Fair*. 'It is stated the Earl of Minto has tried to dissuade his daughter but without avail.' Much, no doubt, to her family's relief Lady Eileen announced in 1914 her engagement instead to her father's old A.D.C., Lord Francis Scott, who had once played her lover in *Truth*. After the war the young couple emigrated to Kenya, where Lord Francis Scott soon became prominent in polo and settler politics, and Lady Eileen noted in her diary the settlers' wives' failure to dress properly or look after their complexions.

Occasionally a true professional swelled the ranks of the gifted amateurs. In 1905 the most dashing couple in Africa were Lillian Decima Moore and Major Gordon Guggisberg, CMG, RE (director of the Gold Coast Survey), whom we have met before on the playing fields of Sekondi. Decima Moore was a pretty, firm-chinned brunette who had made her name singing Gilbert and Sullivan in the '90s, with occasional dips into straight comedy and French farce. (George Bernard Shaw described her as hopelessly British in *La Fille de Mon Argot* in 1892.) Guggisberg was an engineer with matinée-idol good looks, and already celebrated for his love affairs and his prowess at cricket. His first marriage was already over when he met Decima in 1905 (he had eloped to Colombo in 1895 with his colonel's daughter while stationed in Singapore). After a whirlwind courtship, he and Decima had married in August 1905 and set sail almost immediately on the Elder Dempster boat back to Accra. Once arrived in the gloomy Accra cantonment Decima showed her capacity to star on any stage, however unpromising. She transformed decrepit chairs and tables with soap, water, and chintz covers, laid out a few brightly coloured native mats on the floor, helped lay out the new golf course, watched polo and cricket, and kept a diary of all her experiences.

In 1906 she followed her husband on tour and soon had the excitement of being the first white woman into Comassie, the notorious Ashanti capital. In the evening she and her husband entertained the Comassie white community of twenty-eight with little duologues – 'probably the first theatrical performance in Comassie' – and afterwards the Commissioner and she sang for nearly three hours without pause. Even more exciting was the drama she witnessed from her veranda during the day. Two groups of Africans had started to throw stones at each other, amid wild yells and screams, until a small native policeman rushed out and single-handedly pushed them apart. 'One of the pluckiest actions I ever saw.' The first group then returned and broke into a great full-throated triumphant chorus. 'It was the song of defiance

The most dashing couple in West Africa: Decima Moore and Major Gordon Guggisberg.

and I think that nothing I have ever heard has moved me more than that terrific chorus of men's voices, singing in perfect parts, in perfect time, breathing defiance in every note and gradually dying away as the party disappeared down the hill into the native town.'

Her reactions were curiously like Leonard Woolf's. 'It seemed to me more like a scene out of a Drury Lane drama than a bit of real life.'[22]

Decima published a sparkling account of her adventures in 1909 called simply *We Two in West Africa*, which her husband gallantly admitted he would like to have written himself. Sad to say, however, the honeymoon with her handsome surveyor had soon worn off, and so had the lure of the Coast. She returned to the London stage, he to mapping the bush and teaching the natives cricket. In 1912 he was promoted to be director of surveys for the whole of Nigeria, and was soon involved in some steamy exchanges with Lord Lugard himself. Decima did him one good turn, however. During the war she made friends with the famous actress and writer Elinor Glyn and through her with Elinor Glyn's devoted admirer, Lord Milner. After the war Milner promoted Guggisberg to be Governor of the Gold Coast in Sir Hugh Clifford's wake, a feat of professional hurdling which infuriated both Lugard and Clifford.

Decima, who enjoyed the idea of herself as a governor's lady, returned to the Gold Coast to take up her new role. A fierce marital drama was enacted, culminating in a furious scene during the royal visit by Princess Marie-Louise. Decima, who had gone forward to greet the Princess, had to be physically restrained when it was pointed out that her husband, the King's representative, had precedence. The Gold Coast buzzed with the story for years afterwards.

Despite these domestic squalls Guggisberg himself was to prove one of the most successful and progressive of post-war African proconsuls – the two things now being a great deal more synonymous than before the war. Stonewalling imperialism had now given way to a slightly more dashing game. His departure from the Gold Coast was celebrated with a touching tribute to his favourite game. The chiefs of the Legislative Council played a cricket match clad in robes on which his portrait was painted. Under them the inscription read: 'Guggisberg Forever Governor in the Hearts of the Gold Coast People.'[23]

Probably nowhere was cricket and the cricketing spirit more successful than in the mission field. Some of the most famous recruits ever to the missions had been the Cambridge Seven, who enlisted for the China Inland Mission after hearing Moody and Sankey preach in Cambridge in 1883. They included Stanley Smith, stroke of the Cambridge boat, and C. T. Studd, captain of cricket, one of three cricketing brothers as famous as the Lyttletons. C. T. Studd found his way from China to Africa eventually, where he built an open-air cricket-pitch church, twenty-two yards long, in the Congo jungle. Though he suffered from chronic asthma he stayed out there until his death, convinced that St Paul was urging him to keep up the batting till the last.

Tyndale-Biscoe was of the same Cambridge vintage and to some extent took Studd as his mentor. Few missionaries, however, can have preached the gospel of games quite so determinedly. In his autobiography, Tyndale-Biscoe relates cheerfully how he converted his Brahmin pupils to playing football. The original introduction to the game went like this:

The first football team in Kashmir, 1894.

Boys, as T.B. holds up leather football: What is this?
T.B.: It is a football.
Boys: What is the use of it?
T.B.: For playing a game.
Boys: Shall we receive any money if we play that game?
T.B.: No.
Boys: Then we shall not play that game. What is the ball made of?
T.B.: Leather.
Boys: Take it away! Take it away!
T.B.: Why should I take it away?
Boys: Because it is jutha (unholy). We may not touch it, it is leather.
T.B.: I do not wish you to handle it, I want you to kick it and today you are *going* to learn how to kick it, boys.
Boys: We will not play that jutha game.

Undeterred, Tyndale-Biscoe explained the rules, drew a map of a football pitch on the blackboard and, with the help of his Brahmin teachers, all armed with single sticks, shooed the pupils, some of whom were huge bearded boys with wives and children, out onto the public common. After setting his goalposts and positioning his teams properly, he put the football in the middle of the pitch and ordered the centre forward (a boy with a nice black beard) to kick off. Nothing happened. The boy stayed motionless. Tyndale-Biscoe repeated the order. Still nothing. Then he lined up the teachers, still armed with single sticks, and told them as soon as they heard him shout out 'Kick' to rush out from the goal waving their sticks and shouting blue murder for all they were worth. As he called 'kick' for the third time, pandemonium broke out. Down came the teachers shouting and waving their single sticks:

> Off went that ball and in five minutes all was confusion for the boys forgot their places in the field and that they were holy Brahmin and a rough-and-tumble began. As they tried to kick the ball but generally missed it, their clogs flew into the air and their pugaris were knocked off, while their nightgowns flapped in one another's faces – a grand mix-up of clothes and humanity.

Then all of a sudden there was a shriek of horror and the game stopped. A boy had had the unholy leather football kicked bang into his face. Tyndale-Biscoe sent him off briskly to wash in the canal nearby. 'Back came the washed boy and the rest of the players, all of whom to my surprise at once resumed the game and continued till I called time.'[24]

The story, however, had a less jolly sequence. The black-bearded boy who had kicked off at the start of the game was disowned by his family as defiled, and would have been homeless if a 'less bigoted relation' had not taken him in. An English bishop who heard of the incident years later was horrified and sent a letter of remonstration to Biscoe. But the black-bearded boy, now a senior government official, according to Tyndale-Biscoe immediately wrote off to the bishop, testifying to his debt to the game. Football had helped him run straight amid the bribery and corruption of government offices. It took Tyndale-Biscoe ten years more before football and cricket, both using unholy leather balls, found official acceptance, and even then he reported sadly that sportsmanship had remained elusive in Kashmir. Cricket pitches mysteriously contracted or expanded according to whether the opposing team were batting or fielding, and during one tug-of-war between Tyndale-Biscoe's school and the Srinagar state school, he was surprised to see that the end of the rope was firmly anchored on the state-school side to a raised flowerbed. Naturally, when the rope was undone, the C.M.S. school won the tug-of-war.

After this rather hair-raising account of the introduction of football in Kashmir, it is a relief to turn to the happier story of cricket in the Pacific. Enthusiasm there had almost been too great. In 1889 Sir Arthur Gordon reported that all bickering among the tribes in Tonga had ceased since the introduction of cricket. But a few years later *Wisden* reported that the King of Tonga had had to issue a proclamation forbidding play more than one day a week, since the plantations were being entirely neglected by his subjects for the cricket field and they would soon all starve to death.

The last island to be colonised in the Pacific by the English missions was Papua or, later, British New Guinea. Here one of the first arrivals was Charles Abel of the L.M.S. Like Tyndale-Biscoe, Abel was a product of the Moody and Sankey crusade of the 1880s, and a militantly muscular Christian. At home, he had played for

The Rev. Charles Abel's Papuans on the cricket pitch at Kwato, early 1900s.

Hertfordshire. He arrived in Kwato Island in 1891 and immediately set the islanders to fill in a swamp below the site of the mission and lay out a cricket pitch. He had no difficulty in persuading the Papuans to take up the game, though the right attitude sometimes took longer to teach. The Papuans were prone to lie down on the pitch unless actually batting, and when a fielder was told to retrieve the ball, he'd answer, pointing at the batsman, 'No, *he* hit it' – a too literal interpretation of fair play. Abel insisted on strictly formal rules and attire – white pads, boots, etc. The local settler population, mostly Australians, sneeringly dubbed him 'the king of dusky cricket'. They became even more hostile when Abel's sense of fair play led him to denounce the governor to authority in 1904 for a particularly brutal punitive expedition. The governor, who was officially reprimanded, committed suicide under his flagstaff. Abel, undaunted, continued his mission for the next twenty-five years, cricket and Christ increasingly inseparable in his mind.

'You will be pleased when you come back to see the wonderful change in these young converts,' he wrote to one of his friends in 1922. 'Bele is a very attractive youth (and a fine medium bowler), Olaf too is a nice lad (and very clever behind the sticks), Narpie has the family coarseness but M. . . . gives him a good character and he will be the best medium break we have for some time to come.' The Kwato eleven became famous throughout New Guinea. Abel died in a car accident, just as he was arranging to send them to Australia for a cricket tour. After his death the project fell through and was never revived, but cricket had breached racial divisions in Papua at least, and post-war settlers played regularly against the mission team.[25]

It would be easy to claim that, like so many other things, the boundless belief in the civilising effect of games was destroyed by the First World War, but like the Empire itself, for a time it seemed rather to increase. After the horror of the war years the public schools urged their pupils on harder than ever to play the game. In memory of all those who had died a last verse was written for Sir Henry Newbolt's 'Vitae Lampada'.

> And though there is no need to tell
> Their answer to the call,
> Thank God we know they batted well
> In the last great game of all.[26]

In the Colonial Office, the belief that cricket and soundness in colonial administration went together was stronger than ever. In the twenties and thirties Ralph Furse toured the universities and public schools, discreetly putting out feelers for the right sort to serve in Africa or the Pacific or the Far East. When Sir Gordon Guggisberg was on leave from the Gold Coast he would often take him with him, the paragon of a successful cricketing proconsul.

There were of course dissenters at all levels, as always. Here is one schoolboy from Loretto, in 1929:

> Leave rugger, hockey, fives and such
> To those blokes athletic,
> For they lead hardy lives
> And I'm not energetic.
>
> I always was a loafer,
> Away with all these follies,
> O give me but a sofa,
> And a pile of Edgar Wallace.[27]

But even in Edgar Wallace you could not get away from games and the Empire. Wallace's most famous creation, *Sanders of the River*, has his Africans playing rugger in a trice ('fortunately Bowes discovered the little knife before the next scrum was formed'). Sport was to be after all the Empire's most successful export, played in one form or another wherever Englishmen had set foot. It was amateur theatricals that were to be the chief casualty of the post-war period. For how could the Singapore Savage Club, the Perak Players or the Simla Dramatic Society compete with that dazzling new product of Western civilisation, the moving picture show?

In 1935 Robert Bruce Lockhart, whom we have met before, returned to Malaya for the first time in nearly thirty years and decided that the cinema posed a serious threat to the Empire. How could Malays or Chinese or Indians be expected to respect Western values when they saw the kind of behaviour and exposure of white flesh that was now all too common on the screen? Cricket, as always, was safer, a bastion for all that was best about the British Empire in its heyday. 'We have no need to blush for the *gesta dei per Britannos*', wrote Sir Ralph Furse, the grand old man of the Colonial Office in his memoirs in 1962. 'The abolition of slavery, the suppression of cannibalism and tribal warfare, the long campaign against disease and want, the example of justice and fair play, the introduction of cricket, and the rule of law.'[28]

Opposite Winston Churchill as subaltern, and as rising young politician by 'Spy'.

For war by any other name
Is just another British game.

Patriotic song, 1914

9

SOLDIERS

'I wish it were in my power,' wrote the young Winston Churchill in his first book *The Malakand Field Force* in 1898, 'to convey to the reader who has not had the fortune to live with troops on service, some just appreciation of the compensations of war. The open air life, the vivid incidents, the excitements, the generous and cheery friendships, the chances of distinction which are open to all, invest life with keener interest and rarer pleasures.... Besides all this, the chances of learning about the next world are infinitely greater.'[1]

Nine years later, the bumptious young subaltern who had infuriated his commanding officers with his recklessness and talent for self-advertisement had been transformed into the equally bumptious young Liberal Minister at the Colonial Office, who virtuously deplored any tendency to military operations in England's dependent Empire. 'The chronic bloodshed,' he minuted about a proposed punitive expedition against the Munshi tribe in Nigeria, 'which stains the West African seasons is odious and disquieting. Moreover, the whole enterprise is liable to be misrepresented by persons unacquainted with imperial terminology as the murdering of natives and stealing of their lands.'[2]

Nothing illustrates better than Churchill's dramatic conversion both the change in public mood between the late Victorian and the Edwardian age, and the endemic warfare between the Empire's civil and military arm; the 'unsporting attitudes' of those answerable to press and Parliament compared with the dash and enthusiasm of the frontier soldier. Liberal politicians particularly had always been the soldiers' bugbear. Baden-Powell, after a House of Commons debate on the latest Ashanti war, had indignantly compared the Opposition to 'the yapping of jackals at the British lion', then consoled himself by reflecting that this showed up the lions in an even more admirable light. 'They have to carry out their hunting not merely unaided, but handicapped by the incessant yapping at their heals of a pack utterly incapable of hunting for itself.'[3]

Since the Boer War, the lions had felt themselves more beleaguered than ever. The war had proved, in Kipling's famous phrase 'no end of a lesson'. Militarily its reverses had cast a glaring and unflattering light on the entire British Army system. Financially, it had proved disastrously expensive, unlike the 'small wars' the public had learned to expect. And finally it had all seemed rather inglorious after all, particularly in its later stages. Herding Boer women and children into concentration camps and criss-crossing the African veldt with blockhouses and barbed wire might be the only effective way to deal with Boer guerrillas, but it was hardly cricket. Campbell-Bannerman had accused the military of 'methods of barbarism', a phrase which was angrily refuted at the time but which left its mark. The Liberal landslide victory of 1906 showed almost a kind of shame for the jingo spirit of the 'Khaki election' six years before. 'Before the Boer War,' wrote the new Liberal Foreign Secretary, Sir Edward Grey, to President Theodore Roosevelt, 'we were spoiling for a fight. . . . Now this generation has . . . lost a little blood and is sane and normal.'[4] And Lord Morley, the Secretary of State for India, writing to the Viceroy, Lord Minto, warned that anything savouring of 'militarism' would be highly unpopular at home.

Almost as bad from the point of view of the military were the conflicting reports on how the army should be brought up to scratch. The Commission of Enquiry following the Boer War had found almost everything wrong: doddering generals who owed their rank to nothing but seniority; sports-mad officers who made no attempt to study the science of war; recruits of the lowest physical and mental calibre, trained only in barrack-square methods and employed in peace time almost entirely in menial duties – scrubbing out barracks, cleaning uniforms, serving the officers in the mess, tending the cricket grounds. As one critic crisply put it, the British Army was nothing more nor less than a 'gigantic Dotheboys Hall'.[5]

The Royal Commission on the Boer War: St John Brodrick bars the door (*Punch*, 1902).

Two successive Tory Ministers of State for War, St John Brodrick and Arnold Foster, had wrestled unsuccessfully to reform the system before the Tory government fell. Balfour had set up a new Committee of Imperial Defence in 1904 'to survey as a whole the strategical military needs of the Empire', and there was also the framework of a new General Staff to provide a brain for the army.

Much to the Tories' relief, the new Liberal Secretary of State for War was Richard Burdon Haldane, a tough-minded Scottish lawyer, famous for his imperial views and the size of his brain and cigars.

Haldane made it clear that he intended to complete the process of radical reform to create an army fit to defend the Empire. To help him, he claimed, there was already a new school of officer, men of highly scientific training and reflective minds who were as determined as he was that no 'surplus energy should go to waste'. Haldane's eventual proposal for a highly trained, highly mobile expeditionary force of 150,000 troops, backed up by a large territorial army, met with most of his party's approval, largely because he succeeded in cutting the military estimates. Other military pundits were not convinced. 'We have,' wrote that ubiquitous *éminence grise*, Lord Esher, 'an army in excess of our requirements for small wars, and wholly inadequate to the demands of a great war.'[6]

Out in the Empire itself, enthusiasm for any reform was likely to fall on stony ground. The traditional backbone of *Pax Britannica* east of Suez was the Indian Army, complemented by British regiments seconded from home in a ratio of one to two. (Any smaller ratio of English troops to native sepoys had been thought unsafe since the traumatic experience of the Mutiny.) Paid for by India, it was governed from Simla and the India Office in Whitehall, and therefore did not fall directly under War Office control. Its officers were now largely English, except in the lower ranks, and prided themselves on being as much gentlemen as those in British regiments. In practice they came from a slightly less well-heeled social stratum. A subaltern earned three times as much as one in a regiment at home, though even then he would have been hard put to it to live on his pay. As professional soldiers they rated themselves as high, if not higher (only the pick of Sandhurst qualified for commissions) and were fond of comparing their splendid veteran troops, drawn from India's 'martial races' – Sikhs, Jats, Gurkhas – with the raw short-service recruits which made up the British regiments.

Certainly there had been no shortage of active service in the past thirty years: campaigns to Afghanistan; Burma; Egypt; Malaya; China; darkest Africa. The view of where India's defence began could be extended it seemed, if necessary, to cover almost anywhere in the tropics – to the increasing disapproval of the India Office in Whitehall. One colonel of the Uganda Rifles ruefully recalled the freezing reception he received when conducted thither by a nervous Under Secretary from the Foreign Office with Lord Salisbury's request for additional Indian troops to quell a mutiny in Uganda. 'I gathered that we were looked upon as little better than outsiders, almost as conspirators, with fell design upon the safety of the great Indian Empire . . . and that [the officials of the Foreign Office side of the building] were hardly more than imbeciles.'[7] But he got his troops.

Finally, of course, there was India's own North-West Frontier, where Churchill had cut his teeth as a subaltern, a tough training ground by any reckoning. Its jagged hills stretched 400 miles from the Pamirs to Baluchistan, cut by precipitous passes where every rock could conceal a tribal marksman with a highly efficient (stolen) Lee-Enfield rifle. Little chance here of deploying a cavalry charge or even a Maxim gun. The odds tactically and economically were heavily weighted on the enemy's side, as Rudyard Kipling pointed out in his 'Arithmetic of the Frontier'.

Opposite Precipitous passes on the North-West Frontier, a tough training ground for subalterns.

One sword-knot stolen from the camp
Will pay for all the school expenses
Of any Kurrum Valley scamp
Who knows no word of moods and tenses
But, being blessed with perfect sight
Picks off our mess-mates left and right.[8]

The method evolved for controlling the raids by the wild frontier tribesmen into British India was known as 'Butcher and Bolt' – a swift attack on their villages and stock in the steep valleys among the hills. It was the only practical way, it seemed, of dealing with an invisible guerrilla enemy, and even then highly dangerous for the retreating column.

Since Curzon's viceroyalty, however, service on the frontier had been remarkably dull. Determined to break the vicious circle of raids and retaliation, he had withdrawn all British garrisons from forward posts within the tribal areas and replaced them with tribal levies, trained and paid for by the British to act as a kind of militia. He launched the scheme with an impressive durbar in Peshawar, attended by 3,000 vermilion-bearded tribesmen. The results were remarkably successful (at least for a while) and in 1905 Curzon could claim there had been no major fighting for the last five years, and only 106 men killed.

Predictably, his success did not endear him to the Indian Army officers who, from long association, had come to regard the frontier campaigns as the highest form of sport. The army loathed Curzon anyway. His diatribes on its officers' incompetence had quickly percolated to mess rooms and barracks, as had Lady Curzon's reported sneer at Other Ranks, 'the two ugliest things in India are the water buffalo and the British private soldier'.[9] More resented still were Curzon's frequent attacks of what the military caustically dubbed 'poor black man', or as one officer put it, 'his attempts to protect poor Indians from the assaults of brutal English soldiery'. After a punkah coolie had been found dead in the cantonment of the 9th Lancers, Curzon had penalised the whole regiment; all leaves were stopped for an indefinite period. Anglo-India expressed its feelings at the Coronation Durbar a few weeks later by cheering the 9th Lancers wildly when they filed by, and one cavalry subaltern, out of control, nearly mowed down the Viceroy himself during a mock cavalry charge.[10]

After Kitchener's arrival in 1903, Curzon had gratefully resigned the job of army reform to him. To the army it was only a marginal improvement. Lord Kitchener might be England's most famous and respected soldier, the conqueror of the Sudan and the man who had finally brought the Boers to their knees, but he came from a different stable from most Indian Army officers – the Royal Engineers, the army's professional élite – and had seen most of his service with the Egyptian Army. Besides that, he had little in common with the sporting polo-playing ethos of the Indian Army officer and gentleman. Not of course that he did not approve of sport, as we have seen but, as one of his staff noted sadly, 'the Chief spoke of cricket as though it were a medicine to be taken twice weekly by the troops in summer'.[11]

The Indian Army's hero had been Lord Roberts, now Commander-in-Chief in England. Little 'Bobs', as he was known, embodied the code of chivalry: bravery, modesty, courtesy to his officers, devoted care for his men. Kitchener, on the other hand, was a brusque autocrat, with a gaze as stony as an Indian idol's, who relaxed only with a few chosen favourites on his personal staff. He proceeded to trample ruthlessly on some of the Indian Army's most cherished traditions, dismissing out of hand the idea that India was in danger of a second mutiny and breaking up the traditional linkage of native and British brigades, on the grounds of greater economy and efficiency in supply and catering. He closed down many of the smaller garrisons, and proposed instead to concentrate almost the whole weight of India's army in two echelons, pointed towards the frontier.

There were pressing strategic reasons for this. Since 1901, military intelligence had warned of a far more serious danger than raids by Pathans or Afridis. Russian troops were reported to be massing on the northern border of Afghanistan and the new Amir of Afghanistan was an unknown quantity in political terms. Was a Russian takeover in Afghanistan, and then an invasion of India from the north, finally about to happen? The British had dreaded it for years. In Kitchener's view the only safe policy was to extend the railway up to the Afghan frontier, which would allow British troops to arrive in strength – if and when Russia attempted to invade. He would also need another 100–150,000 troops.

Balfour's new Committee of Imperial Defence in London had agonised over the problem. To extend the railway might antagonise the Amir and, besides, how could the five divisions Kitchener talked of be transported from railhead to Kabul? Lord Roberts estimated that at least 234,794 camels would be needed, exclusive of those carrying animal fodder. The Secretary of the Committee of Imperial Defence, Sir George Clarke, recalculated that transport would require 3,056,000 camels, 'a rather startling result', he confessed to Kitchener.[12] Fortunately, from this he drew the conclusion that a major Russian advance from the north would be equally impossible, given the logistics of supply by camel along the narrow defiles of Afghanistan.

At this point in the debate, the Russian threat dissolved for quite other reasons. The Russian Navy was sunk ignominiously by the Japanese at Port Arthur and the Russian government tottered under the impact of the 1905 revolution. By the time the Liberals came to power, early in 1906, Russian responses to English diplomacy had undergone a sea-change. Russia had neither the wish nor the capacity to invade Afghanistan, Grey assured Haldane and the Committee of Imperial Defence. In 1907 a formal treaty saw the end, or at least a truce, in the Great Game which had been played on and off on the North-West Frontier for the last fifty years, and India ceased to figure in the C.I.D.'s deliberations. In public, however, Haldane saw no reason to stress the matter. India's defence was a convenient battle cry with which to get through his annual army estimates and provide for the new expeditionary force, whose destination was never clearly defined.

For Kitchener, the end of the Russian threat spelt an end to his leverage with the government at home, and to a large extent his interest in his command. In any case, he disliked the Liberals intensely, especially the Secretary of State for India, Lord Morley. The Liberal government extended his command for a further two years in 1907 partly, as Kitchener rightly told friends, because they did not know what else to do with him. He spent the last two years of his command agreeably enough, charming Curzon's successor Lord Minto and his family with his affability, shooting tigers, adding to his collection of Oriental porcelain and replanning the decoration of his villa in Simla. A startled visitor found his aides-de-camp engaged in pulping government files to papier-mâché, to make mouldings for Kitchener's ceilings – an act which aptly expressed Kitchener's scorn for 'bumph'. To well-placed friends back in London, such as Lady Salisbury and Colonel Repington (the influential military correspondent of *The Times*), he made it clear that he felt he could now serve India better in an administrative capacity, by succeeding Lord Minto as Viceroy. The bid just failed, despite support in the highest quarters. It was vetoed by Morley, Kitchener's *bête-noire*.

After fifteen months' of conspicuous unemployment at home, more embarrassing to the government than to Kitchener (who bought a country estate and took a prolonged shooting trip up the Nile), a slot was found for him in Cairo, the Empire's second-most prestigious proconsulship. Sir Eldon Gorst, Cromer's successor, was dying of cancer, Egypt was restless, and Cromer advised a strong hand to restore the peace there. Who better to do so than Kitchener, who knew Egypt of old? Rather surprisingly to the Liberals, Kitchener succeeded brilliantly in doing just that. He arrived in a grey frock coat and hat, only a little bulkier than when he had left Egypt twelve years before, and threw himself into his first non-military command with all his old relentless energy, organising vast drainage and irrigation schemes and pushing through radical law reforms to benefit the fellahin whom, like Lord Cromer, he saw as the real Egypt. To live with him, wrote one of his staff, was to feel like the Jules Verne men, 'dosed with oxygen at a double rate'.[13] It was still his passion to direct everything himself down to the smallest detail, which necessitated tactful footwork on the part of his staff.

Back in India, meanwhile, his successor as Commander-in-Chief was finding Kitchener's style of military government impossible to follow. The victory over Curzon six years before had left Kitchener, when Commander-in-Chief, responsible for all aspects of military planning and supply, and also the Viceroy's only military adviser. As Lord Roberts had warned Kitchener at the time, few men had his power of organisation and could advise and plan at the same time. By 1912 the Viceroy was reporting that the whole system of military administration was collapsing in chaos.

Kitchener's restless energy and his failure to find a military role large enough to interest him under the Liberals reflected on a grander scale the increasing dilemma of any ambitious young officer. In 1906 a revised edition of a best-selling book on military theory was reprinted, entitled *Small Wars, Their Principles and Practice*. Its author, Colonel Callwell, like Kitchener Anglo-Irish and a product of Woolwich, had been much admired both in Europe and at home as one of England's few able

ove Lord Kitchener (*second right*), bored, at Simla. By 1907, the Russian threat to India had evaporated.
low Interior of Kitchener's house, Calcutta. His A.D.C.s were made to dust his porcelain collection.

military theorists. But somehow the enthusiasm had gone out of the book. It no longer bore the official War Office imprimatur and it no longer spoke confidently of the inevitability of small wars as a fact of Empire, small wars being defined as campaigns against uncivilised or barbarous peoples. Most of its examples were still drawn from the 1880s and '90s and the Boer War was barely mentioned, though in one chapter Colonel Callwell rather sadly admitted that his hopes that the cavalry would come into their own on the open South African veldt had not been fulfilled – it was mounted infantry on the Boer model which had won the day.

The book repeated, with only minor changes of emphasis, the points made in the 1896 edition: the tactics needed to lure a guerrilla opponent into open fight where superior arms and discipline could be used to effect; the necessity of keeping always on the offensive, any defensive position being 'fundamentally unsound'; how to harry an invisible enemy if necessary by economic warfare, rounding up his stock or burning his crops; how to keep supply lines under control and not allow the army to become a mere escort for its food on extended campaigns; when to use the extended line for advance; when to resort to the 'elastic square'.

Having dropped his chapter on the role of the cavalry, Colonel Callwell added two new chapters: 'Hill Fighting' and 'Bush Fighting'. The first was written with special reference to the North-West Frontier where, despite Curzon's tribal militias, there seemed good reason to expect further trouble. The second was clearly written with the new African Empire in mind, though for Callwell (like most officers), bush fighting rated a poor second to hill fighting. First of all, nature itself was usually a formidable enemy; theatres of bush warfare 'are almost always unhealthy, noisome, fever-stricken tracts of country where officers and men become enervated by the heat and where a disciplined army is soon decimated by disease'. Secondly, the denizen of the tropical forest was 'it must be confessed, rather a poor creature as a fighting man'. He had neither the love of war nor the sporting instincts of the hill men. Indeed, his fighting spirit seemed to decrease in direct proportion to the thickness of the bush. Perhaps, noted Callwell, this was just as well.

> Were the inhabitants of recent wars in West Africa brave fanatics like the Sudanese, or were they supplied with magazine rifles, as were many of the Afridis in 1897, it is not easy to see how operations could have been brought to a successful issue without a deplorable loss of life.[14]

Still, for an officer eager to see active service, tropical Africa after the Boer War must have seemed to offer better prospects than anywhere else in the Empire. There were still huge areas where *Pax Britannica* was more a statement of aspiration than a fact. In the west, the new West African Frontier Force (the W.A.F.F., pronounced 'Wuff'), founded by Chamberlain in 1897, was still involved in almost continuous campaigns – first against the Fulani emirs of northern Nigeria, latterly against pagan tribes and the forest-dwellers around the Niger Delta. This was the 'chronic bloodshed' which Churchill had so piously deplored. Hugh Trenchard, who had arrived to join the Southern Nigerian Regiment in 1903, led annual campaigns

{aking soldiers out of tribesmen, Uganda. 'The denizen of the tropical forest is rather a poor creature as a fighting man,' 'rote Colonel Callwell.

against the Ibos in the huge, largely unmapped, quadrilateral between the Cross and Niger rivers, and ended his career as Commander with an unofficial expedition into the north against the Munshis, famous for their ferocity.

In the east, on the Horn of Africa, the English had been engaged in a running battle with Mohammed Bin Abdullah Hassan, popularly known as the Mad Mullah, who had sworn to drive the English or any other Christians out of Somaliland. He had eluded four campaigns against him by retreating across the waterless Haud, where it was too expensive and difficult to follow him, and teased his opponents by summarising their problem with admirable clarity in letters addressed to the British public.

> I like war but you do not. . . . If the country was cultivated or contained houses or property, it would be worth your while to fight. The country is all jungle and that is no use to you. If you want wood or stone you can get them in plenty. There are also many ant heaps. The sun is very hot.[15]

Further south, however, there were more than ant heaps to fight for, and just how much one young officer could 'like war' can be seen by the fascinating diary kept by Richard Meinertzhagen of his campaigns in East Africa for the years 1902–1906.

Richard Meinertzhagen as a young officer in the King's African Rifles, Nairobi, 1903.

To classify Meinertzhagen as a typical Edwardian subaltern would of course be to wrong him. For one thing he was extraordinarily intelligent, and for another, like Kitchener, he was a loner – cut off, or so he believed, from his mother's affection as a boy, passionately devoted to an older brother who had died aged eighteen, and convinced that his family regarded him as cannon fodder, a 'black sheep'. His diaries, which he kept from the age of twelve onwards, show an odd mixture of arrogance and extreme sensitivity which had him in constant hot water with his superiors. As we have seen, he had come to East Africa to join the King's African Rifles, a new imperial unit, partly because he had quarrelled with his commanding officer in the Royal Fusiliers while stationed in India; partly also because he was fascinated by the prospect of observing and shooting African game and partly perhaps for financial reasons. His pay in the K.A.R. was four times higher than in his English regiment and the cost of living was cheaper (after four years in Africa, he had saved over £4,000).

But without a doubt Meinertzhagen's main motive in coming to Africa was to teach himself his profession – by fighting. An African tribesman would do as well as any. Like nearly all his contemporaries, Meinertzhagen's code was a strange mixture of social Darwinism (the nation's right to impose itself on lesser breeds) and belief in the moral benefits of British rule. As a soldier, militarily he accepted wholeheartedly what was known in India as the 'Punjab Principle' – a shot in time saves nine. Swift and drastic punishment was the best way to ensure peace. Kipling had once described the British Army in one of his Indian short stories as 'blackguards commanded by gentlemen to do butchery with efficiency and dispatch'.[16] Meinertzhagen would not have dissented. In Africa, where the army was infinitely more thinly spread than in India, the principle seemed even more applicable. He wrote on his first posting away from Nairobi, in Kikuyu country:

> Here we are, three white men in the heart of Africa with twenty nigger soldiers and fifty nigger police ... administering a district inhabited by half a million well armed savages who have only recently come in touch with the white man. The position is most humorous.[17]

In fact his first military duty was to arrest an Englishman, one of the wrong sort who seemed especially attracted to East Africa. He was a 'missionary' called Smith, a carpenter by trade who had been telling the Kikuyu girls they could not be true Christians until they had slept with a Christian.

Most of Meinertzhagen's diary, however, shows him engaged on shooting either animals or Africans in dizzy succession. He confessed later that his arrival in Africa had brought on a kind of bloodlust. His first action was against a Kikuyu village where a policeman had been murdered.

> I strongly advised immediate and drastic action in the shape of surprising the village this very night and arresting the murderers – Hemstead agreed with me but McLean demurred, so I pointed out the evil effect on the native mind of allowing the crime to go unpunished.

Having won them round, Meinertzhagen staged a dawn raid on the offending village and found the inhabitants dancing round in full war paint.

> There was a rush ... into the surrounding bush and we killed about 17 niggers. Two policemen and one of my men were killed. I narrowly escaped a spear which whizzed past my head. Then the fun began. We at once burned the village and captured the sheep and goats. After that we systematically cleared the valley in which the village was situated, burned all the huts and killed a few more niggers who finally gave up the fight and cleared off.[18]

This application of the Punjab Principle seemed highly successful. A deputation from the village came begging for mercy and next day the two men who had murdered the policemen were handed over. They claimed they had been misled by the local medicine man and were sentenced to six months' hard labour. Meinertzhagen's diary notes, however, that the same village revolted two months later and more troops had to be sent to punish them.

Meinertzhagen's next punitive operation was even more drastic. This time it was a white settler who had been murdered in a peculiarly horrible way. He had been pegged down in the centre of a village with his mouth open and urinated on until he was drowned. Meinertzhagen gave orders that every living thing in the village should be killed without mercy, except children. This he admitted he found 'a most unpleasant duty', but justified it on the grounds that it was the women who had instigated the white settler's death. Not surprisingly, perhaps, he soon had trouble imposing the normal code of chivalry in war that no women or children should be killed. A year later he recorded having to shoot five of his own troops, whom he had found spearing women and children during a lightning raid on an Irryeni village. It was, he wrote, 'the only thing possible under the circumstances, though contrary to military law. War is necessarily brutal, but it need not be made too brutal. Without iron discipline black troops and undisciplined levies would get disastrously out of hand.'[19]

For the Kikuyu or the other East African tribes with whom Meinertzhagen was dealing, it must have been difficult to distinguish between the code and practice of white man's warfare and that of their own traditional tribal wars; especially since Meinertzhagen had recruited levies of Masai spearmen to his force, who carried out enthusiastically the principal punishment meted out to dissident tribes: capturing their stock. Personally, Meinertzhagen much disliked this kind of economic warfare. 'I want a good fight in the forest, not to take part in a cattle or goat lifting competition.' Besides which, travelling with a huge caravan of cattle and goats made campaigning almost impossible. When he returned to his base at Fort Hall after a prolonged campaign against the Irryeni, he compared his own column's 'bag' favourably with that of his brother officers.

> Our total captives were 782 cattle and 2150 sheep and goats. We killed 796 of the enemy, [whereas] they had raked in 602 cattle and 4500 sheep and goats, without firing a shot.[20]

And he ventured to doubt whether the latter were the enemy's stock at all.

In fact, Meinertzhagen's seemingly rather illogical preference for killing the enemy rather than confiscating their stock was perfectly in line with the code outlined by Callwell in his book on Small Wars. He wrote that:

> The objection was one of principle. To filch the property of irregulars is not the true spirit of waging war against such opponents; the proper way to deal with them is to kill them or wound them, or at least hunt them from their homes and then to destroy or carry off their belongings.[21]

The belief that war should take some higher form than cattle-stealing also links up, in Meinertzhagen's case, with passionate dislike of what he felt to be the commercial exploitation of Africa. He had several sharp exchanges with the High Commissioner, Sir Charles Eliot, on the unwisdom and injustice of importing white settlers.

Ironically, Meinertzhagen's second tour in East Africa was to be spent largely in enforcing the kind of policy he most disapproved of. After a short leave in England

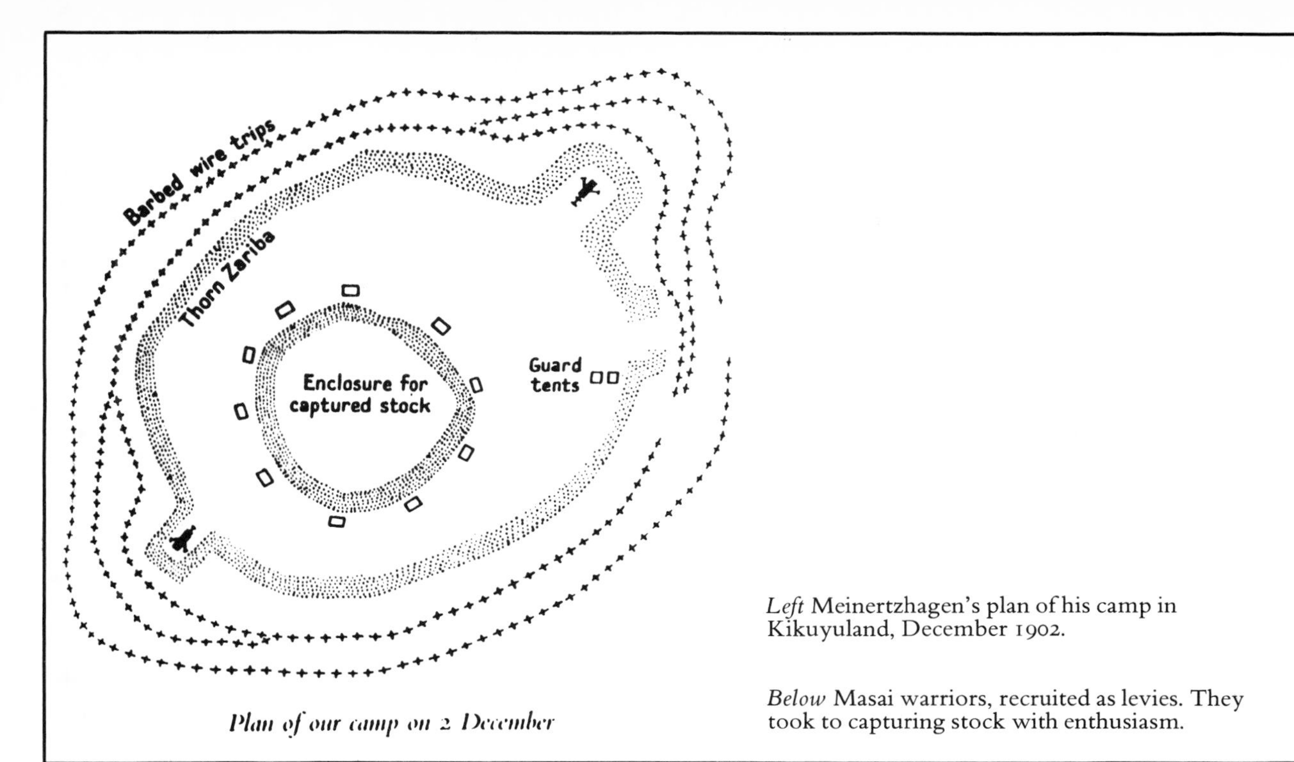

Left Meinertzhagen's plan of his camp in Kikuyuland, December 1902.

Below Masai warriors, recruited as levies. They took to capturing stock with enthusiasm.

he returned in March 1905 to find himself promoted to Captain and posted to a remote fort in the north-east of the Protectorate, among the Nandi, a Nilo-Hamitic tribe like the Masai, who were notoriously 'troublesome'. The British had already sent three expeditions to punish them for attacking the Uganda Railway which bisected their tribal lands. Soon after Meinertzhagen arrived, they had killed a missionary and one of his own African soldiers who had unwisely ventured out alone to buy himself a new wife. Meinertzhagen attributed the outbreak of trouble to a particularly corrupt district officer called Mayes, who confiscated cattle from the natives on the slightest pretext to feather his own nest, and also, much to Meinertzhagen's disapproval, kept half a dozen Nandi concubines. (Meinertzhagen eventually reported him to the Sub-Commissioner for corruption and he was dismissed to another post.)

But by now it was clear that the Nandi were spoiling for a fight, rather like Meinertzhagen himself, who confessed to suffering from acute depression, isolated as he was in Nandi Fort among hostile tribesmen without any chance of physical or intellectual outlets. To occupy himself he organised his first intelligence network, using local tribesmen to keep him informed of the activities of the Nandi's hereditary medicine man and leader, Koitalel, who was reported to be 'teaching his people all sorts of nonsense, persuading them that our bullets turn to water when fired at a Nandi, that we dare not fight them, etc'.[22]

From his spies' reports Meinertzhagen became convinced that by disposing of Koitalel, he could nip a major Nandi rising in the bud and prevent a prolonged campaign which would cause much suffering and devastation among the non-belligerents. (He had been touched when the old Nandi who had been supplying him with eggs and milk confided to his care his three nubile daughters for safety during the coming months, and was much relieved that his motives for keeping them were not misunderstood by his fellow officers.) He therefore sent word to Koitalel requesting a meeting, which he felt sure would result in some kind of personal duel in which one would be killed. The two men met in a patch of open ground, both having concealed their forces behind them. According to Meinertzhagen it was Koitalel who made the first hostile move and he only narrowly escaped being speared.

Whatever the sequence, Koitalel and twenty-two of his entourage were left dead, leaving the rest of the Nandi temporarily stunned, while Meinertzhagen and his company trekked home 'as fast as our legs would carry us, pursued by a swarm of angry warriors'. 'Thus may all the king's enemies perish,' wrote Meinertzhagen triumphantly, his only regret being that Koitalel's wives 'will certainly be burned with him, as is the custom'. He sent a brief wire to headquarters in Nairobi, announcing his success, and was soon rewarded with congratulatory telegrams from, among others, Frederick Jackson, the High Commissioner, and the news that his fellow officers had recommended him for the V.C.

Koitalel's death did not, however, prevent the full-scale military campaign which the authorities had decided was necessary to teach the Nandi a lesson. A field force of 1,500 troops, 1,600 Masai and Somali levies, 4,160 porters, 2 armoured trains and

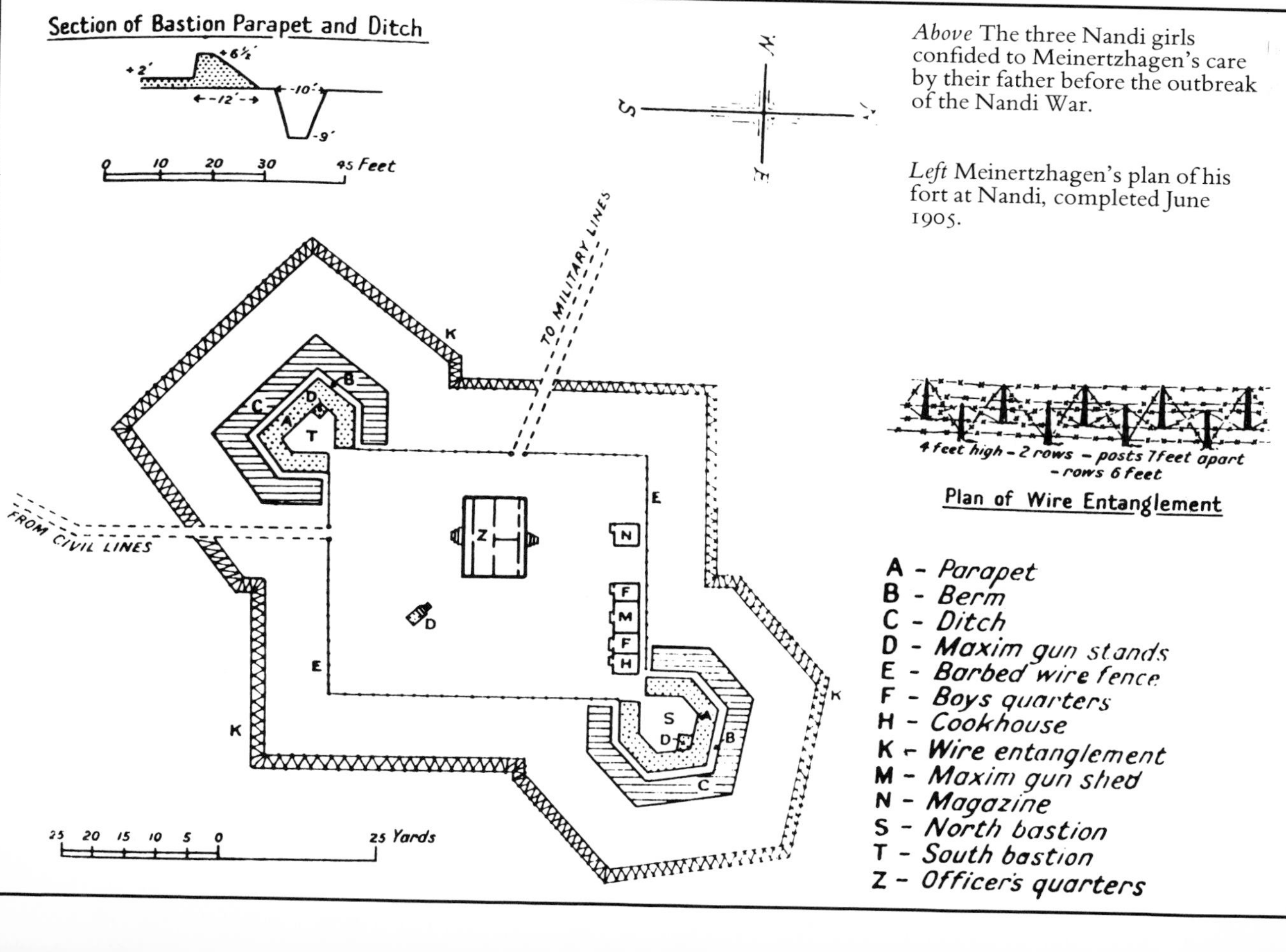

Above The three Nandi girls confided to Meinertzhagen's care by their father before the outbreak of the Nandi War.

Left Meinertzhagen's plan of his fort at Nandi, completed June 1905.

10 machine guns arrived at Nandi Fort. Three weeks later the Nandi had lost 500 of their warriors, 10,000 cattle and 70,000 sheep and goats. The government had also decided that they must be moved away from the railway to a new reserve, and Meinertzhagen was detailed to mark out its limits, which he noted were far too small and would not allow for any expansion of population. Predictably, groups of Nandi were soon breaking out of the reserve and Meinertzhagen spent several months hunting out groups who had taken refuge in the forest and in caves. His fears that the land they had lost would be given to white settlers proved correct. One large block of 5,000 acres went, as we have already seen, to Lord Kitchener.

At this point the see-saw of Meinertzhagen's own career went sharply down, thanks to his old enemy, the district officer Mayes. Mayes had sent an official complaint to the Colonial Office that Meinertzhagen had killed the Nandi leader by treachery. After three courts of enquiry, all of which cleared him, Meinertzhagen was astonished to be told in Nairobi that the Colonial Office had asked that he should be removed from East Africa, since his action had resulted 'in the reputation of the British government for fair dealing and honesty being called into question'.[23] In May 1906, after a last dinner with his old mess mates in Nairobi ('buckets of champagne and later a rag'), Meinertzhagen sadly caught the train to Mombasa, while the K.A.R. band gave a mournful and idiosyncratic rendering of 'Auld Lang Syne'.

Meinertzhagen was much consoled back in London by a personal interview with Haldane at the War Office. Haldane told him that if it had not been for the Colonial Office's extraordinary view of his case, the recommendation to give him the V.C. might have gone forward and that 'none of this wretched business would count against [him] as far as the War Office was concerned'.[24] He rejoined his old regiment, the Royal Fusiliers, to find the officer he had quarrelled with back in 1902 still in command, but was agreeably surprised to find how much more efficient and professional the regiment had become. He spent the next few years being rotated round the Empire, from South Africa to the forests and sugar-cane plantations of Mauritius and then to a hill station in the Himalayas. In 1912 he took the entrance exam to Kitchener's new staff college at Quetta and passed in top. He found the lectures on military theory as absorbing as military practice, though, as he wrote in his diary late in 1913, 'Work at the staff college makes me realise what a ghastly business the next war is going to be.'[25]

By 1913 few intelligent officers had many doubts about where the next war was likely to occur – when it would occur was another matter. Ambitious subalterns looking for active service at the beginning of 1914 found the prospects remarkably bleak. There was still the occasional flare-up on the North-West Frontier, but for most soldiers in India there was only barrack-room routine or tricky policing work, tightly controlled by the civil powers.

Almost the only place left east of Suez which could provide a decent small war was now Somaliland. Attempts to deal with the Mad Mullah had been one of the Liberals' most notable failures. Since 1906 they had pursued a policy of 'coastal

The Somaliland Camel Corps on the move, early 1914.

concentration', leaving the unfortunate 'friendly' tribes of the interior to the mercy of the Mullah's raiders. In 1909 they had sent that much respected soldier and administrator Sir Reginald Wingate, Governor of the Sudan, to advise on how to deal with the Mullah. After fruitless attempts at negotiation, Wingate had reported that he saw no alternative to a major military operation. But instead, the Liberals had set up a tiny police force called the Somaliland Camel Constabulary to try and hold back the Mullah's forays from the coast.

In August 1913, the head of the Camel Constabulary unwisely allowed himself to be lured outside his normal range and almost the entire force was wiped out. The event made headlines in England and the government was forced to declare the raising of a new force under military control. There was a rush of ambitious officers to serve in its ranks, and most of them disembarked at Berbera in May and June 1914. Then in early August the news broke – the real war was elsewhere. Somaliland overnight became a sideshow, and officers were soon scrambling to disentangle themselves from the Somaliland Camel Corps and get back to the centre of things.

The outbreak of war caught even the Empire's most famous soldier unawares. Kitchener was on leave in England and on 1 August was hurrying to catch the Channel boat, which was the first step back to Egypt. He was stopped, just as he had feared, by a telegram from Asquith asking him to report back to London. The government needed him at the War Office, a post which he had turned down six years before and always dreaded. It would be the grave of his reputation, he had once told Lord Esher prophetically. But as he installed himself there was a general sigh of relief. England's greatest professional was in charge – the man who could be trusted to make the machinery of war turn smoothly. Within a few days, Sir Charles Callwell, now promoted to head of military operations, reported that

Lord Kitchener calls for volunteers, 1915. Conscription became compulsory the following year.

things had begun to hum. Elderly War Office messengers were seen running down the War Office passages with coat-tails flying, to summon staff officers to Kitchener's sanctum.

In the Cabinet, even Churchill was awed to silence by Kitchener's presence, as 'he proclaimed in soldierly sentences a series of inspiring and prophetic truths'.[26] The war, Kitchener told the Cabinet, would not be a short one, as they hoped. Nor would it be won at sea by British dreadnoughts. It would be fought on land with enormous armies, which he proposed to set about recruiting immediately. Kitchener's instructions, sent out to Haldane's expeditionary force now embarking for France, had a familiar note. On this new experience they would encounter many temptations, especially wine and women. All of them must be resisted.

In some parts of the tropics, the King's proclamation that the British Empire was now at war was greeted by the authorities almost with relief. This should clear the air. The Indian rajahs' response was magnificently loyal. They offered their revenues, their regiments, their lives. What, one cabled, 'Can I do for my king?' 'I was reading it out and I found such a lump in my throat that I could hardly go on', wrote that veteran Indian Army officer, Lord Lugard, from Nigeria.

> Truly our rule has been wonderful. Peace brings sedition and bombs and agitation. But when the Empire has to fight for life, all these are swept aside. Here in Nigeria the heads of the tribes in German territories are coming over to

> declare their desire to be under our rule. It is times like these that make us proud to be of the race of Englishmen.[27]

In India, even Annie Besant declared her conviction that to fight for the Empire was a moral duty. The struggle against Germany reflected a struggle in higher worlds between the White Brotherhood and the Lords of the Dark Face, whose servants the Germans were. (Mrs Besant's strong anti-German line caused a temporary split in the Theosophical Society.) Further east, reactions were more down-to-earth. The griffins of the great commercial houses of Hong Kong and Singapore had been drilling regularly for the last few years in the Hong Kong and Singapore volunteer forces after their games of polo and golf and cricket. 'Hong Kong Ready', declared the *South China Mail*. Any enemy would find the colony ready to accord him the warmest of receptions.

As for the commercial repercussions, leading businessmen 'regard the present deadlock with some little satisfaction; provided it is not unduly protracted, they consider it a splendid means for reducing the huge accumulation of stocks at Shanghai and Hong Kong which have glutted the market for many months'.[28]

In the staff college at Quetta, Meinertzhagen had heard the news during a 'most apathetic' game of polo, and was suddenly depressed by the noisy elation among his brother officers in the mess. The holocaust ahead would offer none of the conditions he understood and loved – wide horizons, freedom, fresh air and exercise. It would let loose on the world

> all the criminal and scientific methods of destruction. Is that what I have been working for the past fifteen years? And now the moment has come, do I shrink back in horror and disgrace myself? In a war of this nature, personal feelings must be suppressed, and I am merely a pawn in the Great Game, but it is going to be too horrible.

The next day the professional soldier has resurfaced. The immediate problem was to get himself to the main theatre of war.

> It has been my bad luck to have missed most of the small wars in which I might have taken part. When I joined the army I deliberately chose India as giving me the best chance for active service. Then I went to the King's African Rifles as I thought I had a better chance there than in India. True, I did see a certain amount of service in Africa and gained a lot of invaluable experience. But no sooner do I go to Africa than my British battalion is the one selected in all India to go on that unique Tibet expedition, and now I come to the staff college in order to make certain I am employed in a Great European War, and here I am 'work as usual', anchored in Quetta with my country bleeding to death.[29]

Meinertzhagen need not have worried. The following week he was told to report to Bombay. He was to be sent to German East Africa, with a large contingent of

General von Lettow-Vorbeck (*second right*) at Moshi, Tanganyika, just before the outbreak of war.

troops under General Aitken, as intelligence officer. It was the theatre of war he had most hoped to be sent to after Europe. He had spent some weeks in 1906 reconnoitring the German troops along the border in Tanganyika, and his hypercritical mind was already picking holes in the British invasion plan before they arrived at Mombasa. It was folly to attempt to invade German East from the coast. Much better concentrate inland at Taveta, on the protectorate's southern border, and build a railway across the Serengeti to occupy Kilimanjaro. 'Our position would secure British East from invasion and would give us healthy country for our men.' Nor did he have any faith in the troops accompanying them – 'the worst in India'. 'I tremble to think what may happen if we meet with some serious opposition.' The two battalions had no machine guns and the service chiefs were 'nearer to fossils than active energetic leaders of men'.

He presented his views on paper to General Aitken, who brushed them aside, and told Meinertzhagen that the German troops were

> ill trained ... and bush or no bush he means to thrash the German before Christmas. Fine words, but I know the German. His colonial troops are second to none. They are led by the best officers in the world, he knows the country and understands bush warfare and his men are not prone to malaria as ours are. And finally, he will be operating in his country and can choose the time and place for attacking our converging forces. ...[30]

As they so often did, Meinertzhagen's prophecies proved depressingly accurate. The British attempt to invade Tanga on the German East African coast proved a

Selous's regiment, the 25th Royal Fusiliers on the march, 1915. They were the last white unit to survive the bush.

fiasco. Withering machine gun and shell fire among the tangled mangrove roots along the beaches broke the Indian troops' morale and caused hideous casualties. For the next four and a half years the lumbering Allied army was to pursue in vain a game of hide-and-seek against a tiny German force led by General von Lettow-Vorbeck. Von Lettow-Vorbeck's declared aim was to tie down as many Allied troops as possible and by 1918 he had nearly half a million pursuing him through the Tanganyika bush. The British had never encountered this kind of bush-whacking before, at least not against this kind of enemy. The veteran Frederick Selous wrote:

> The black troops are not only as brave as any Zulus, but splendidly led and well armed and supported with any number of machine guns. I would much sooner have to fight against Germans from the Fatherland than these well trained and elusive blacks.[31]

Selous's own regiment, 'The Old and Bold', were to be the last white unit to survive the bush. They were finally cut to pieces at the last pitched battle of the campaign at Beho-Beho, just before von Lettow-Vorbeck escaped across the Rovuma river into Mozambique.

Since most of the Indian troops proved as susceptible to the rigours of bush warfare, malaria, dysentery, blackwater fever as the white ones, the African forces were hastily expanded – including Meinertzhagen's old regiment, the K.A.R., and the W.A.F.F. from West Africa. In West Africa the campaign against the Germans in Togoland and the Cameroons (where Joyce Cary had been fighting) had proved

comparatively short and easy, though none of the German African tribes had come over to the British, as Lugard had hoped. The Nigerian and Gold Coast regiments were hurriedly embarked to sail round the Cape to the other side of the continent, proudly watched by their respective governors, Lord Lugard and Sir Hugh Clifford. Their cheerful faces and splendid physique did wonders for the morale of the rest of the British Army, and in combat they proved the nearest thing yet to a match for the German askaris. They also carried with them a psychological weapon. The Germans, Lord Cranworth wrote, believed quite unfairly that the West Africans would not only kill them but eat them.

Most of the East African settlers had joined up at the start of the war, galloping into Nairobi wild-west style on their rough ponies, and noisily refuting the Governor's unpatriotic claim that the colony had no interest in the present war. They were hastily formed into a regiment, the East African Mounted Rifles, and had the honour of the first engagement of the campaign, an attack on the German gunboats at Kisii on Lake Victoria. Then they were set to guard the railway, strung out in the low-lying bush country to the south, where the perennial enemies, mosquitoes and tsetse fly, quickly thinned the ranks.

Early in 1915 there were rumours, however, of a new danger that might strike suddenly at their backs. Nyasaland to the south, long regarded as one of the most peaceful protectorates in tropical Africa (thanks to its long record of missionary activity), had been shaken by a serious native rising in which several settlers' families and missionaries had been killed. It was led by a mission-educated youth, John Chilembwe, who had gone to America and then returned to set up his own native church. He had declared a general rising against all Europeans. Most of the settlers requested extended leave and hurried back to their own farms.

The more restless spirits in East Africa, meanwhile, had struck out on their own. The elephant hunter, 'Karamoja' Bell, had headed immediately for Europe to learn how to fly, and then got himself posted back to the East African campaign with a squadron of obsolete B.E.Q.S.s seconded from the Western Front. He spent many exhilarating hours skimming over the bush, trying to pepper the concealed German machine gun posts with a repeating rifle and scoring considerably worse than in his former encounters with elephants.

Lord Delamere had vanished on a mule into the Masai Mara to recruit the tribesmen as scouts, the only role, he rightly guessed, the proud Masai were likely to undertake. Berkeley Cole, his brother-in-law, had raised a troop of Somali scouts to patrol the frontier further east, and he was joined by most of the settlers' old Etonian élite, including the irrepressible Lord Cranworth. They painted their ponies zebra-fashion with iodine to blend into the landscape, and spent five months leading a glorious cowboy existence, riding across a vast game reserve full of herds of almost tame game, before being brought sharply back to reality by a vicious fight with the Germans at Mbuyuni. Cranworth's zebra-striped mule, to his horror, bolted headlong through the German lines, and he then had to charge them in reverse.

Opposite Wounded West Africans in Tanganyika, 1917. They proved the British Army's best troops.

Pony camouflaged as zebra for Cole's Scouts, Tanganyika border, 1914.

After the battle, Cole's scouts were disbanded, to be absorbed into regular army units in German East or volunteer for the Western Front back in France. The guard on the frontier was handed over to an elderly staff officer seconded from India – Colonel Kitchener, the Commander-in-Chief's elder brother, a rather ludicrous, though likeable figure, noted Meinertzhagen, who 'has clothed himself with the cloak of his brother's genius and ... emits hot air by the cubic yard'.

From June 1916 the Colonel provided a ghostly echo from the main theatre of war, by becoming the second Lord Kitchener. His brother had been drowned in the icy waters of the North Sea, *en route* to inspect the Russian Front. The Empire's most famous soldier had sunk just in time, before the cracks in his heroic façade began to show. In private, among his Cabinet colleagues, his standing as an effective war lord had ebbed steadily since 1915. By the autumn they had been as eager to shunt him back to Egypt as they had once been to recall him.

The Cabinet's other old soldier – Winston Churchill – was already a public political casualty of the war. He had been pushed out of the Admiralty and the War Cabinet in turn, chief scapegoat of the Dardanelles fiasco. Africa, he decided, was the place to rebuild his reputation. He proposed to the Cabinet that he should be appointed Governor-General and Commander-in-Chief of British East Africa. He would raise an army of Africans and attack the Germans 'with armoured cars'. The Cabinet rejected the plan as laughable and Churchill sadly embarked for the Western Front with the rank of major.

Richard Meinertzhagen found himself back in Europe early in 1917, seconded to the War Office, Kitchener's last disastrous post. Meinertzhagen had made himself a brilliant reputation in the East African campaign as Chief Intelligence Officer,

Masai tribesmen recruited as scouts for the East African campaign, 1915.

where he evolved a highly original method of collecting information about the enemy's strength and movement. He called it the D.P.M. – Dirty Paper Method – since it depended largely on salvaging jettisoned documents from the enemy's latrines. Unfortunately, much of his information was disregarded by the campaign's early commanders. 'Here I am in the rottenest sideshow imaginable,' he wrote bitterly. 'Rotten troops and rotten leaders.'[33]

A few months in the War Office at the height of Haig's Somme offensive, which cost the British Army 420,000 lives in five months, was enough to cure Meinertzhagen of any belief in leadership at the centre either. In December he was relieved to be posted to another sideshow – the Palestinian campaign, this time as Chief Intelligence Officer to Allenby, the first general for whom he soon had unstinted praise. He set up his D.P.M. system again to report on Turkish activities and in October carried out in person one of the war's most daring coups. He rode up alone to within sight of the Turkish lines, near enough to be shot at, then, wheeling about, apparently wounded, he dropped a bloodstained haversack in mid-flight. The haversack contained carefully forged plans of an Allied attack on the Turks' western front, among other personal documents; it fooled the Turks sufficiently to allow Allenby's real offensive a few weeks later at Beersheba to go through relatively unopposed.

Even more inventive was Meinertzhagen's plan for disposing of Turkish resistance at Gaza. He had made repeated drops of cigarette packs containing mild propaganda handouts, in preparation for a final drop just before the British offensive, in which he planned to shower them with cigarettes heavily laced with opium. Allenby vetoed the plan as against the code of war, but Meinertzhagen went ahead

Richard Meinertzhagen disguised as an Arab in Southern Palestine, 1917.

without permission and was pleased to find the tactic brilliantly successful – most of the prisoners taken were scarcely coherent. A few days later he tried out one of his own doped cigarettes. The effect was 'sublime . . . all energy gone, lovely dreams and complete inability to act or think'.[34]

Much to Meinertzhagen's disappointment, he was then recalled to the War Office and spent the last few months of the war pinned down in France, on official staff duties. In August 1918 he managed to contrive one glorious break-out. After giving a lecture to the cavalry corps at Dieppe, he drove over to Amiens, where a major Allied offensive was under way, and attached himself to a friendly Canadian armoured car unit. He persuaded them to drive him to the front line, ahead of the infantry. Many of the Germans who had left their trenches on the approach of tanks were hiding in shell holes in the standing corn, where they could be spotted by low-flying Allied aircraft. 'On our getting near their hiding places, they would bolt like rabbits and the game was not without its element of sport.' Meinertzhagen accounted for twenty-three himself, with a Hotchkiss gun. Finally they ran down a car containing two German officers. One was shot dead, the other bolted. Meinertzhagen leapt out and gave chase with his knobkerrie, a relic of his East African campaigns. He was just catching up with his prey when his companion in the car bowled the officer over with a shot from a Hotchkiss gun. 'Another yard,' wrote Meinertzhagen, and 'I should certainly have had him on the head.' By the evening he was back on duty at G.H.Q. 'It was surely,' he wrote with some satisfaction, 'some kind of record for a G.S.O.I. at the War Office.'[35]

Opposite The British Lion triumphs in Tanganyika (*Punch*, December 1918).

10

WINNERS/ LOSERS

~~GERMAN~~ EAST AFRICA.

The British flag has never flown over a more powerful and united Empire.

Lord Curzon, 18 November 1918

A few months after the Great War had begun, Richard Meinertzhagen in Nairobi asked himself what England was actually fighting for. It was 'certainly not for Belgium, not for sea power, not for more possessions'. It was, he finally decided, 'because we have to struggle for existence. We have to show the world that we who are fittest shall survive.'[1]

By 1918 survival of the fittest hardly seemed a respectable enough reason. 'We have', wrote Meinertzhagen grandly in his diary on the day of the Armistice,

> fought for the idea of Christianity, truth and justice; we have warred against the idea of might is right, necessity has no law and God

> marches with the big battalions.... We have fought for freedom and democracy, for equal rights of the small and the weak, we have crushed the idea of Imperial Despotism and the right of rulers to override the will of the people.[2]

Probably Meinertzhagen did not remember his earlier diary entry, or see anything incompatible between what he had just written and the continuation and expansion of the British Empire. Indeed he was to spend the next year proselytising hard for the annexation of some of the territories left over after the break-up of another imperial despotism, Turkey. Turkish Sinai should, he felt, be annexed immediately by right of conquest, to give Britain a strategic base, an access to the Mediterranean and the Red Sea. Palestine could best be kept under British control by encouraging the Jews to make it their national home. The Jews were, in his experience (some of them had worked for him in Egypt in his intelligence service), 'virile, brave, determined and intelligent', unlike the Arabs who were lazy, decadent and 'produced little beyond eccentrics influenced by the romance and silence of the desert'. Meinertzhagen's enthusiasm for a new Middle Eastern empire was shared by no less a person than the King-Emperor George V, he discovered, when he called on him in 1918 to report progress in the East African and Palestine campaigns.

> He seemed to take it for granted that German East Africa, Palestine and Mesopotamia would come under the British Crown at the end of the war, and outlined his ideas on the subject. He particularly desired Palestine for biblical reasons. He made some remarks about the final crusade.[3]

At Westminster and Whitehall 'thinking imperially' was back in the air. The war had disinterred two of the most ardent Edwardian empire-builders from the grave in which the Liberal landslide had apparently buried them for good ten years before. Lord Curzon had been recruited to the inner War Cabinet in May 1915; Lord Milner in December the following year; and many of Milner's old South African Kindergarten now held key government posts – Leo Amery, Lionel Curtis, Philip Kerr, John Buchan. There were committees to discuss '*territoria desiderata*', and there was cheerful talk of the Indian Ocean becoming at last a 'British lake'. Egypt had already been formally annexed as a protectorate at the outbreak of war and would soon, Lord Milner predicted, be as much a part of the Empire as India or Nigeria. For the moment, the first priority was naturally the struggle in Europe, but if 'when all was over', wrote Leo Amery to Lloyd George, 'the British commonwealth emerges as greater than ever in area and resources ... who has the right to complain?'[4]

The people who might complain, of course, were Britain's new and most powerful allies, the Americans. Since Roosevelt's day they had shown little enthusiasm for associating themselves with the White Man's Burden, and on 4 July 1918 President Wilson had made a much publicised speech, announcing that self-determination would be the moral imperative of the peace.

'Are we to give up Arabia, Palestine and the German colonies,' wrote Lord Derby, the Minister of War, indignantly to Balfour four days later, 'and to give

'The Last Crusade' – The British enter Jerusalem (*Punch*, December 1918).

Ireland, Egypt and even India such governments as the people there can be said to want?'[5] And Meinertzhagen wrote off Wilson as an irresponsible and conceited dreamer 'whose mind soars at altitudes beyond our ken'.

In the event, the Paris peace negotiations after the war proved thoroughly satisfactory from the empire-builders' point of view. England acquired all the buffer states she wanted in the Middle East – Palestine, Transjordan, the Persian Gulf states and Mesopotamia. The route to India had never seemed so secure. And in Africa the Cape-to-Cairo dream was reality at last, with Tanganyika now closing the gap between Nyasaland and Uganda. True, the new territories were not strictly colonies; they were to be held under a mandate from the new League of Nations. But, as Amery noted confidently, it was unlikely that any mandate would 'impose

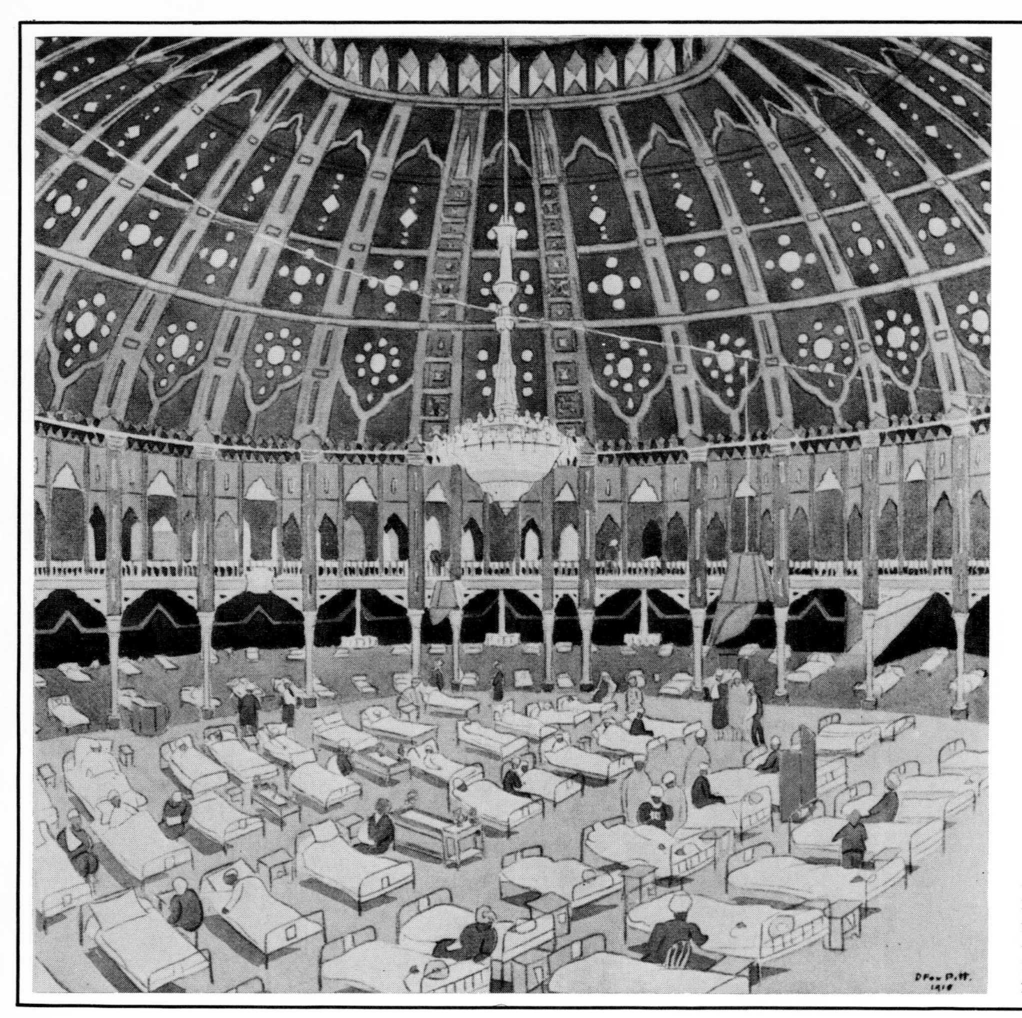

Indians wounded on the Western Front in hospital at the Dome, Brighton, 1918. India made a massive contribution to the war in men and money.

conditions upon us we have not been in the habit of imposing upon ourselves ... whenever we dealt with subject peoples'.[8]

The euphoria did not last long, however. Spring 1919 produced a crop of revolts from subject peoples, most of which had their seeds in government pledges made during the war. The Egyptian nationalists, for example, had been promised that England would review restoring self-government to Egypt after the war, and the Egyptian fellahin had not enjoyed the British military occupation. The final straw was Curzon's high-handed refusal to meet an Egyptian delegation in Paris, despite the pleas of the British High Commissioner in Cairo, Sir Reginald Wingate. There were mass riots and assassinations of a number of British officers. The Cabinet hastily rethought their attitudes and sent Lord Milner out to investigate. The immediate scapegoat was the unfortunate Wingate, who was removed from office and never received another government post.

A few weeks later there were reports of serious rioting throughout the Punjab, this time in protest against the Rowlett Acts which had been brought in to empower the government to arrest any suspected agitators. It seemed a poor reward for India's massive contribution in men and money to the war effort, and a

Brigadier-General Dyer. Born and trained in India, he applied the 'Punjab Principle' with disastrous results at Amritsar, April 1919.

contradiction of England's promise of 'gradual development towards self-governing institutions' made in 1916. The riots convinced the nearest Anglo-Indian general that here was a clear case where the Punjab Principle was called for. He applied it to a large, excited but unarmed crowd in the Jalianwallah Bagh at Amritsar, killing 375 people and wounding another 1500. The massacre marked the end of the hope that the new system of provincial power-sharing (or 'dyarchy'), set up a few months before, would work. What horrified anglophile Indians was Dyer's unrepentant admission that he had gone down to the Jalianwallah Bagh with the deliberate intention of shooting, 'to create a sufficient moral effect from a military point of view throughout the Punjab'. What horrified the English in India was that the government should openly dismiss and disgrace a soldier acting, albeit foolishly, on its behalf. It was 'time to close ranks'. Clubs and messes in India and England set up subscription boxes for Dyer to demonstrate their solidarity. In England the *Morning Post* collected £26,000 for his support. Even in Westminster, Conservative sympathy ran so high for Dyer that it was only quelled by an impassioned speech by Churchill, pointing out that Dyer's action was of 'quite un-English frightfulness'.

The Prince of Wales, heavily guarded, on his tour of India, 1920. He wrote privately that the tour was a failure.

To try to mend fences, the government wheeled out that well-tried expedient – a royal tour. This time Prince Charming himself, the young Prince of Wales. The tour was not a success. Gandhi chose the day the Prince arrived at Bombay to launch his new civil disobedience campaign, and the Prince's progress was dogged by riots and general strikes, except in the safety of the princely states. He reported to the Indian Secretary of State, Edwin Montagu, that the Raj's morale was at rock bottom.

> ... They one and all say the same thing, that they won't let their sons come out here to earn a living in the Indian Army, Indian Civil Service etc etc, and that nor now would they ever recommend these services to any good fellow.... India is no longer a place for a white man to live.[7]

The immediate post-war recruiting figures bore him out. Over two-thirds of the successful applicants to the Indian Civil Service were Indians, rather than the fifty per cent the government of India had intended. Within ten years 'Indianisation' had spread so far into all the old services – forestry, agriculture, even the army – that the English I.C.S. man out in a district could feel as lonely as his early twentieth-century colleague in the wilds of Africa. The deserted bungalows seemed to cry out 'Ichabod, Ichabod', wrote one officer wistfully. And those few Europeans who remained now had to be grateful for admission to the Indian clubs 'which provided good tennis', but fell sadly short 'in matters of bridge, billiards and the bar and other indoor amusements'.[8]

In 1920 Anglo-India received another jolt to its self-esteem. 233 enthusiastic young Anglo-Indian officers had been recruited to run the new colonial administration in Mesopotamia. After only a year the Arabs rose in fury, interrupting G.H.Q.'s annual retreat to a delightful new hill station in the Persian hills. One million Arabs, claimed T. E. Lawrence bitterly, had been alienated by the installation of an administration which was no good to anyone except the administrators. Sadly, the government of India agreed that the experiment must be dismantled. Instead, Mesopotamia was handed over to T. E. Lawrence's friend, Prince Faisal, who promptly renamed it Iraq.

Still, there were plenty of other places where a young empire-builder could look for a job. Ceylon and Burma were being 'Indianised' almost as fast as India itself, but in Malaya you could still find something not so far removed from the old I.C.S. ideal, 'plains for hacking about on horseback, and open hill country to scramble about in and a chance of some *shikar*. All this without any fear of Indianisation hanging over one's head.'[9] Then there was the huge range of African territories, now more numerous than ever with the addition of Tanganyika, parts of Togoland and the Cameroons. In Winston Churchill's view, tinged with happy memories of his journey fifteen years before, Africa was 'the' place. As he told Parliament in 1921

> In the African colonies, you have a docile tractable population who only require to be well and wisely treated to develop great economic capacity and utility, whereas the regions of the Middle East are unduly stocked with peppery pugnacious proud politicians and theologians who happen to be at the same time extremely well armed and extremely hard up.[10]

A sweeping Churchillian exaggeration. Africa had had its post-war troubles too, with strikes in the copper belt, riots in Nairobi and, on the Horn of Africa, the military had only just settled the hash of that peppery theologian, the Mad Mullah. This time they finally achieved it by using some of Lord Trenchard's aeroplanes to drop a bomb on his camp. The Mullah, who had come out of his tent in his best robes to greet what he took to be an aerial envoy from the Sultan of Turkey, escaped by a hair's breadth but died of Asiatic flu a few months later. (The whole expedition, Amery pointed out, had provided a valuable example of how order could be kept in remote parts of the Empire at reasonable cost.)

Bringing back the wounded from Somaliland, 1921. Airpower dramatically cut the cost of imperial campaigning after 1918.

The darker the prospects for the Raj in India and the Arab states, the rosier the prospects for the African services, a reversal of fortune which gave at least one old African hand a certain grim satisfaction as he recalled 'the ineffable disdain of I.C.S. officers when they visited East Africa on shooting trips before the war'.[11] Even the Labour party did not foresee anything like self-government for the 'non-adult races' in Africa, except after several decades of careful apprenticeship. Their expert on imperial matters was now the ex-A.G.A. from Hambantota, Leonard Woolf. He had been recruited by Beatrice and Sidney Webb just before the war and spent most of it writing treatises on international government. He ended with a virulent indictment of European economic imperialism in Africa, partly the result of his friendship with that fiery castigator of the 'Congo System' – E. D. Morel. But he admitted that to withdraw now would lead only to more cruel exploitation.

But the book that struck just the right note about Africa was Sir Frederick Lugard's, which appeared in 1922. Grandly named *The Dual Mandate in British Tropical Africa*, 640 pages long and two guineas in price (a considerable outlay compared with Woolf's pamphlet for the Labour party at twopence), it proved unexpectedly a best-seller, partly because it reassured the public that things were not as unpleasant as Leonard Woolf's pamphlet made out. Real progress, claimed Lugard, had been made in Africa by trial and error; the people's very discontent was 'a measure of their progress'. In the second half of the book Lugard restated, in essence, what Chamberlain had claimed twenty years before. The tropics were the heritage of mankind; they must be developed equally for the benefit of the natives

Indirect Rule personified: model of a Nigerian emir at the British Empire Exhibition, Wembley, 1924.

who lived there, the ruling power and the world. No one had the right to their exclusive exploitation, but neither

> have the races who inhabit them a right to deny their bounties to those who need them. . . . The merchant, the miner and the manufacturer do not enter the tropics on sufferance or employ their technical skill, their energy and their capital as 'interlopers' or as 'greedy capitalists', but in the fulfilment of the Mandate of civilisation.[12]

But there was a new slant to it all. This time the dependent countries were to be developed on their own lines – no more attempts to create brown or black Englishmen; that had been the mistake in India. Instead, the Englishman's task was to advance tribal peoples slowly, within the framework of their own cultures and social systems. Extreme caution was to be the keynote. Going too fast with native tribes was more likely to lead to disappointment, if not to disaster, than not going fast enough.

Lugard's preferred method of achieving this was of course Indirect Rule, as he had practised it in Nigeria. The colonial power could then become a kind of scaffolding, supportive not obtrusive, which in some future time, a great way off, could be removed without causing structural damage. The best kind of scaffolding was the public-schoolboy with his almost passionate conception of fair play, of protection of the weak and of playing the game. Neither the 'prig' nor the 'bookworm' nor the 'bounder' need apply. (The first two categories would certainly have excluded Woolf, and the second perhaps even Joyce Cary.) It all sounded very like the kind of young men Ralph Furse at the Colonial Office had been recruiting since just before the war and was to recruit for the next thirty years. Furse later described his method as one of the '*arcana imperii*'. (The nearest he could get to describing it was to compare it to choosing a first-class hunter at Tattersall's.) It was not always easy, despite a network of contacts in universities and public schools. There were a lot of 'defeatist ideas' about, and 'materialism, selfishness and self-indulgence' were rampant. He noted sadly that it was the families with the tradition of service who had been hardest hit by war and the economic squeeze. Many younger sons of county families had even been forced to go into trade.[13]

For the new recruits who got past Furse, Lugard's Dual Mandate was to be the new colonial gospel and Indirect Rule its first commandment. Where suitable native authorities were in short supply, the colonial governments applied themselves to creating them – ironically, just at the time when Lugard's old recruits started to voice public criticism of his system. Before the British takeover in Northern Nigeria, wrote Captain Fitzpatrick, one of Cary's old senior officers from Bauchi Province, in the *National Review*, the system had been one of 'autocracy tempered by assassination'. Now the emirs were maintained by British bayonets, without which they would not last one week. And the so-called Native Authorities were instruments of oppression hated by the people.[14]

Lugard's warnings on the dangers of going too fast were reinforced by a new kind of imperial pundit, the Anthropologist. From the late twenties, anthropology lectures by the great Bratislov Malinowski or R. S. Rattray were *de rigeur* for all new recruits who came away dazed with the knowledge that almost anything that interfered with tribal structures could prove fatal. What then were they there for at all? 'It does seem rather strange that we won't let these poor devils have any of the comforts or conveniences that we couldn't do without ourselves,' says a puzzled prospector in one of Cary's African novels. 'Why, we don't even teach them English, we behave exactly as if English books and English ideas would poison them.'[15]

To cynics the new stress on indirect rule and anthropology was simply a convenient way for the colonial governments to avoid spending any money. Like Chamberlain's dream of developing England's 'tropical estates', the Dual Mandate remained more aspiration than actuality. It was clear to the post-war government, especially the Treasury, that it was no part of *its* mandate from the *British* native to splash around money in Africa or the other colonies. The spirit was willing, wrote the Under Secretary at the Colonial Office, Leo Amery, sadly, 'but the flesh in terms of money is sadly weak'.[16]

What little *was* done for the Africans' 'economic and moral development' was mostly the result of a strange alliance which would not have seemed possible in the quarrelsome days before the war. The Protestant missions, thanks largely to the efforts of the brilliant and tactful Dr J. H. Oldham, who had been appointed Permanent Secretary to the Conference of Missionary Societies, had emerged from the war keener than ever to resolve their liturgical differences. At the second Kikuyu conference in 1918, Bishop Frank Weston startled the delegates by presenting a list of brilliantly simple proposals for a United Church. (Unfortunately there was still one dissenting mission, the American-led African Inland Mission, who feared that the U.M.C.A. might prove dangerous Modernists. They had evidently missed the great drama of Frank Weston's '*Ecclesia Anglicana*'.)

In 1920 the missionaries commissioned a group of American educationalists to advise on a joint policy for African education and, especially, on how to avoid the disruptive effects on the African social structures which were the chief charge, as they were well aware, levelled against them by the administrators. In 1922 Oldham drew the attention of the Colonial Under Secretary to the Commission's report. Ormsby-Gore was so impressed that he proposed setting up immediately a joint advisory body between the colonial governments and the missions. At a famous 'Derby day meeting' in 1926, attended by Lugard, the Archbishop of Canterbury and all the African colonial governors, the missions formally agreed to work together with the colonial administrations. Two years later even the Roman Catholic missions declared themselves prepared to join in.

By 1930 the rambling network of mission stations in the bush had been transformed into bustling primary schools with government subsidies and official inspectors. Secondary schools, according to the policy of indirect rule, were largely reserved for chiefs' sons, which would make possible, wrote one education officer, 'the full realisation of the British ideal to delegate authority to those who by heredity ought to possess and exercise it'.[17] Still, the old antipathies died hard. 'Many officials confessed in unofficial moments,' wrote Evelyn Waugh on a visit to East Africa in 1931, 'that if they had their way they would like to clear all the missionaries out of the country.'[18]

The people who fitted least happily into the scenario of the Dual Mandate were the East African settlers. Once again the problem had been exacerbated by war and government miscalculation. Alarmed in 1916 that the black soldiers and carriers recruited in thousands for the East African campaign might draw their own conclusions about the white man's invulnerability and even acquire a taste for killing him, the government had decided to double the settler population. Early in 1919 ballots were set up in London and in Nairobi to allot plots of vacant land to ex-officers. The result, coupled with the fact that many former settlers had returned from the war to find their lands had reverted almost to bush, was a louder-than-ever clamour for native labour from the reserves. Since vast numbers of Africans had died as combatants or carriers during the East African campaign and more still in the flu epidemic that followed, the labour was not forthcoming. We have seen already Frank Weston's and the East African bishops' battle with the Colonial Office over the Forced Labour Bill, which Churchill rescinded in 1921. The episode only strengthened the settlers' belief that they must win more control of their own political affairs. Kenya had become officially a Crown Colony in 1920, with an enlarged legislative council. Surely self-government must follow soon. Rhodesia had been granted it in 1922.

The problem was, it transpired, not so much the Colonial Secretary (Churchill still had romantic views about the settlers), but the Secretary of State for India. The Indian settlers in Kenya outnumbered the Europeans two to one. To deny them voting rights in a new self-governing constitution would, it was only too plain to the India Office, provide yet one more stick for Gandhi to attack 'British imperialism' with. By 1923 the settlers were desperate enough to plan to kidnap their governor, Sir Robert Coryndon, and hide him at a remote farmhouse (with a convenient trout stream) until the government submitted to their demands. Instead they were persuaded to send a delegation to put their case at Westminster. In January it arrived, headed by Lord Delamere, still wearing his hair to his shoulders and dressed in battered settler's clothes and flanked by his two Somali servants. He received the press and other influential visitors at a palatial house in Grosvenor Place which he had booked specially for the occasion, and soon the London papers resounded with the Kenya debate.

The white settlers, argued Delamere, had made Kenya what it was, hacking their farms from virgin bush. The Indians had merely followed in their wake as traders; and were anyway from the lowest class, mostly untouchables at home. Meanwhile the Indian delegation, supported by the most famous of Anglo-Indian missionaries and Gandhi's friend, C. F. Andrews, presented their rival claim. *They* had been in East Africa for over 200 years. Sensing the battle would be a close one, Delamere's delegation threw in for good measure the government's responsibility towards Kenya's African population. Any increased Indian immigration would be directly against their interests; the Indians would form an impenetrable barrier to the Africans' advance.

The claim rebounded disastrously. The government suddenly saw its way out of the dilemma and announced that Kenya was primarily after all an African territory in which African interests were paramount. Any further move towards self-government for the immigrant population, white or brown, could not therefore be envisaged. The only thing which made it possible for Delamere to calm his

The Joint Parliamentary Enquiry on Closer Union (for Uganda, Kenya and Tanganyika), 1925. The Committee included (*reading from top left*) Lord Cranworth (*seventh*), Leo Amery (*eighth*), Lord Lugard (*fifteenth*) and Lord Passfield (Sidney Webb) (*sixteenth*).

embattled followers at home was the report of the intense fury of the Indian delegation.

Though Delamere periodically extracted by skilful lobbying and charm various concessions from the successive commissions sent out from England to report on the Kenyan problem, from then on he never really had a chance of winning. The pro-African lobby, primed and mobilised by Oldham and Lugard with the Archbishop of Canterbury as a powerful go-between to the Colonial Office, blocked him at every turn. In 1925 he tried another tack. This time a plan for Closer Union (a federation of the three East African states – Tanganyika, Kenya and Uganda – with its administrative and political centre at Nairobi). It was dished by the Tanganyikan governor, Sir Donald Cameron, an ex-disciple of Lugard's, and by what Amery described as 'mischievous lobbying' by Oldham and Lugard himself. By then, Delamere had to deal with a Labour Colonial Secretary, Lord Passfield (the former Sidney Webb) who had little sympathy for Delamere's basic tenet – that the best way of raising the African was by involving him in white settler farming and providing him with examples of a stable civilised community at first hand, rather than a few remote and transitory district officers.

What was unfortunate for Delamere's cause was the notoriety of at least one section of his civilised white community in the Highlands. The Muthaiga Club outside Nairobi was soon the Mecca for every randy upper-class Englishman south of Suez.

When I observe the situation out here and see how people with the greatest equanimity and social success conduct themselves, [reported Karen Blixen from her farm in the Ngong Hills in a long serious letter to her brother in Denmark] I am certain the old negative sexual morality has had its day. It may be of course that to a certain extent the country is outside the normal bounds of law and order. There is quite simply nothing that one cannot freely undertake in this direction. . . .[19]

Although Karen Blixen herself was soon deeply and hopelessly in love with one of the most dashing of Kenya's displaced English aristocrats, Dennis Finch-Hatton, and liked and admired Lord Delamere, she could not help feeling slightly revolted by the White Highlands' frenetic high life.

The upper classes haven't improved in the slightest since the revolution. When they're not *afraid* of the lower classes they're really completely without shame; the natives can be starving here and dying of starvation . . . and the champagne flows in torrents at their races and so on – Lord Delamere recently held a dinner for 250 people at which they drank 600 bottles and they just do not *see* it; the ladies here are quite capable when they hear that the natives cannot get *posho* [mealies] of asking why they do not eat wheat or rice instead, just like Marie Antoinette. . . .[20]

Karen Blixen went home to Denmark the same year that Delamere died – 1931. Both in different ways were casualties of the Great Depression which wrecked the settlers' economic hopes as well as their political ones. Their farm crops – coffee, maize, flax, wheat, butter – fell by half their previous value in one year and then by half again. It was soon cheaper to burn Kenyan coffee beans as fuel in the Uganda Railway engines than export them from Mombasa. Delamere died hugely in debt, having mortgaged most of his Vale Royale estate. He was buried on the stony hillside above his ranch, Soysambu, overlooking Lake Elmenteita.

Even the price of ivory slumped. Most of the few remaining white elephant-hunters traded in a precarious living for a game warden's salary – poachers turned gamekeepers at last.

What died with Delamere and the hunters was at least one vital element in the old Edwardian Empire – its sense of freedom, its savagery. In a sense the Empire really had been about 'a sense of space in the blood', as John Buchan had put it a generation before. Of course it was also about having your cake and eating it. Civilisation *and* the African bush or the Malayan jungle, champagne for dinner *and* lions in the morning. 'The English gentleman is half barbarian too – that is . . . just the value of him',[21] the most famous of imperial journalists, G. W. Steevens, had written in 1899. It was its inconsistencies which had given the imperial idea much of its appeal. What made the twenties and thirties so much flatter and duller was that the Empire was now run by such thoroughly tame, civilised Englishmen. There were no heroes and very few villains.

Lord Delamere just before his death in 1931. He was buried on his farm, Soysambu in Kenya.

Although India and the Middle East were still seething with troubles, by the thirties the British faith in what they were doing in Africa and Malaya and Papua New Guinea and all that assorted ragbag of colonial territories acquired in the eighties and nineties was as high as ever. Out in the African bush or up-country Pahang, Furse's young men still trudged or bicycled under the noonday sun, lecturing chiefs and *penghulus* on sanitation and erosion and the need to keep the native Treasury accounts more carefully.

These days, thanks to wives, wirelesses and a better class of hut, fewer of them went mad or took to the bottle or native concubines as they had in Joyce Cary's or Bruce Lockhart's day. Foreign observers were usually deeply impressed by them: 'Not since the heroic days of Greece has the world had such a sweet, just, boyish master,' wrote the American philosopher, George Santayana. 'It will be a black day for the human race when scientific blackguards, conspirators and fanatics manage to supplant him.'[22] Out in the missions, more missionaries than ever were now hard at work, turning out native teachers and medical orderlies. It might not be as romantic as the old days of tramping for thousands of miles across Africa, but at least the results were more clearly quantifiable, unlike the elusive process of implanting the faith. Even the settlers (with the exception of the fast Muthaiga Club set) were quiet these days under the sensible leadership of Lord Francis Scott.

In sheer size the Empire was larger than ever. It had reached its apogee in 1923. By 1930 you could go round the world by the new British Imperial Airways without setting foot on anything but British soil. But no one at home seemed much to care. Like the eminent Victorians discredited by Woolf's friend Lytton Strachey, the Empire had become rather a joke. Only Big White Carstairs and Colonel Blimp in the *Daily Express* worried about the White Man's Burden. There were only three serious students of colonial affairs between the wars, lamented Sir Ralph Furse in his memoirs, and one of them was a *woman* (Marjorie Perham).

Oddly, the last place to provide the old kind of imperial thrills was Hollywood. Early in the 1930s the movie moguls had realised that the retreat from the Khyber Pass and Livingstone's death made splendid colourful alternatives to Custer's Last Stand or the Alamo. And of course there was Tarzan, who first appeared on film just after the First World War. A truly imperial mixture of white aristocrat and noble savage, not very articulate perhaps, but then the English seldom were. It was a sign of the times that when George V's dying words were reported by *The Times* in January 1936 to be 'How is the Empire?', the wits should rephrase them as 'What's on at the Empire'.

The people who did care passionately *how* the Empire was, of course, were the old

Left Sir Frank Swettenham, aged ninety-one.

Opposite Tarzan: the authentic imperial mixture of white aristocrat and noble savage, first filmed in 1918.

empire-builders themselves. Seasoned perhaps by their early exposure to tropical wind and rain, a little yellow, a little sallow still, with hallways thick with fine heads stuffed by Rowland Ward, a rare antelope skin in front of the fire perhaps, a glass case or two of curios, a signed portrait of Chamberlain on the mantelpiece, most of them lived on long enough to watch over the imperial conscience until the Second World War.

There was Sir Frank Swettenham in his handsome flat in Stanhope Gate, keeping a careful watch on the affairs of the Malay States and denouncing any attempt to dismantle his federation. At eighty-six, Bruce Lockhart reported that he was still as mentally alert as colonial servants half his age. At ninety-one he published his autobiography, *Footprints in Malaya.* The Second World War had just begun, and he thanked heaven that at least Singapore was safe. The British had spent £60 million on making it the most powerful naval base in the East. By a sad irony the Japanese overran it a few months after the book appeared. He died at the age of ninety-six. Almost as long-lived was Sir Reginald Wingate of the Sudan, who had retired home to Scotland but kept a house on the Red Sea as well for a little winter sun. He lived till the age of ninety-one. Then there was Sir Henry Hesketh 'Juju' Bell. He had retired finally to the Bahamas, where he edited his diaries as *Glimpses of a Governor's Life*, the wittiest of all proconsular memoirs. He died in 1952, aged eighty-seven.

Lord Lugard (*centre*) with a delegation of Nigerian emirs at his house in Surrey.

The most active of retired proconsuls was undoubtedly Sir Frederick Lugard, from 1925 Lord Lugard. From Abinger in Surrey he travelled ceaselessly up to London to sit on colonial committees and boards: the League of Nations Mandate Commission; the Advisory Committee on African Education; Lord Leverhulme's Congo company 'Les Huileries du Congo Belge' (which Lugard insisted should look after the welfare of its workers in the true Port Sunlight tradition). Then at home he struggled to revise his book, *The Dual Mandate*. He never finished it. Events in Africa were moving too fast, he confessed sadly in 1939, and each time he got to the end, he found his early chapters were out of date. He died in April 1945, aged eighty-six.

Finally, the smallest and oddest of all, Sir Harry Johnston, Lugard's contemporary. Always unlucky, he suffered an attack of mustard gas during the war while lecturing on Africa to the troops on the Western Front and never really recovered. He died impoverished in 1927, at a mere sixty-seven, having turned out during his twenty-six years' premature retirement a formidable number of books on Africa and Empire. By chance one of them was to win him a strange kind of immortality. It caught the attention of Edgar Wallace, who incorporated Johnston's adventures into that most famous classic of colonial life, *Sanders of the River*.

Edgar Wallace's book was filmed in 1935 by Alexander Korda as a lavish tribute to British colonial rule. By a nice piece of historic irony, one of the extras who pleads with 'Lord Sandy' to stay with his people forever was Jomo Kenyatta, the man who was to put paid finally to the Kenyan settlers' dream of White Man's Country.

Left Sir Harry Johnston, whose early adventures inspired Edgar Wallace's *Sanders of the River*. This was filmed (*below*) by Alexander Korda in 1935 with Leslie Banks playing Chief Commissioner Sanders. Jomo Kenyatta played one of the extras.

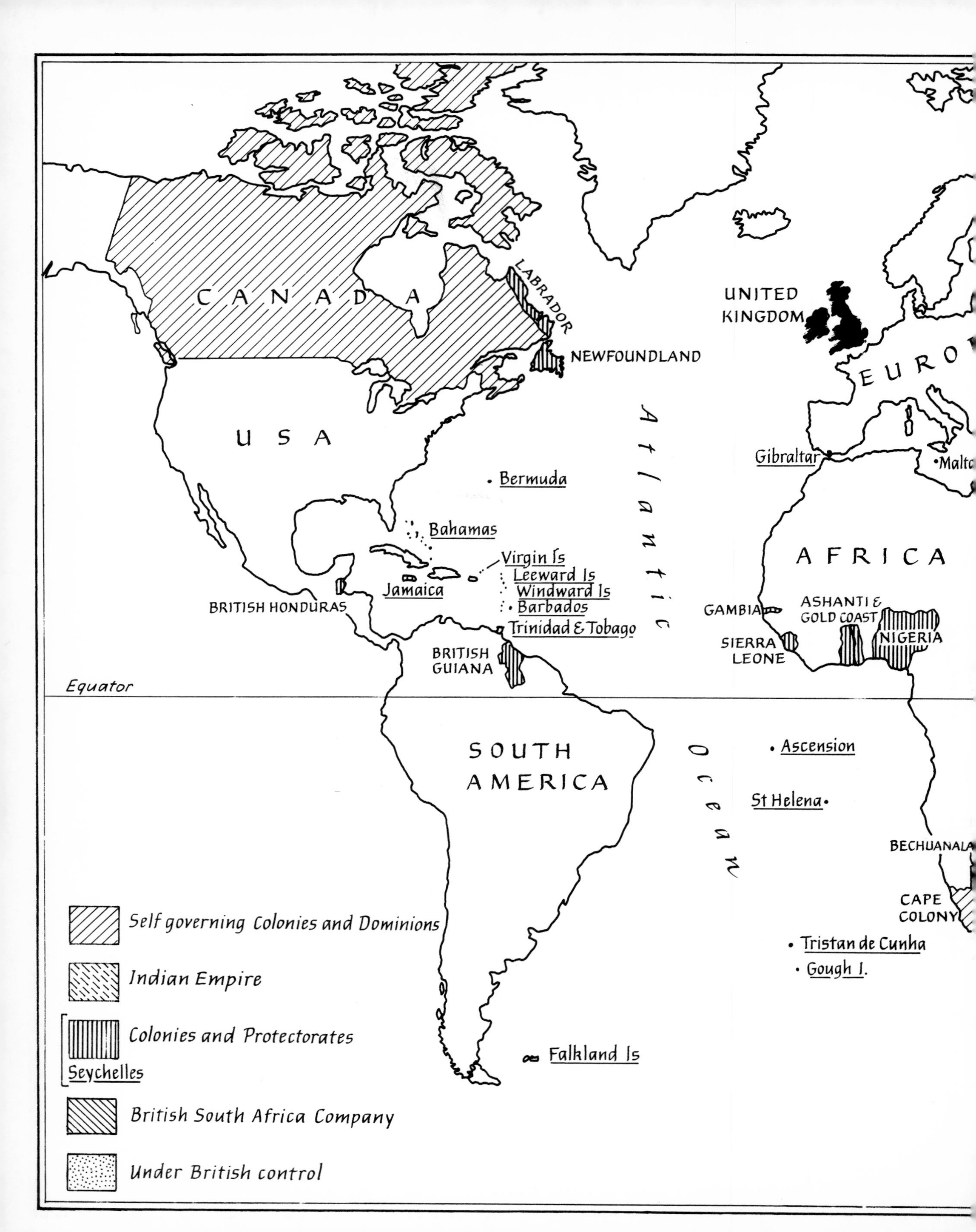
CANADA
LABRADOR
NEWFOUNDLAND
UNITED KINGDOM
EURO
USA
Atlantic
Ocean
Gibraltar
•Malta
Bermuda
Bahamas
Virgin Is
Leeward Is
Windward Is
Barbados
Jamaica
Trinidad & Tobago
BRITISH HONDURAS
AFRICA
GAMBIA
ASHANTI & GOLD COAST
NIGERIA
SIERRA LEONE
BRITISH GUIANA
Equator
SOUTH AMERICA
Ascension
St Helena
BECHUANALA
CAPE COLONY
Tristan de Cunha
Gough I.
Falkland Is
Self governing Colonies and Dominions
Indian Empire
Colonies and Protectorates
Seychelles
British South Africa Company
Under British control

THE BRITISH EMPIRE in 1901

BIOGRAPHICAL NOTES

Abel, Rev. Charles: born 1863 in London into family of staunch congregationalists. Emigrated to New Zealand aged eighteen to work as farm cadet, but ran away to live in the bush among the Maori. Worked briefly as trader, then as stevedore in Sydney docks. Returned home aged twenty-two to train as missionary. Ordained in 1890 and sent by London Missionary Society to Papua New Guinea. Pioneered an industrial mission on Kwato Island opposite the China Straits, where he remained for the next thirty-five years 'beating spears into cricket bats'. Successfully prevented white settlement in his district and fought long battle with white 'diggers' after gold was discovered nearby. After the First World War he found financial support for his mission mainly in America, helped by the son of the great revivalist preacher, Dwight Moody. Knocked down by a car while on leave in England and died at Woolwich in 1930.

Baden-Powell, Lord (Robert): born 1857, son of Oxford professor of geometry who died when he was three; brought up by strong-minded mother who encouraged interest in natural history. Educated at Charterhouse, failed Balliol, but placed second on cavalry list and gazetted to 13th Hussars in India in 1876. Made his name as reconnaissance officer and expert at polo and pig-sticking. From 1884 served mainly in Africa, fighting in Zulu and Matabele wars and as chief planner of the Ashanti campaign, 1896 (described in his book *The Downfall of Prempeh*). In 1897 made colonel of the 5th Dragoon Guards in India and instituted training course described in his *Aids to Scouting* (1899) which was much admired. Caught with two regiments in Mafeking at outbreak of Boer War, and held siege for 217 days, emerging as national hero. Made Major-General in 1900 and created new South African constabulary. In 1903 made Inspector-General of Cavalry, and was inspired by the Boys Brigade to found his Boy Scouts. The first trial camp was held in 1907 and *Scouting for Boys* was published in parts in 1908. In 1910 he retired from the army with the King's approval to devote himself full time to the movement. In 1912 married Olive St Clair who helped set up the Girl Guides. During First World War he founded the Wolf Cubs (inspired by Kipling's Mowgli) and, after it, the Rover Scouts for Boy Scouts above age. At the First International 'jamboree' in 1920 he was elected Chief Scout, and spent the next twenty years promoting the scouts worldwide. Created baron in 1929. Caught in Kenya where he was convalescing at outbreak of Second World War and died at Nyeri in 1947.

Bell, Sir Henry Hesketh: born 1864 in West Indies, educated in Brussels and Paris. Rose from clerkship in Barbados government office to be treasurer of the Bahamas. Caught Chamberlain's eye as administrator in Dominica and appointed High Commissioner of Uganda, 1906, where he set up cotton-growing industry and helped to bring sleeping sickness epidemic under control. Knighted 1908.

Governor of Northern Nigeria from 1909 to 1911, then drastically demoted after quarrel with Colonial Office to governorship of Leeward Isles. In 1916 appointed governor of Mauritius, where his Anglo-French background proved ideal. Was retired, protesting, in 1924 but received his coveted G.C.M.G. and in 1926 won the Royal Empire Society's gold medal for his study of colonial systems in the Far East. Retired to France and finally to the Bahamas. Died on visit to London in 1952.

Bell, Walter 'Karamoja': born near Edinburgh in 1880. Left school at fourteen to make his way to Africa on a cargo ship. Worked briefly on the Uganda railway, then rushed off to join Klondike gold rush. Returned to Africa with a group of Canadian volunteers to fight in Boer War; and remained there hunting elephant in the African interior until the First World War, perfecting the use of the high-velocity rifle. At outbreak of war, he went back to England to learn how to fly and was sent to East Africa as a fighter pilot. Later transferred to Egypt and to Salonika. After the war, he returned to Africa and continued to make a successful living out of hunting elephant until the slump in 1932. Died 1954.

Berkeley, Hubert: born 1864 into cadet branch of famous Berkeleys of Berkeley Castle, and grandson of an Irish peer on his mother's side. Joined navy as midshipman, but jumped ship (it is said) after a voyage up the Malay coast. Served as police inspector in the Dindings, joined Perak civil service in 1889 and first appointed to Upper Perak on Siamese border in 1891. Remained there (with the exception of the First World War years) until 1927, creating a semi-feudal state and becoming legendary hero of the M.C.S. Retired finally to a family estate in Worcestershire, and died aged eighty in 1944.

Besant, Annie: born in London, 1847. Brought up by her mother as devout Christian (her father had died early) and at the age of seventeen married a clergyman. Left him six years later to join the National Secular Society and became close friend of Charles Bradlaugh. Her *Gospel of Atheism*, published with him, made her notorious and lost her custody of her daughter. Joined Fabian Society in 1885, but abandoned it for Theosophy in 1893 after meeting its mesmeric founder, Mme Blavatsky. From 1895 she lived and preached full-time in India and in 1898 founded the first Hindu college at Benares. In 1909 she split the Theosophical Society by claiming that her adopted son Krishnamurti was the vehicle of the world teacher or Messiah (he disclaimed this in 1932), and shifted her H.Q. to Adyar. During Hardinge's viceroyalty (following Minto's) she enjoyed a relative honeymoon with the English Raj, but in September 1916 she initiated her Home Rule for India League, proclaiming herself an 'Indian tom-tom' to wake the sleepers; and was interned for inflammatory speeches. After the British declaration in August 1917 of India's right to progress to 'responsible government' she was released and elected next year to be first President of the Indian National Congress. But she lost the leadership to Gandhi the following year after denouncing his civil disobedience campaign, both before and after Amritsar. Her popularity in India never recovered though she campaigned hard in England for Indian Home Rule. Aged eighty-three, her energies finally failed and she retired to Adyar until her death in 1933.

Blunt, Wilfrid Scawen: born 1840, the son of a Sussex landowner. Joined diplomatic service aged eighteen, but left it in 1869 to marry Lady Anne Noel, Byron's granddaughter. Spent next ten years travelling in North Africa and the East, and founded a famous Arab stud in Sussex with brood mares presented to him by an Arab emir. Bought an estate (Sheyk Obeid) outside Cairo in 1881. The crushing of Arabi Pasha's revolt in 1883 and a visit to India made him a passionate anti-imperialist, and he spent the rest of his life denouncing the wickedness of the British Empire to the world and his large circle of friends (who included Curzon and Winston Churchill), but without much success. Notorious for his amorous adventures; his wife finally separated from him to live at Sheyk Obeid while he retired to Sussex with an adopted 'niece'. Published just before his death in 1922 two highly edited volumes of his diaries.

Brooke, Sir Charles: born 1829 in Somerset, nephew of Sir James Brooke, the first White Rajah of Sarawak. Resigned from the navy to join him there in 1852, and spent next twelve years living alone among the headhunting Dyak tribesmen. Succeeded James as Rajah in 1868 and reigned as a highly efficient despot over his little kingdom for next forty-eight years. Disapproved strongly of New Imperialist doctrines of Chamberlain's era and refused concessions to commercial and plantation companies which he saw as harmful to his subjects. After his death in 1916, the tradition of personal rule was continued by his son, Vyner Brooke; but after the Second World War and the devastation caused by the Japanese invasion, the third White Rajah handed Sarawak over to the Colonial Office, much to many of his subjects' distress.

Cary, Joyce: born 1888 in Londonderry, and brought up between London and his grandmother's house in Donegal (described in his semi-autobiographical novel *A House of Children*). Educated at Clifton College, then went to Paris to study art. After two years decided to go to Cambridge instead to read law, but spent much of his time reading philosophy and came down with a Fourth. Enlisted as medical orderly in the Montenegrin war and then worked briefly for Horace Plunkett in Ireland. Joined Nigerian service in 1913; drafted into the army from 1915 to 1916 and wounded at Mount Mora during Cameroons Campaign. Married during leave and returned to Nigeria in 1917. Resigned early 1920 and settled with wife in Oxford for the rest of his life. Published first novel in 1932 only after ten years' intensive writing and reading; then wrote more easily, sixteen novels in twenty-five years. Returned to Africa briefly during Second World War to write script for a government film, and afterwards revised and expanded an earlier pamphlet he had written for the Liberal party on colonial rule in *The Case for African Freedom*, 1946. Died after long painful illness, stoically borne, in 1957.

Churchill, Sir Winston (early life): born 1874, elder son of Lord Randolph Churchill, educated Harrow and Sandhurst, commissioned in 4th Hussars, 1895, and brilliantly combined – much to many of his senior officers' displeasure – the career of soldier and journalist for the next five years, fighting in Cuba (unofficially), on the North-West Frontier, at Omdurman and in South Africa, where he made himself famous by escaping from the Boers. Elected as M.P. for Oldham, 1900, but resigned from the Tory whip three years later over Joseph Chamberlain's Tariff Reform proposals and joined the Liberals. Appointed Colonial Under Secretary in 1906, made his African Journey, 1907, and married the beautiful Clementine Hozier the following year. Rose to be First Lord of the Admiralty in 1911, but was forced to resign in 1915 and made chief scapegoat for the disastrous Gallipolli campaign. Rejoined army as commander of a battalion on the Western Front. Brought back into cabinet by Lloyd George as Minister for Munitions in 1917 and became Secretary for War, 1918–21, then Colonial Secretary, 1921–2. Defeated at Dundee in 1922 election by Labour candidate, E. D. Morel; but won seat as Conservative at Epping two years later, and became Chancellor of the Exchequer, 1924–9. Published in 1930 the most delightful of all his books, *My Early Life*, which distils the excitement of the imperial high noon.

Clifford, Sir Hugh: born 1866, grandson of Lord Clifford of Chudleigh. Educated at private Catholic school. Enlisted in Malay Civil Service aged seventeen to join his father's cousin, Sir Frederick Weld, who was already there as governor. Sent alone to Pahang aged twenty to 'persuade' the Sultan to accept a British adviser (a process vividly described in one of his stories) and, from 1896 to 1899, returned there as Resident. Made a minor literary reputation in the '90s with his stories and novels about Malaya and became close friend of Joseph Conrad (who did his best to prune Clifford's purple prose-style). Briefly governor of British North Borneo Company, 1901, but resigned in disgust at their commercial methods, retaining a lifelong suspicion of 'plantation systems' (which partly explains his later quarrel with Lever). Served as Colonial Secretary in Trinidad, 1903–7, where his first wife was tragically killed. From 1907 to 1912 deputy governor in Ceylon; 1912–19 governor of the Gold Coast; 1919–24, governor of Nigeria; 1925, governor of Ceylon; returned to Malaya as governor, 1926, but resigned through illness soon after. Died in 1941.

Cranworth, Lord (Bertram Gurdon): born 1877, son of Norfolk M.P. who was made a baron in 1899. Educated at Eton and Trinity College, enlisted in Boer War, 1901. Inherited title in 1902 and emigrated with family to British East Africa in 1906. Published *A Colony in the Making*, 1912, which encapsulates the old-Etonian view of White Man's Country. Joined his friend Berkeley Cole's Scouts at outbreak of war (Meinertzhagen described them as hopelessly undisciplined); then fought gallantly on Western Front, winning M.C. and *Croix de Guerre*. Returned to Norfolk estate after war, but spoke for Kenyan settlers in the House of Lords and served on Committee for Closer Union, 1929. Published memoirs (*Kenya Chronicles*), 1939. Vice-Lieutenant of Suffolk from 1947. Died 1964.

Cromer, Lord (Evelyn Baring): born 1844, educated at Woolwich, commissioned in 1858 and became A.D.C.

to High Commissioner of Corfu. Returned to Staff College, followed by the War Office, where he earned a brilliant reputation, but resigned to go with his cousin Lord Northbrook, the Viceroy, to India as private secretary, 1872. Sent by Lord Goschen to Egypt in 1876 as first British Commissioner to the *Caisse de la Dette*, but resigned after a clash of views on policy with the French; and returned to India. Sent back to Egypt by Gladstone to pick up the pieces after the British Army had crushed Arabi's revolt in 1883; and remained for next twenty-four years as British consul-general, reorganising Egypt's finances and administration from top to bottom. Known in Cairo society, half affectionately, as 'le Grand Ours' because of his massive physical presence and his lack of small talk, but much resented by the young King Abbas Hilmi for his autocratic manner (his Anglo-Indian colleagues had long before nicknamed him overBaring). After his return to Egypt with his second wife in 1901 he faced increasing opposition from nationalists, and resigned pleading failing health a year after Denshawai. Refused all official posts; published his account of 'Modern Egypt' in 1908 which was enthusiastically received in England but not in Egypt. From 1912 he reviewed enthusiastically for the *Spectator* – later published as *Political and Literary Essays* – lecturing his readers on everything from vivisection to free trade. Appointed chairman, 1916, of the Dardanelles Commission but collapsed after first meeting and died in January 1917.

Curzon, Lord (George Nathaniel): born 1859 at Kedleston Hall in Derbyshire, educated at Eton and Balliol, Oxford where he won nearly every available prize but failed to get a First. Spent next six years mainly travelling in Asia (with brief interlude working in the India Office) and wrote three brilliant travel books stressing Russia's threat to the British Empire as an expanding power. In 1895 married beautiful and unselfish American heiress, Mary Leiter, and entered full-time politics as Salisbury's under secretary at the Foreign Office and his spokesman in the Commons. Labouchère described his manner there as 'a divinity addressing black beetles' but he impressed the House by his hard work. In 1898 Salisbury appointed him Viceroy of India, the post he had always wanted. He was much acclaimed for his reforms during his first few years, but after that increasingly at odds with Anglo-India, the Indian nationalists and Balfour's government at home. Resigned after clash with Kitchener over control of the army in India in 1905, and spent next eleven years in the political wilderness, privately desolated by the death of his wife in 1906. Brought into coalition government in 1916 after fall of Asquith, and then became part of Lloyd George's inner war cabinet. Helped draft declaration of India's right to 'responsible government' in 1917, but bitterly opposed proposals for 'dyarchy'. Became acting foreign secretary in 1919 during Balfour's absence at the Paris Peace Conference, then full foreign secretary under Bonar Law. In 1923 he believed he would be offered the premiership as Bonar Law's successor, and broke down in tears when told that the King had chosen Baldwin. But he rallied and served loyally as Lord Privy Seal until his death in March 1925. Buried at Kedleston after a state funeral in Westminster Abbey.

Delamere, Lord (Hugh Cholmondely): born 1876, educated at Eton and inherited his father's title and estate in Cheshire aged seventeen. Spent next few years mainly hunting at home and shooting big game in Somaliland; stumbled into the 'white' highlands in 1897 from Abyssinia and returned five years later to settle permanently with his young wife, Lady Florence Cole (described by Meinertzhagen as 'very beautiful and charming and quite unfitted for this savage country', she died in 1914). Granted 99-year lease on 100,000 acres at Njoro by Sir Charles Eliot. Elected first President of the Farmer and Planter's Association in 1903 and remained leader of the European settlers until his death, pioneering experiments in crops and stockfarming and fighting recurrent battles against the colonial authorities. Became legendary for his wild exploits and puckish charm which, however, concealed, as one fellow settler noted, a Draconian will. Post-war, he dreamed of establishing a chain of European self-governing colonies from Kenya to the Cape, and organised a series of unofficial conferences in southern Tanganyika at his own expense. Was blocked largely by Lugard's disciple, Sir Donald Cameron, Governor of Tanganyika. Died of angina in 1931, mainly from the strain of re-organising his farms to meet the catastrophic fall in prices, and was buried at his ranch at Soysambu.

Eliot, Sir Charles: born 1862, educated at Cheltenham and Balliol, where he took a double first in classics and won a series of scholarships. A brilliant linguist, fluent in Finnish, Sanskrit, Pali, Hebrew, Syriac, Turkish and Persian, he served in the diplomatic service mainly in the Near East until his appointment as High Commissioner to East Africa in 1900. Resigned in 1904 after row with Foreign Office over white settlement and went back to academic life. From 1912 became vice-chancellor of Lugard's new university in Hong Kong. His last post was as ambassador to Japan, where he wrote a massive study of Hinduism and Buddhism, and stayed on to live after his retirement. Died at sea in 1931.

Furse, Sir Ralph: born 1882, son of a crippled agnostic with passionate belief in empire (mother died just after his birth). Educated at Eton and Balliol; left army to join the Colonial Office as recruiting officer in 1910 and returned after the First World War. Married the daughter of the poet Sir Henry Newbolt, and recruited his brother-in-law to the Colonial Office in 1919. Together they transformed the colonial services between the wars, recruiting by personal interview, mainly from Oxford and Cambridge, but with emphasis on 'character' rather than brains. Furse retired in 1948, Newbolt in 1954 after what Furse called 'a first-wicket partnership' of twenty-nine years. Newbolt died in 1966, Furse in 1973 aged ninety-one.

Girouard, Sir Percy: born 1867, son of an eminent Canadian lawyer, educated in Montreal, sent on scholarship to the Royal Military College in England and commissioned in Royal Engineers. Quickly won reputation as a brilliant railway engineer, was picked by Kitchener in 1898 to mastermind the Sudan campaign, and became reigning favourite on Kitchener's staff. Planned and organised vital railways for South African war. Appointed High Commissioner of Northern Nigeria to succeed Lugard in 1907 and Governor of Kenya in 1909, where he became immensely popular with settlers and restored the country to solvency. But resigned after bitter row with Harcourt in the Colonial Office over his attempt to shift the Masai from their traditional grazing ground on the Laikipia plateau and free it for white settlement. Took directorship of Vickers Armstrong; recruited as Director-General of Munitions in 1915 but resigned after row with Lloyd George. Died in London in 1932.

Guggisberg, Sir Gordon: born in Toronto, but educated largely in England. Commissioned in Royal Engineers in 1889, and sent to Singapore where he eloped with his colonel's daughter, who soon found him too imperious and divorced him. Appointed by Colonial Office to survey the Gold Coast and Ashanti in 1902. Married the actress Decima Moore while on leave, 1905; and soon after promoted in turn to be Director of Survey in S. Nigeria then Surveyor-General of the new unified Nigeria. Rejoined his regiment in 1914 and rose to be brigadier-general. In 1919 appointed as Sir Hugh Clifford's successor as Governor of the Gold Coast, much to Clifford's disgust. Built deep-water harbour at Takoradi and founded the nucleus of Accra university, Achimota College. In 1928 he reluctantly accepted the governorship of British Guiana, mainly in order to qualify for a governor's pension, but soon fell desperately ill and had to return to England. Spent last year of life dreaming of a return to Africa, 'to do something for the Empire' but died in Sussex in 1930.

Hine, Bishop John: born 1857, son of a Nottingham manufacturer. Sent to school at University College, London, went on to read medicine at University College Hospital and joined a practice at Oxford where he became an extra-mural student. Applied to read theology full time in 1885 and was ordained two years later. In 1889, he became the U.M.C.A's first (much needed) medical missionary at Likoma Island on Lake Nyasa; and was made Bishop after the death of his friend Bishop Chauncy Maples in the lake. Transferred with regret to Zanzibar in 1901 and retired, exhausted and ill, in 1904. Returned to take up the new diocese of Northern Rhodesia in 1910, retiring just before the outbreak of the war, and spent rest of his life in England, mainly as Bishop of Grantham, where a carving of him and his beloved cats adorns the church. Died in 1934. His letters reveal him as a man of great charm and dry humour, but a confirmed misogynist.

Holt, John: born in Lancashire in 1841, left village school at age of fourteen to be apprentice at Laird's shipping office in Liverpool. In 1862, excited by his reading about Africa, he enlisted on one of Laird's ships as purser and found a job as shop assistant on Fernando Po. Left in sole charge after his employer's death from fever, he slowly expanded his trading activities as far south as Angola and inland up the Congo and Benue rivers, far beyond any other European trader. Returned to England in 1875 and set up his company in Liverpool where he soon became a leading figure and spokesman on African affairs. Backed Morel with moral and financial support throughout the campaign for Congo reform. In business he remained fiercely independent, a tradition handed on to his son after his death in 1914.

Jackson, Sir Frederick: born in 1860 and educated at Shrewsbury and Cambridge where he rowed for his college but took no degree. Spent next seven years shooting in Kashmir and then East Africa, starting at Lamu with his friend Rider Haggard. In 1888, when his private income failed, he joined the new Imperial East Africa Company and led an expedition into Kikuyuland and Uganda on their behalf. Played key role in British intervention during Uganda's civil war, and was seriously wounded trying to quell a mutiny of Sudanese troops. In 1900, became deputy commissioner to Sir Charles Eliot, but opposed his white settlement policy. From 1907 Lt.-Governor of B.E.A. and from 1911, Governor of Uganda. Seen by contemporaries as a 'chevalier sans peur et sans reproche'. Wrote the East African section of the Badminton Library and had almost completed on his death in 1929 a massive study of East African birds.

Johnston, Sir Harry: born in London in 1858; educated at Stockwell grammar school where he showed a precocious gift for drawing and natural history. Won scholarship to art school and also studied anatomy and zoology. In 1879 sent to Tunis to convalesce and learnt Arabic. Returned to Africa as companion to the young Earl of Mayo and stayed on to explore the Congo basin, where he met and charmed Stanley. In 1884 led a scientific expedition to Kilimanjaro and made treaties with local chiefs which were later used as basis for British claims in East Africa. In 1885, he joined the Foreign Office as vice-consul in the Cameroons and deposed King Ja-Ja (who was blocking European trade into the interior), exceeding official instructions but catching Salisbury's interest by his bravado. In 1889, Salisbury appointed him British consul to Portuguese East Africa; where he extended British 'influence' into a vast area north and west of the Zambezi, helped by Rhodes's money, and defeated the Arab slavers based at the north end of Lake Nyasa. After a brief period as consul in Tunis, Salisbury sent him back to East Africa as High Commissioner for Uganda in 1900, but after his return in 1902, and Salisbury's death, he was never given another official post and spent the next twenty-five years living mainly by his pen. Visited United States in 1908 at invitation of President Roosevelt, and revised many of his opinions on African development after meeting leading American negroes. Died in 1927.

Jones, Sir Alfred: born in Wales in 1845, and apprenticed like Holt to Liverpool shipping company aged fourteen. Attended night school and rose to become manager. In 1876, proposed himself to run the Elder Dempster Steamship Co., which he did with brilliant success, establishing a monopoly over the entire West African shipping trade and setting up large mills to process palm-oil in Liverpool itself. Saved Canaries from bankruptcy by helping to establish banana trade and building large resort hotels; and undertook the same process in the West Indies at Chamberlain's request (he founded Fyffes to market Jamaican bananas). Opened first bank in British West Africa and in 1899, the Liverpool School of Tropical Medicine (a complement to Chamberlain's in London). Knighted 1901. His links with the Congo went back to the days of the Congo Association, which had welcomed Leopold as a fellow free trader in the 1880s, and he remained

British Consul-General for the Congo until his death. Casement and E. D. Morel saw him as a 'poisonous serpent' but Holt believed he had genuinely hoped to influence Leopold to change his methods. He died, unmarried, of a heart attack in 1907.

Kingsley, Mary: born 1862, only daughter of Dr George Kingsley (and niece of Charles). Educated at home in London and devoted her youth to helping her father with his natural history studies. After her parents' death, she resolved 'to learn her tropics' at first hand and selected West Africa as the nearest place. Made her first journey there alone in 1893 and returned for more ambitious scientific exploration in 1894. Her prim exterior and Victorian bonnet concealed a great original, and her book, *Travels in West Africa*, was an immediate bestseller thanks to its humour and racy style. She was soon in constant demand as an authority on West Africa and became a close friend of the Liverpool traders, in particular John Holt – 'the one man, to my mind, who would save Sodom and Gomorrah'. Her second, more serious book, *West African Studies*, set out to explain West African customs and dispel the harsher racial views current at the time; and also pleaded eloquently against extending the 'Crown colony system' as expensive and offensive to Africans. Died of enteric fever nursing Boer prisoners at Simonstown in June 1900. The Royal African Society was founded by her friends in her honour.

Kitchener, Lord (Horatio Herbert): born in 1856 and brought up on spartan principles in Co. Kerry, where his father, a retired English colonel, had bought an estate. Educated in Switzerland, fought briefly as volunteer in the Franco-Prussian war, commissioned in Royal Engineers in 1871. Began a long career in the East when he was lent by the Army to the Palestine Exploration fund as engineer; and quickly made reputation for his drive and thoroughness. At Cromer's request he was appointed Sirdar (C.-in-C.) of the Egyptian army in 1892 and, after meticulous planning, led the campaign to re-conquer the Sudan. Caused great outcry in England by his desecration of the Mahdi's tomb, but regained popularity when he set up Gordon College at Khartoum (viz. Kipling's poem 'Kitchener's School'.) Posted to South Africa early in 1900 as second-in-command to the veteran Lord Roberts, and succeeded him as C.-in-C. from November until the peace was finally signed with the Boers in 1902. Took up command of the army in India at Curzon's request early in 1903 and pushed through a major programme of reforms, including founding of a staff college at Quetta. Promoted to Field-Marshal on his return in 1909, but left without a job until at Cromer's suggestion he was appointed Consul-General in Egypt in 1911. Recalled at outbreak of war to be Secretary of State for War; but soon overwhelmed by triple task of recruiting new armies, organising munitions and planning overall strategy. Viciously attacked in May 1915 by the press for the shortage of munitions, and from November, recognising his own shortcomings, he handed over the main military organisation to Sir William Robertson. But he remained a public idol until his dramatic death by drowning in June 1916, when the ship carrying him on a mission to Russia hit a mine just off Scapa Flow. He was mourned at a huge state memorial service in St Paul's cathedral.

Leverhulme, Lord (William Hesketh Lever): born in Bolton, Lancashire in 1851. Brought up on strict non-conformist principles, he joined his father's grocery business aged sixteen and became a partner at twenty-one. From 1884, he began trading on his own, specialising in soap, and by 1888 had built his own soapworks and model workers' estate, Port Sunlight, on the Mersey. By 1900, his factories and trading interests were already spread worldwide and he had begun steps to ensure supplies of tropical oils, investing first (unsuccessfully) in the Pacific and on an increasing scale in West Africa during the next twenty-five years. His Congo venture – set up in 1911 by a deal with the Belgian government – remained his most cherished project, rivalled only by his attempt after the First World War to bring prosperity to two remote islands in the Outer Hebrides, Lewis and Harris. Here, however, he was blocked by the crofters and was finally forced to withdraw by the financial crisis caused by his ill-judged bid for the Niger Company. Outside business, he remained a lifelong Liberal (he was swept briefly into the House of Commons by the Liberal landslide election of 1906, rather to his consternation) with strong views on the need for pensions, graduated income-tax and shorter working hours. Became also a passionate art-collector – his museum at Port Sunlight, built to commemorate his wife in 1913, contained a vast and eclectic collection of porcelain, furniture and paintings bought by himself. He made his last speech in his home town of Bolton to an audience of Sunday School children shortly after his return from the Congo; and died of pneumonia a few days later in May 1925.

Lockhart, Robert Bruce: born 1887, son of a Scottish headmaster, won scholarship to Fettes College but spent next five years 'in the worship of athleticism', then sent to study in Paris and Berlin. Set out to Malaya to become a rubber planter in 1908; returned home after acute malaria in 1910, and joined the Consular Service. As acting Consul-General in Moscow during the war, he played a key role in efforts to keep Russia in the war during and after the Revolution, and at one point was imprisoned in the Kremlin as a spy (see his *Memoirs of a Secret Agent*). From 1919 to 1922 he worked as commercial secretary to the British Legation in Prague and became a close friend of Dr Benes and Jan Masaryk. From 1928, he worked mainly as a Beaverbrook journalist. He rejoined the Foreign Office in 1939 as liaison officer with the exiled Czech government; then took over directive of Political Warfare Executive which co-ordinated propaganda to the enemy. Knighted in 1943. After the war returned to writing, and married for the second time in 1948. He died at Hove in 1970. His enthralling diaries, published after his death, reveal his chronic susceptibility to amorous adventure.

Lugard, Lord (Frederick): born 1858 to missionary parents; lost mother when he was seven. Educated at Rossall School and Sandhurst. Commissioned in 9th Foot, and fought almost immediately in Second Afghan War, followed in 1885 by Suakin campaign and as military transport officer in Third Burmese War. Sailed for Africa on a tramp ship after a crushing disappointment in love in 1888 and enlisted with the African Lakes Company to fight the slavers on Lake Nyasa, where he was badly wounded. Sent to Uganda in 1890 by the

Imperial East Africa Company, and secured treaty with King Mwanga. Returned home to write a massive history of the campaign, *The Rise of our East African Empire*, and to lobby for a formal annexation of Uganda. Recruited by Sir George Goldie and subsequently by Chamberlain to block French expansion in the Nigerian hinterland during the '90s; and appointed first High Commissioner for the new Protectorate of Northern Nigeria from 1900. Married 1902 Flora Shaw, the brilliant ex-colonial editor of *The Times*. To be with her, he accepted in 1907 the governorship of Hong Kong; but returned at the Liberals' request to carry through amalgamation of Northern and Southern Nigeria in 1912. Met fierce opposition in the South for his attempt to extend his system of Indirect Rule by chiefs. Retired rather embittered, but became after publishing his massive *Dual Mandate in Tropical Africa* the most admired authority on African affairs. Served on Mandates Commission from 1922–36, and a host of other committees. Created baron in 1928, just before his wife's death; and died at their home in Abinger, in 1945. His reputation after his death has remained as controversial as in his lifetime.

Meinertzhagen, Richard: born 1878, son of Daniel Meinertzhagen, a merchant banker; his mother was Beatrice Webb's sister. Brought up at Mottisfont Abbey, Romsey in Kent, and educated at Harrow. After a brief, much disliked, experience of the City, he joined the Royal Fusiliers who were stationed in India. Transferred to the King's African Rifles after a quarrel with his commanding officer in 1902 and spent next four years fighting tribes in East African highlands. Returned to old regiment in 1907 and entered staff college at Quetta three years later. Drafted to East Africa as Chief Military Intelligence Officer at outbreak of First World War, then to Palestine where his exploits became legendary for daring and ingenuity. Military delegate to the Paris Peace conference in 1919, which he found deeply disillusioning. Chief political adviser in Palestine from 1919 to 1920 where he took a strong pro-Zionist line and quarrelled with Allenby. Recruited by Churchill for the Colonial Office (Middle East department) in 1921 and became a close friend of T. E. Lawrence, who described him in his *Seven Pillars of Wisdom* as 'a silent laughing masterful man with an immensely powerful body, and a savage brain'. (Meinertzhagen, Ralph Furse recounts, was so irritated by Lawrence's showing-off that he once picked him up bodily and shut him in one of the Colonial Office cupboards). Married after a whirlwind courtship in 1921 fellow ornithologist Annie Jackson (she was killed in a shooting accident seven years later) and resigned from the army in 1925 to devote himself to his family and ornithology. His *Birds of Arabia* (1930) became a classic. Retained into old age his taste for fighting and his fervent Zionism. Died in London in 1967.

Miller, Walter: born 1873 in Devon. Studied medicine at St Bartholomew's Hospital in London where he became a leader of the Students' Christian Movement, joined the Church Missionary Society in 1897, and became a brilliant Hausa scholar in preparation for the Sudan Party mission. After its initial fiasco at Kano, he returned to work outside Zaria and became one of the few missionaries admired by English officials. But he made few converts and his first attempt to set up a Christian village turned to tragedy when all its inhabitants were wiped out by sleeping sickness. In 1929, he transferred his mission on the C.M.S.'s orders to a site outside Kano, but reported the walls of 'mud and religion' still impenetrable. Retired from Nigeria in 1935 but returned two years later and died there in 1952.

Morel, Edmund Dene: born 1873 in Paris, son of a French civil servant, but sent by his English mother to school in England. Joined Sir Alfred Jones's company, Elder Dempster, as shipping clerk aged eighteen and soon became an authority on West African history and affairs, writing regularly for the London and Liverpool press. In 1901 he resigned from Elder Dempster to write full-time and started his own paper, the *West African Mail*, funded by the Cadbury family, John Holt, and his old employer Jones (who still hoped to moderate his attacks on the 'Congo system'). Founded the Congo Reform Association in 1904 and remained its secretary and driving force until 1913. The campaign left him deeply hostile to Sir Edward Grey and 'secret diplomacy' and at outbreak of war, he helped to found the Union for Democratic Control. He was much attacked at the height of the war, partly because of his known friendship with Roger Casement who was executed for gun-running in 1915, and was briefly imprisoned for a trivial publishing offence. But became rising star in the Labour party after 1918 and defeated Winston Churchill at Dundee in the 1922 election. Died aged only fifty-one in 1924, cutting short a rising political career.

Paice, Arnold: born at Egham in Surrey in 1879 and entered tea trade after leaving school. Served with Berkshire Yeomanry in South Africa from 1900 to 1901 and went back to farm after the war. In 1907 he took the boat to East Africa with his stock and after three years working for other settlers in the Naivasha district trekked over the Aberdares and became the first white farmer in the Nanyuki district. Died on his farm in 1963.

Roosevelt, Theodore: born in New York, 1858, educated at Harvard. After chronic ill-health in childhood he set out on a deliberate course of toughening himself by buying a ranch in Dakota. Became famous for his books on hunting and pioneer life. Made a well-planned entry into Republican politics in 1894 and was appointed Assistant Secretary to the navy. Resigned to lead a volunteer force, the 'Rough Riders', to the Cuban War. Stood successfully as President McKinley's running-mate in the presidential election of 1900 and became President a year later when McKinley was assassinated. He galvanised American politics by his tough line at home and abroad and was swept back to power with a huge majority in 1904, but stood down in 1909 claiming at fifty to be too old to stand. He spent the next year travelling and hunting mainly in Africa; his outspoken speeches, praising British administration in East Africa and the Sudan, but criticising its vacillations in Egypt, caused a furore in England. Decided to re-enter politics in 1912 but his intervention as an independent or 'Bull Moose' candidate split the Republican vote and let in the Democrat, Woodrow Wilson. In 1914, he went on a last safari into the Brazilian jungle, but narrowly escaped dying from tropical infections and never fully recovered. Denounced Woodrow Wilson's stand on neutrality at outbreak of the First World War and besieged the War Office with requests to raise a regiment and fight. He was refused, to his bitter disappointment, and died in January 1919.

Scott, Lord Francis: youngest son of 6th Duke of Buccleuch, born 1879. Left Oxford early to enlist in Boer War. From 1905 to 1910, served as A.D.C. to the Viceroy, Lord Minto, in India and married his daughter Lady Eileen Eliot in 1915. Badly wounded fighting at Mons which left him permanently in pain. Emigrated to Kenya with his wife in 1920 and bought 3,500 acres at Rongai from Lord Delamere. Dour, reserved, he became Lord Delamere's alter ego and succeeded him as the settlers' leader in 1930. 'In politics and polo', wrote one governor of Kenya, 'he rode straight as a die.' Created K.C.M.G. in 1937. Defeated by Michael Blundell in the post-war election, and retired rather bitterly to his house in Rongai. Died in Kenya in 1952.

Scott, Thomas: born 1832 in Scotland, brought out to Singapore to work in his brother-in-law James Guthrie's company and rose to be its senior partner. Member of first legislative Council and leader of merchants who pushed for expansion into the Malay States. Founded Tanjong Pagar Dock Company which built the main docks at Singapore. Bought up with two partners the bankrupt estate of Heslop Hill in Perak, one of the earliest estates to yield rubber. By the end of the century had retired, mainly to his house in Angus, and died in 1902.

Selous, Frederick: born 1851, son of the chairman of the London Stock Exchange. Educated at Rugby (where he spent most of his time shooting in surrounding woods). Emigrated to South Africa aged nineteen to live as hunter and ivory trader; and spent next ten years exploring Southern Africa as far north as Matabeleland. His first book, *A Hunter's Wanderings in Africa*, earned him immediate fame (though some attacks for the length of its lists of dead game) and commissions to shoot specimens for the Natural History Museum and private collectors. In 1890 acted as intermediary for Cecil Rhodes with Lobengula, King of the Matabele, to negotiate mineral rights – which eventually led to Lobengula's loss of his lands – and guided Rhodes's pioneer column into Mashonaland. Settled briefly in the new Rhodesia and fought in both Matabele wars, but after his marriage retired to England, returning to Africa only for hunting trips (though he confessed privately he would have liked to settle in Kenya). At outbreak of First World War, volunteered for service and was finally given commission in the 25th Royal Fusiliers, a volunteer force of assorted East African friends. Killed by a German sniper in Tanganyika, January 1917. His splendid private collection was left to the Natural History Museum, where a bronze plaque commemorates him.

Swettenham, Frank: born in Derbyshire in 1850, youngest son of a reclusive Scottish lawyer. Followed his older brother to the East as a cadet in the Straits Settlement Service in 1871. In 1873 he was sent, as a fluent Malay speaker, to persuade the Malay rulers of Perak and leading Chinese tin-miners to submit their chronic disputes to British arbitration (the so-called Pangkor Engagement) and succeeded brilliantly. In 1875 he was sent as adviser to the Sultan of Selangor who described him as 'very clever at gaining the hearts of Rajahs with soft words, delicate and sweet'; but narrowly escaped death a few months later in Perak when a less tactful adviser, James Wheeler Birch, was murdered. During the next ten years he rose to become in turn Resident of Selangor and Perak, and finally Resident-General and High Commissioner of the new Federation of Malay States (Perak, Selangor, Negri-Sembilan and Pahang) based in Singapore. Resigned to general surprise in 1904 'after thirty years of exceptionally trying service', refusing the Colonial Office's offer to make him Governor of Kenya; and spent the rest of his long life in England, much in demand at country houses. His book, *British Malaya*, first published in 1906, ran into six editions. He married for the second time aged eighty-nine, wrote his autobiography aged ninety-one and died in 1946 aged ninety-seven.

Swire, John Samuel: born in Liverpool, 1825, where he spent his first forty years in the family import and export business. Made an early and fruitful alliance with T. H. Ismay of the White Star Line, but did not enter China trade seriously until after the American Civil War when Swire's re-routed their ships to export textiles to China and Japan, in brief partnership with a Yorkshire mill-owner named Butterfield. In 1866, he went out to Shanghai in person when Swire's agent proved inefficient and set up his own trading company, grandly named Taikoo (the Great and Ancient), within a week. By the 1880s, he had branches in Yokohama, Hong Kong and all the major ports along the China coast, and had secured a third share of the valuable Yangtse river trade after fierce in-fighting between his company and Jardine's. To eliminate the same fighting on a wider scale, he set up an annual shipping conference for the Far Eastern routes, dominating their proceedings with his dour Yorkshire personality until his death in 1898. ('It is so equitably arranged,' he wrote after one, 'that every man is dissatisfied.') Succeeded by his sons, who maintained more temperately the famous feud with Jardine's.

Trenchard, Lord (Hugh): born in 1873, son of a country solicitor, whose business failed when Hugh was still at school. Scraped into the militia at his third attempt and served first in India, where his colleagues found him grim and taciturn. Made his name in Boer War as commander of a flying column, but was left half paralysed by a bullet in the chest, until he knocked his spine back into shape by bobsleighing down the Cresta Run. Commanded Southern Nigerian Regiment from 1904 to 1910, until invalided home. Volunteered for flying school in 1913 and rose by a mixture of stubbornness and organisational talent to become 'Father of the Royal Air Force' (a title he much disliked) successfully securing its independence from the two 'wicked uncles', the army and navy, after the First World War. (He was helped by the visible success of his scheme of 'air control' for dissident tribesmen in Iraq which, as in the campaign against the Mad Mullah of 1921, slashed the cost of 'imperial policing'.) He was brought back almost as soon as he had retired in 1929 to reorganise the English police; and died loaded with honours aged eighty-three in 1956.

Tucker, Bishop Alfred: born in 1849 and brought up mainly in the Lake district where he and his brothers became famous for their feats of hillclimbing. Both his parents were landscape artists, and he began as an art student at Oxford then changed course to read theology and became a curate at Durham. Appalled by the news of the massacre of Christian converts in Uganda, he offered himself for missionary service in 1890 and was consecrated as Bishop of Eastern Equatorial Africa to succeed the murdered Bishop Hannington. Arrived in December 1890 to find Uganda 'like a volcano on the verge of an eruption'. Returned to England to urge strongly that Britain must retain her influence, and to raise money to keep the struggling I.B.E.A. company alive. After the formal annexation of East Africa, his huge diocese was divided in two, and he was confirmed as Bishop of Uganda. He left after eighteen years as Bishop, having set up Africa's first self-supporting, self-governing Anglican church, and returned to Durham as canon. Died suddenly at Lambeth on his way to attend the first meeting of the synod to discuss the Kikuyu 'heresy' in June 1914.

Tyndale-Biscoe, Canon Cecil Earle: born 1863, son of an Oxfordshire squire, educated at Bradfield College and Cambridge, where he coxed the college boat to the head of the river. Ordained in 1890 and two years later was sent to Kashmir to take over the C.M.S. school in Srinagar, where he remained for the next fifty-five years. His ideas on character-building and community service influenced many other missionaries, notably A. G. Fraser, who founded Achimota College on the Gold Coast with Guggisberg in the '20s. He left India in 1947 to live with his son in Rhodesia (his wife died before they reached there) and died in 1949.

Weston, Bishop Frank: born 1871 in London, son of a tea-broker. Educated at Dulwich and Trinity College, Cambridge, where he took a First in theology. Ordained in 1895 and joined the U.M.C.A. mission three years later in Zanzibar. After nine years here, working mainly as head of a training college for African priests, and two books on theology, he succeeded John Hine as Bishop of Zanzibar. After the drama of the Kikuyu controversy of 1914, he defended his views in two more books, both of which the public found incomprehensible. After the war, however, he surprised his fellow bishops at the second Lambeth conference by his well-reasoned arguments in favour of mission unity. In 1923 he returned to London again for the second Anglo-Catholic congress, and dazzled audiences by his oratory, only to cause another outcry when it was discovered he had sent simultaneous greetings to the Archbishop of Canterbury and the Pope. Returned unrepentant to Africa, but contracted blood-poisoning while tramping through his diocese and died in a hut at Hegongo in November 1924.

Wingate, Sir Reginald: born in Scotland, 1861, son of a textile merchant. Made brilliant reputation at Royal Military College and was posted to Egypt where he became a fluent Arabist and A.D.C. to Sir Evelyn Wood, Sirdar of the Egyptian army. Took part in Gordon relief expedition of 1884, and became Director of Military Intelligence which provided vital information for the planning of Kitchener's Sudan campaign. Succeeded Kitchener as Governor of the Sudan in 1900 and transformed the country in the next sixteen years into a showpiece of successful colonial rule (Roosevelt praised him to the skies after his visit in 1909), skilfully using his influence with the King to extract government grants for his huge country. At outbreak of First World War helped to organise Arab revolt. In 1916, made High Commissioner of Egypt, but his warning that Egypt would rise after its harsh military occupation was disregarded with the result he predicted. He was made the chief scapegoat and never given another government post. Died in Scotland in 1953.

Woolf, Leonard: born 1880, son of a London barrister, educated at St Paul's school and Trinity College, Cambridge, where he became a close friend of Lytton Strachey and the other future 'Bloomsberries'. Joined the Ceylon Civil Service as an Eastern Cadet, 1904, and resigned seven years later when he came home on leave. Published his first novel, *The Village in the Jungle*, in 1912 (it was compared to Kipling) and married Virginia Stephen the same year. Joined the Fabians in 1913 and spent war years studying and writing for them on international politics (many of his ideas were incorporated into the League of Nations charter). Wrote savage indictment of 'economic imperialism', published in 1920 as *Empire and Commerce in Africa*, partly influenced by E. D. Morel. It was hailed by Lytton Strachey as 'magnificent' but its attack on Lugard in particular brought hostile reviews and a mammoth refutation by Lugard himself in his book, *The Dual Mandate*. After war, worked mainly as editor of successive political reviews, and as publisher of the Hogarth Press, which he and Virginia had founded in 1917. Wrote several more serious books on politics and, in old age, a remarkable autobiography whose second volume, *Growing*, recounts his life in Ceylon. Returned to Ceylon in 1962 to a hero's welcome, but also to some attacks in the Colombo press for his former 'imperialist' behaviour. (Woolf was stung by one in particular from an old headman from Hambantota which claimed he had also been a bad shot!) Died in Sussex in 1969.

PHOTOGRAPHIC CREDITS

Acknowledgments and thanks are due to the following for permission to reproduce illustrations: (Private collections) Mrs Pippa Boyle: 85; Lord Cranworth: 78, 203 (below); Dr Peter Davies: 126 (top and below); the John Holt Group: 127 (top); Robin Bruce Lockhart: 88 (left and right); R. G. McNair Scott: 117; Alan Morkill: 67; the Scout Association: 147, 172; John Swire & Sons: 115, 119, 121; the Theosophical Society: 97 (right); Unilever: 136, 137; UAC International Ltd: 124, 139. (Libraries) Bodleian Library: *Cary MSS* 59 (307. Fol. 125), 60 (309. Fol. 127), 61 (307. Fol. 133), 62 (305. Fol. 57), 63 (top) (309. Fol. 31), 63 (below) (307. Fol. 61); BBC Hulton Picture Library: 12, 24, 30, 127 (below right); Church Missionary Society: 102; Foreign and Commonwealth Office Library: 41, 52, 53, 92, 93, 120, 179, 199, 220, 225; Indian Institute: *Minto MSS* 23, 32, 181; India Office Library: 17 (top), 144, 221, 222; Imperial War Museum: 112–113, 193, 207, 208, 210, 211, 214, 215; National Army Museum: 123, 141, 170, 197 (below); National Film Archive: 232 (copyright London Films), 235; National Portrait Gallery: 11, 31, 233; Rhodes House: *Lugard MSS* 42; *Cholmondeley MSS* 74; *Foran MSS* 77, 158, 162; *Meinertzhagen MSS* 146, 200; Royal Commonwealth Society: 20, 21, 25, 35 (left), 37, 38, 43, 45, 47, 49, 66, 73, 80, 86–7, 103, 116, 142, 143, 154, 176, 178, 205 (top), 212, 216; School of Oriental and African Studies (Council for World Mission) 187; United Society for the Propagation of the Gospel: *U.M.C.A. archive* 105, 107, 108, 109; Victoria and Albert Museum: 97 (left).

The following illustrations are taken from books and magazines: Correlli Barnett, *Britain and her Army* (1970): 168; W. D. M. Bell, *Wanderings of an Elephant Hunter* (1923): 161; Abel Chapman, *On Safari* (1909): 163; Randolph Churchill, *Winston S. Churchill*, Vol. I (1966): 189 (left); P. A. Cohen, *China and Christianity* (1963): 94; *Colour* (magazine) (1918): 220; Lord Cranworth, *A Colony in the Making* (1912): 82, *Kenya Chronicles* (1939): 69, 229; Malcolm Foster, *Joyce Cary* (1969): 58; Ralph Furse, *Aucuparius* (1962): 175; J. L. Garvin, *Life of Joseph Chamberlain*, Vol. III (1934): 17 (below); Carruthers Gould, *Westminster Cartoons* (1903): 13; Elspeth Huxley, *White Man's Country* (1935) Vol. I: 75; Vol. II: 231; *Illustrated London News*: 132; Harry Johnston, *Britain Across the Seas: Africa* (1909): 91; Mary Kingsley, *West African Studies* (1896): 127 (below left); Philip Magnus, *Kitchener, Portrait of an Imperialist* (1958): 197 (top); John Marlowe, *Cecil Rhodes* (1972): 71; H. Maynard Smith, *Frank, Bishop of Zanzibar* (1926): 112; Richard Meinertzhagen, *Kenya Diary* (1959): 203 (top), 205 (below); Walter Miller, *Reflections of a Pioneer* (1932): 95; E. D. Morel, *History of the Congo Reform Movement* (1968): 128; Decima Moore, *We Two in West Africa* (1909): 183; G. Spater and Ian Parsons, *The Marriage of True Minds* (1969): 55; Frederick Pedler, *The Lion and the Unicorn in Africa* (1974): 133; Margery Perham, *Lugard: The Years of Authority* (1956): 234; *Review of Reviews*: 9, 19 (left), 173; Ronald Ross, *Memoirs* (1923): 14; Alan Ross, *Ranji* (1983): 167; Mary Soames, *A Churchill Family Album* (1982): 39; Frank Swettenham, *British Malaya* (1907): 26; Frank Swettenham, *Footprints in Malaya* (1942): 44; C. E. Tyndale-Biscoe, *Against the Stream* (1930): 99, 101, 185; *Vanity Fair*: 28, 29, 152, 189 (right); Leo Weinthal, *The Cape to Cairo Railway* (1923): 165, 166, 235 (top); Ronald Wingate, *Wingate of the Sudan* (1955): 51 (left). The map on pp. 236–7 was drawn by Neil Hyslop. Every effort has been made to trace copyright owners of these illustrations, and we apologise for any errors or omissions.

Endpapers: 'South Africa: the ideal' from J. G. Millais's *A Breath from the Veldt* (1899).

SELECT BIBLIOGRAPHY

Most of the books I have drawn on are quoted in the Notes to the Text (below). These are a few books which I have found most useful for background material and which have led me on to other sources.

E. A. Ayandele, *The Missionary Impact on Modern Nigeria* (Longmans, 1966)
John Gallagher, *The Decline, Rise and Fall of the British Empire* (Cambridge University Press, 1982)
L. H. Gann and Peter Duignan, *The Rulers of British Africa, 1870–1914* (Croom Helm, 1978)
Elspeth Huxley, *White Man's Country, Lord Delamere and the Making of Kenya* (Chatto & Windus, 1935)
Ronald Hyam, *Britain's Imperial Century, 1814–1914* (Batsford, 1976)
V. G. Kiernan, *The Lords of Human Kind* (Weidenfeld and Nicolson, 1969)
R. V. Kubicek, *The Administration of Imperialism: Joseph Chamberlain at the Colonial Office* (Duke University Press, 1969)
Peter Mansfield, *The British in Egypt* (Weidenfeld and Nicolson, 1971)
Philip Mason, *A Matter of Honour* (Jonathan Cape, 1974)
Charles Miller, *The Lunatic Express* (Macdonald, 1972), *The Battle for the Bundu* (Macdonald, 1974)
James Morris, *Pax Britannica* (Faber, 1968), *Farewell the Trumpets* (Faber, 1978)
Roland Oliver, *The Missionary Factor in East Africa* (Longmans, 1952)
Frederick Pedler, *The Lion and the Unicorn in Africa* (Heinemann, 1974)
Bernard Porter, *Critics of Empire* (Macmillan, 1968), *The Lion's Share* (Longman, 1976)
A. P. Thornton, *The Imperial Idea and its Enemies* (Macmillan, 1959)
Derek Wilson and Peter Ayerst, *White Gold: The Story of African Ivory* (Taplinger, 1976)
George Woodcock, *The British in the Far East* (Weidenfeld, 1969)

NOTES TO THE TEXT

1 PILLARS

1. *The Times*, 21 June 1900.
2. Winston Churchill, *The River War* (London, 1899), vol. I, pp. 18–19.
3. *The Nineteenth Century*, January 1900.
4. Kenneth Rose, *Superior Person* (London, 1969), p. 227.
5. Kenneth Rose, *George V* (London, 1983), p. 65.
6. *Blackwoods*, March 1901.
7. Robert Taylor, *Lord Salisbury* (London, 1975), p. 173.
8. 'Recessional', *Rudyard Kipling's Verse: Definitive Edition* (Hodder and Stoughton, 1940), p. 329.
9. Kenneth Young, *Arthur James Balfour* (London, 1963), p. 129.
10. Ronald Hyam, *Britain's Imperial Century, 1815–1914* (London, 1976), p. 111.
11. Sir Ralph Furse, *Aucuparius: Recollections of a Recruiting Officer* (London, 1962), p. 26.
12. Alex Johnston, *Life and Letters of Sir Harry Johnston* (London, 1929), p. 226.
13. David Dilks, *Curzon in India* (London, 1969), vol. I, p. 98.
14. J. A. Hobson, *Imperialism: A Study* (London, 1902), p. 117.
15. 'The Islanders', *Kipling's Verse*, p. 301.
16. Kenneth Rose, *The Later Cecils* (London, 1975), p. 301.
17. John Jolliffe (ed.), *The Letters of Raymond Asquith* (London, 1980), p. 86.
18. Marjorie Perham, *Lugard: The Years of Adventure* (London, 1956), p. 104.
19. Rose, *Superior Person*, p. 190.

2 RULERS

1. *Review of Reviews*, 1900, p. 441.
2. Dilks, *Curzon in India*, vol. I, p. 220.
3. McDonnell MSS, 12 March 1903.
4. Eunice Thio, *British Policy in the Malay Peninsula, 1880–1940* (University of Singapore, 1969), pp. 183–6.
5. Johnston, *Life and Letters of Sir Harry Johnston*, pp. 258–9.
6. Perham, *Lugard: Years of Authority* (London, 1956), p. 104.
7. Ibid., p. 84.
8. Dilks, *Curzon in India*, vol. II, p. 247.
9. John Marlowe, *Cromer in Egypt* (London, 1970), p. 302.
10. Wilfrid Scawen Blunt, *Diaries*, 17 February 1900 (Alfred Knopf Inc., New York, 1922).
11. Ibid., 18 May 1901, vol. II, p. 23.
12. Anthony Stockwell, 'Clifford in Trinidad', *Caribbean Quarterly*, March 1978.

NOTES TO THE TEXT

13. Ronald Hyam, *Elgin and Churchill at the Colonial Office* (London, 1968), p. 15.
14. Ibid., p. 502.
15. Ibid., p. 199.
16. Perham, *Lugard: Years of Authority*, p. 244.
17. Stockwell, op. cit.
18. Winston Churchill, *My African Journey* (London, 1908), p. 8.
19. Ibid., pp. 86–7.
20. Hesketh Bell, 'On Her Majesty's Service', *Love in Black* (London, 1911).
21. Hesketh Bell Diaries (TS) (Royal Commonwealth Society Library), p. 147.
22. Hesketh Bell, *Glimpses of a Governor's Life* (London, 1946), p. 170.
23. Churchill, *My African Journey*, pp. 209–11.
24. Hesketh Bell MSS (letter to aunt), 14 June 1908.
25. Bell, *Glimpses of a Governor's Life*, p. 203.
26. Holt MSS, E. D. Morel to John Holt, 21 September 1910 (Rhodes House Library, Oxford).
27. Hesketh Bell Diaries, July 1912.
28. Perham, *Lugard: Years of Authority*, p. 388.
29. Guggisberg MSS (Rhodes House Library).
30. I. F. Nicholson, *The Administration of Nigeria* (London, 1969), pp. 173–6.

3 BUILDERS

1. Sir Donald Mackenzie Wallace, *The Web of Empire* (London, 1902), p. 101.
2. Hugh Clifford, *In Court and Kampong* (London, 1899), p. 251.
3. Ibid., p. 2.
4. Rose, *Superior Person*, p. 343.
5. Philip Woodruff, *The Men Who Ruled India* (London, 1963), vol. II, p. 92.
6. J. de Vere Allen, 'The Malayan Civil Service, 1874–1941', *Comparative Studies in Society and History*, April 1970.
7. Woolf to G. E. Moore, 14 October 1904, quoted by G. Spater and Ian Parsons, *A Marriage of True Minds: an intimate portrait of Leonard and Virginia Woolf* (London, 1977), p. 44.
8. Colin Crisswell, *Rajah Charles Brooke* (London, 1978), p. 121.
9. Robert V. Kubicek, *The Administration of Imperialism* (London, 1969), p. 59.
10. Richard Meinertzhagen, *Kenya Diary* (London, 1957), p. 132.
11. Lord Cranworth, *A Colony in the Making* (London, 1912), p. 76.
12. Francis Hall MSS, 25 April 1899 (Rhodes House Library).
13. Churchill, *My African Journey*, pp. 26–7.
14. Henry Seaton, *Lion in the Morning* (London, 1963), p. 9.
15. Robert O. Collins, 'The Sudan Political Service', *African Affairs*, July 1971, p. 294.
16. Perham, *Lugard: Years of Authority*, p. 81.
17. Journal of R. P. Nicholson (Rhodes House Library).
18. Robert Heussler, *The British in Northern Nigeria* (London, 1968), p. 37.
19. Perham, *Lugard: Years of Authority*, p. 264.
20. Joyce Cary MSS, 13 September 1916 (Bodleian Library).
21. Marjorie Perham quoted in L. H. Gann and P. Duignan, *African Proconsuls* (New York, 1978), p. 210.
22. T. H. R. Cashmore, *Your Obedient Servants* (Rhodes House Library).
23. Leonard Woolf MSS, 8 January 1905 (Sussex University).
24. Ibid., 21 April 1906.
25. Ibid., 23 June 1907.
26. Ibid., 3 March 1907.
27. Leonard Woolf, *Growing* (London, 1970), p. 193.
28. Ceylon Diary, 28 March 1909, quoted by T. J. Barron, 'Before the Deluge', *Journal of Imperial and Commonwealth History*, p. 47.
29. Woolf, *Growing*, p. 251.
30. Woolf MSS, 23 April 1913.
31. 'Mankind and the Jungle', *Blackwoods*, June 1913.
32. Molly Mahood, *Joyce Cary's Africa* (London, 1964), p. 10.
33. Malcolm Foster, *Joyce Cary: A Biography* (London, 1969), p. 92.
34. Cary MSS, 5 May 1917.
35. Ibid., 7 June 1917.
36. Ibid., 3 July 1917.
37. Joyce Cary, *The Case for African Freedom* (University of Texas Press, 1962), p. 204.
38. Cary MSS, 22 September 1917.
39. Cary, *The Case for African Freedom*, p. 216.
40. Cary MSS, 9 November 1918.
41. Cary, *The Case for African Freedom*, p. 115.
42. Malcolm Foster, *Joyce Cary*, pp. 152–3.
43. Cary MSS, 29 May 1919.
44. Woolf, *Growing*, pp. 158–9.
45. Cary MSS, 30 May 1919.
46. Malcolm Foster, *Joyce Cary*, pp. 206–7.
47. Ibid., 4 October 1919.
48. Cary, *The Case for African Freedom*, p. 14.
49. J. S. Read, 'A District Officer of Bygone Days', *Malaya*, 1960.

4 SETTLERS

1. A. P. Thornton, *The Imperial Idea and its Enemies* (London, 1959), p. 89.
2. Hyam, *Elgin and Churchill at the Colonial Office*, p. 409.
3. Julian Amery, *Life of Joseph Chamberlain* (London, 1951), vol. IV, p. 261.
4. Elspeth Huxley, *White Man's Country* (London, 1935), vol. I, p. 120.
5. Charles Eliot, *The East African Protectorate* (London, 1905), p. 80.
6. Churchill, *My African Journey*, p. 56.
7. Lord Cranworth, *Kenya Chronicles* (London, 1939), p. 262.
8. Arnold Paice MSS, 9 September 1907 (Royal Commonwealth Society Library).
9. Lord Cranworth, *A Colony in the Making* (London, 1912), p. 180.
10. Cranworth, *Kenya Chronicles*, p. 36.
11. Mary E. Stewart, *Everyday Life on a Ceylon Estate* (London, 1905), p. 9.
12. Woolf, *Growing*, p. 85.
13. Richard Winstedt, *Start from Alif* (London, 1969), p. 105.
14. Ibid., p. 109.
15. John G. Butcher, *The British in Malaya, 1880–1941* (London, 1979), p. 85.
16. Winstedt, *Start from Alif*, p. 18.
17. Robert Bruce Lockhart, *Memoirs of a British Agent* (London, 1932), pp. 20–6.
18. Robert Bruce Lockhart, *Return to Malaya* (London, 1937), p. 236.
19. Ibid., p. 198.
20. Isak Dinesen (Karen Blixen), *Shadows in the Grass* (London, 1960), p. 17.
21. Lord Altrincham, *Kenya's Opportunity* (London, 1955), p. 73.
22. Lady Frances Scott diaries, 25 February 1920.
23. Ibid., 25 January 1920.

NOTES TO THE TEXT

5 PREACHERS

1. David Wetherell, *Reluctant Mission* (University of Queensland Press, 1977), p. 44.
2. Roland Oliver, *Sir Harry Johnston and the Scramble for Africa* (London, 1957), p. 182.
3. Michael Gelfand, *Lakeside Pioneers* (London, 1964), p. 164.
4. *The Times*, 20 June 1900.
5. E. A. Ayandale, *The Missionary Impact of Modern Nigeria* (London, 1966), p. 134.
6. Ibid., p. 147.
7. Ibid., p. 151.
8. *Tyndale-Biscoe of Kashmir, An Autobiography* (London, 1951), p. 50.
9. Ibid., p. 77.
10. Gelfand, *Lakeside Pioneers*, p. 234.
11. Mrs Arthur Colville, *2,000 Miles in a Machilla* (London, 1911), p. 47.
12. Griff Jones, *Britain and Nyasaland* (London, 1964), p. 55.
13. John McCracken, *Politics and Christianity in Malawi, 1875–1940* (London, 1977), p. 137.
14. John Hine MSS, 9 September 1910, U.M.C.A. archives (United Society for the Propagation of the Gospel, London).
15. Ibid., 25 June 1897.
16. John Hine, *Days Gone By* (London, 1924), p. 89.
17. Ibid., p. 94.
18. John Hine MSS, 1 February 1902.
19. A. G. Blood, *History of the U.M.C.A.* (London, 1957), vol. II, p. 4.
20. John Hine MSS, 14 November 1909.
21. Ibid., 9 September 1910.
22. Robert Rotberg, *Christian Missions and the Creation of Northern Rhodesia 1800–1924* (Princeton, New Jersey, 1965).
23. John Hine MSS, 7–9 September 1910.
24. Frank Weston MSS, May 1913 (U.M.C.A. archives), quoted in Gavin White, *Kikuyu 1913 – An Oecumenical Controversy* (unpublished thesis, 1970, Senate House Library, London University).
25. *The Times*, 11 October 1913.
26. John Hine MSS, December 1913, quoted by Gavin White, op. cit.
27. *The Times*, 13 December 1913.
28. Grogan and Sharp, *Cape to Cairo* (London, 1902), p. 366.

6 TRADERS

1. Woolf, *Growing*, p. 17.
2. John Drabble, *Rubber in Malaya 1876–1922* (London, 1973), p. 7.
3. Capt. G. Casserly, *Land of the Boxers* (London, 1903), pp. 190–3.
4. S. Cunyngham-Browne, *The Traders* (London, 1971), p. 155.
5. Sheila Marriner and Francis Hyde, *The Senior: John Samuel Swire 1825–98* (London, 1967), p. 70.
6. Charles Drage, *Taikoo* (London, 1970), p. 176.
7. Ibid., p. 150n.
8. Ibid., p. 92.
9. Perham, *Lugard: Years of Authority*, p. 320.
10. Ibid., p. 170.
11. John Holt to E. D. Morel, 7 January 1906, Morel MSS (London School of Economics).
12. Mary Kingsley to John Holt, 24 February 1900, Holt MSS (Rhodes House Library).
13. Holt MSS, 1871 and 1888.
14. Morel MSS, 31 December 1901.
15. Ibid., May 1904.
16. Holt MSS, 27 October 1905.
17. Ibid., extract from James Irvine's statement for Elder Dempster, 30 October 1905.
18. John Holt to Grattan Guinness, 3 November 1905, Holt MSS.
19. E. D. Morel, *History of the Congo Reform Movement*, ed. W. Roger Louis and Jean Stengers (London, 1968), p. 263.
20. Holt MSS, 31 August 1910.
21. Holt MSS, 5 September 1910.
22. Charles Wilson, *History of Unilever* (London, 1964), vol. I, pp. 160–3.
23. D. K. Fieldhouse, *Unilever Overseas: The Anatomy of a Multinational 1895–1965* (London, 1978), p. 460.
24. Morel MSS, 1 September 1910.
25. Ibid., 13 February 1913.
26. Wilson, *History of Unilever*, vol. I, pp. 174–6.
27. Ibid., p. 158.
28. Ibid., p. 187.
29. Ibid., p. 253.
30. William P. Jolly, *Lord Leverhulme: A Biography* (London, 1976), p. 229.
31. Frederick Pedler, *The Lion and the Unicorn* (London, 1970), p. 188.

7 HUNTERS

1. Kenneth Rose, *Superior Person*, p. 338.
2. John Buchan, *A Lodge in the Wilderness* (London, 1906), p. 93.
3. Adam Lindsay Gordon, quoted by E. H. Baxter, *From Shikar and Safari* (London, 1931), p. 1.
4. Somerset Maugham, *A Writer's Notebook* (London, 1949), p. 278.
5. Ted Morgan, *Churchill, 1874–1915* (London, 1982), p. 194.
6. Maj-Gen. J. G. Elliot, *Field Sports in India, 1800–1947* (London, 1975), p. 25.
7. Meinertzhagen MSS, *Diaries*, vol. II, p. 17 (Rhodes House Library).
8. Robert Baden-Powell, *Pig-sticking or Hog-hunting* (London, 1924), pp. 33–9.
9. Poulteney Bigelow, 'The Latterday Fighting Animal', *Anglo-Saxon Review*, March 1900.
10. Abel Chapman, *On Safari* (London, 1908), p. 4.
11. J. G. Millais, *The Life of Frederick Courtenay Selous*, D.S.O. (London, 1919), p. 359.
12. Francis Hall MSS, November 1899 (Rhodes House Library).
13. R. Oliver, *Sir Harry Johnston and the Scramble for Africa* (London, 1957), p. 295.
14. Lord Cranworth, *Kenya Chronicles*, p. 107.
15. Elspeth Huxley, *The Flame Trees of Thika* (London, 1959), p. 43.
16. Theodore Roosevelt, *African Game Trails* (London, 1909), pp. 4–5.
17. Cranworth, *A Colony in the Making*, p. 236.
18. Frederick Jackson, *Early Days in East Africa* (London, 1930), p. 381.
19. G. C. Schillings, *With Flashlight and Rifle* (London, 1906), vol. I, p. xv.
20. W. D. M. Bell, *Wanderings of an Elephant Hunter* (London, 1958), p. 110.
21. Ibid., p. 114.
22. John Boyes, *The Company of Adventurers* (London, 1928), p. 93.

NOTES TO THE TEXT

23. Roosevelt, *African Game Trails*, p. 388.
24. *The Times*, 4 March 1909.
25. Millais, *Life of Frederick Selous*, p. 304.
26. *The Times*, 9 January 1917.

8 PLAYERS

1. Robert Baden-Powell, *Indian Memories* (London, 1915), p. 168.
2. Martin Gilbert, *Servant of India* (London, 1966), p. 196.
3. Philip Mason, *A Matter of Honour* (London, 1974), p. 386.
4. Meinertzhagen, MSS, *Diaries*, vol. II, pp. 19–21.
5. Meinertzhagen, *Kenya Diary*, p. 10.
6. Andrew Boyle, *Trenchard* (London, 1962), p. 88.
7. Decima Moore and Major F. G. Guggisberg, *We Two in West Africa* (London, 1909), p. 36.
8. Quoted by Mark Girouard, *The Return to Camelot* (London, 1981), p. 233.
9. Verses on Games, *Kipling's Verse*, p. 359.
10. 'The Islanders', *Kipling's Verse*, pp. 302–3.
11. Blunt, *Diaries*, vol. I, p. 391.
12. Furse, *Aucuparius*, p. 37.
13. Hesketh Bell MSS, diary 1899.
14. Quoted by J. A. Mangan, *Athleticism and the Victorian and Edwardian Public School* (London, 1981), p. 9.
15. J. G. Butcher, *The British in Malaya, 1880–1941* (Kuala Lumpur, 1979), p. 76.
16. Woolf, *Growing*, p. 69.
17. Hyam, *Britain's Imperial Century*, p. 157.
18. Tyndale-Biscoe, *Autobiography*, p. 157.
19. Joyce Cary, *The African Witch* (London, 1936), pp. 158–61.
20. Lady Minto, *India, Minto and Morley* (London, 1934), p. 321.
21. Lady Minto's Indian Journals, July 1909 (Indian Institute, Oxford).
22. Moore and Guggisberg, *We Two in West Africa*, p. 183.
23. R. E. Wraith, *Guggisberg* (London, 1967), p. 255.
24. Tyndale-Biscoe, *Autobiography*, p. 129.
25. Wetherall, *Reluctant Mission*, p. 210.
26. Girouard, *Return to Camelot*, p. 235.
27. Mangan, *Athleticism*, p. 217.
28. A. H. Kirk-Greene, *New Society*, 10 November 1977.
29. Furse, *Aucuparius*, p. 309.

9 SOLDIERS

1. Reprinted in *Frontiers and Wars* (London, 1962), pp. 115–16.
2. Hyam, *Elgin and Churchill at the Colonial Office*, p. 208.
3. Robert Baden-Powell, *The Downfall of Prempeh* (London, 1898), Introduction.
4. James Joll, *Europe Since 1870* (London, 1973), p. 85.
5. L. S. Amery, *History of the South African War* (London, 1902), vol. II, p. 33.
6. Hyam, *Britain's Imperial Century*, p. 121.
7. Trevor Ternan, *Some Experiences of an Old Bromsgrovian* (London, 1930), p. 2.
8. 'Arithmetic of the Frontier', *Kipling's Verse*, p. 45.
9. Frank Richards, *Old Soldier Sahib* (London, 1936), p. 76.
10. Sir George Younghusband, *40 Years a Soldier* (London, 1923), p. 235.
11. Philip Magnus, *Kitchener* (London, 1958), p. 238.
12. John Gooch, *The Plans of War* (London, 1975), pp. 215–22.
13. Lord Edward Cecil, *The Leisure of an Egyptian Official* (London, 1921), p. 186.
14. C. E. Callwell, *Small Wars: their Principles and Practice* (London, 1906), pp. 349–65.
15. Douglas Jardine, *The Mad Mullah of Somaliland* (London, 1922), p. 122.
16. Angus Wilson, *The Strange Ride of Rudyard Kipling* (London, 1977), p. 84.
17. Meinertzhagen, *Kenya Diary*, p. 32.
18. Ibid., p. 39.
19. Ibid., p. 144.
20. Ibid., p. 146.
21. Callwell, *Small Wars*, p. 147.
22. Meinertzhagen, *Kenya Diary*, p. 208.
23. Ibid., p. 327.
24. Ibid., p. 334.
25. Meinertzhagen, *Army Diary* (London, 1960), p. 53.
26. Magnus, *Kitchener*, p. 283.
27. Perham, *Lugard: Years of Authority*, p. 531.
28. Colin N. Crisswell, *The Taipans: Hong Kong's Merchant Princes* (London, 1981), p. 217.
29. Meinertzhagen, *Army Diary*, p. 78.
30. Ibid., pp. 82–4.
31. Millais, *Life of Frederick Selous*, p. 330.
32. Meinertzhagen, *Army Diary*, p. 116.
33. Ibid., p. 120.
34. Ibid., p. 224.
35. Ibid., p. 241.

10 WINNERS/LOSERS

1. Meinertzhagen, *Army Diary*, p. 140.
2. Ibid., p. 238.
3. Meinertzhagen, *Middle Eastern Diary* (London, 1959), p. 11.
4. Bernard Porter, *The Lion's Share* (London, 1975), p. 248.
5. Max Beloff, *Britain's Liberal Empire, 1897–1921* (London, 1969), p. 269.
6. Porter, *The Lion's Share*, p. 249.
7. Corelli Barnett, *The Collapse of British Power* (London, 1972), p. 154.
8. R. D. Macleod, *Impressions of an Indian Civil Servant 1910–1937* (London, 1938), p. 134.
9. Robert Heussler, *British Rule in Malaya* (London, 1983), p. 186.
10. Porter, *The Lion's Share*, p. 288.
11. C. W. Hobley, *Kenya from Chartered Co. to Crown Colony* (London, 1929), p. 13.
12. Lugard, *The Dual Mandate in British Tropical Africa* (London, 1922), p. 61.
13. Furse, *Aucuparius*, p. 258.
14. Michael Crowder, *The Story of Nigeria* (London, 1966), p. 258.
15. *An American Visitor*, quoted by Molly Mahood, *Joyce Cary's Africa*, p. 137.
16. Porter, *The Lion's Share*, p. 282.
17. Richard Symonds, *The British and their Successors* (London, 1966), p. 189.
18. Evelyn Waugh, *Remote People* (London, 1931), p. 204.
19. Isak Dinesen, *Letters from Africa, 1914–1931* (London, 1982), pp. 290–1.
20. Ibid., p. 240.
21. G. W. Steevens, *With Kitchener to Khartoum* (London, 1899), p. 167.
22. Quoted by Furse, *Aucuparius*, Prologue.

INDEX

Abel, Rev. Charles, 186–7, **187**, 238
Aberdare Mountains, **80**, 81
Accra, 182
Admiralty, 214
Afghanistan, 192, 195
Africa, 26–8, 219; administration, 47–54, 57–66; after the First World War, 223–31; big game shooting, 143, 149–66; First World War, 208–14; military campaigns, 192, 198–208; missionaries, 92–3, 94–6, 102–14, 227; Scramble for Africa, 10, 27, 93; settlers, 70–81, 82, 90; sports, 171, 180, 182–4; traders, 122–40; *see also individual countries*
African and Eastern Trading Company, 139–40
African Association, 125
African Church Synod, 103
African Inland Mission, 227
African Lakes Company, 107
Aga Khan, 179
Aitken, General, 210
Albert, King of the Belgians, 136
Algoa Bay, 151
Aliyu the Great, 94–5
Allenby, General, 215
Amai, 87–9
Amery, Leo, 23, 28, 218, 219–20, 227, **229**
Amritsar, 221
Andrews, C. F., 228
Arabs, 30, 122, 218, 223
Arnold, Dr, 171
Ashanti, 182
Ashanti wars, 190
Asia, administration of colonies, 18; *see also individual countries*
Asquith, H. H., 207
Asquith, Raymond, 22
Assam, 81, 145
Australia, 9, 18, 187

Baden-Powell, Robert, 50, 101, **147**, 148–9, 150, 155, 164, 168, **172**, 174, 190, 238
Baker, Mr, 163
Balfour, Arthur, 14, 15, 29, 32, 130, 191, 195, 218
Bank of England, 14
Banks, Leslie, **235**
Bathurst Trading Company, 138
Bauchi Province, 58, 60, 226
Beersheba, 215
Beho-Beho, 211
Belgaum, 145
Belgian Congo, 126, 128–31, 134, 135–8, **137**, 140, 153, 160, 184
Belgium, 135, 160, 217
Bell, Sir Henry Hesketh, **35**, 36–8, **37**, 38–40, **38**, 41–2, 77, 102, **142**, 175, 233, 238
Bell, Moberley, 51
Bell, Walter 'Karamoja', 160–2, **161**, 164, 177, 213, 238
Benares, 98, 100
Benue river, 27
Berbera, 207
Berkeley, Hubert, **66**, 67–8, **67**, 238
Besant, Annie, 96–8, **97**, 102, 209, 238–9
Binks, 'Pop', 157
Blackwoods magazine, 12, 32, 36, 43, 56
Blantyre, **92**, 93, **93**, 104, 106
Blavatsky, Mme, 97, 101
Blixen, Karen, 90, 230
Blunt, Wilfrid Scawen, 29–32, **31**, 34, 174, 239
Boer War, 10, 12, 14, 15, 18, 76, 94, 153, 173, 190, **191**, 198
Boers, 24, 125, 149–50, 190
Bombay, 222
Borgu, 59, 61–5
Boxer rising, 94, **94**, 116, 120
Boy Scouts, 100–1, 174
Boyes, John, 155–7, 162, **162**
Bradlaugh, Charles, 96, **97**, 98
Brahmins, 97–8, 101, 184–6, 199
Brazil, 83
Bright, John, 20, 26
Brighton, **220**
Brisbane, 91
British Army, 190–2, 194, 201, 213, 215
British Central Africa (Nyasaland), 16, 104, 154
British East Africa (Kenya), 16, 48–9, 71–81, 90, 111, 113, 143, 155, 210
British Empire Exhibition, **225**
British Guiana, 70
British Imperial Airways, 232
British New Guinea, 186–7
British North Borneo, 70
British West Africa, 138, 140
Brodrick, St John, 29, 191, **191**
Brooke, Sir Charles, 46–7, 239
Brooke, Vyner, 47
Buchan, John, 22, 142, 218, 230
Buddhism, 102
Bulawayo, 151
Burma, 16, 46, 192, 223
Bussa, 59–61, **59**, 63
Butterfield and Swire, 118–19, 121
Buxton, Sidney, 157
Byron, Lord, 30, 90
Cairo, 29, 30, 178, 196
Calabar, 171
Calcutta, 16, 28, 116
Callwell, Sir Charles, 196–8, 202, 207–8
Cambridge Mission, 98
Cambridge Seven, 184
Cameron, Sir Donald, 229
Cameroons, **41**, 58, 211, 223
Campbell-Bannerman, H. C., 29, 32, 35, 190
Canada, 9, 18
Canary Islands, 122, 126
Cardi, Charles Napoleon de, 133–4
Cardross, Lord, 77
Caribbean, 70
Cary, Gertrude, 58, 64
Cary, Joyce, 53, 54, 57–66, **58–63**, 180, 211, 226, 231, 239
Casement, Roger, 130
Catholic Church, 227
Catholic White Fathers, 102, 108
Cavalla River Company, 138
Cawnpore, 145
Cecil, Lady Maud, 20–2
Central Africa, 26, 48, 92, 122
Ceylon, 34, 42, 54; administration, 46, 54–7, 66–7, 223; planters, 81, 82–3, 122; sports, 180–1; traders, 115–16
Chamberlain, Joseph, 9, 10, 13–20, **13**, **17**, **19**, 27, 28, 33, 36, 47, 54, 72–4, 76, 120–2, 125, 126, 134, 175, 198, 224, 227, 232
Chamberlain, Neville, 36
Chapman, Abel, 155
Chilembwe, John, 213
China, 121, 178; Boxer rising, 94, **94**, 116, 120; military campaigns, 192; opium trade, 121–2; traders, 117–18, 119–20
China Inland Mission, 184
Chittagong, 145
Chun Koo Leang, **121**
Church of England, 92
Church Missionary Society, 40, 94–6, **94**, 98, 101, 102–3, 186
Church of Scotland, 111
Churchill, Lady Randolph, 64–5
Churchill, Sir Winston, 10, 33, **34**, 35–6, 38–9, **39**, 48–9, 50, 54, 71, 76, 102–3, 114, 158, 189–90, **189**, 192, 198, 208, 214, 221, 223, 228, 239
Clarke, Sir Andrew, 117
Clarke, Sir George, 195
Clifford, Sir Hugh, **21**, 22, 32, 34, 36, 42, **42**, 43–5, 54, 56, 57, 65, 96, 140, 184, 213, 239
Clifford, Lady, **51**

INDEX

Cole, Berkeley, **69**, 79–81, 90, 213–14, **214**
Colombo, 54, 56, 57, 83, 116, 182
Colonial Office, 33, 34, 35, 39, 226; administration of Africa, 27, 40–2, 47–8, 50; administration of Malaya, 25; Chamberlain and, 15, 16–18, **19**; and cricket, 175, 188; Forced Labour Bill, 228; and Lever, 134–5, 138, 140; and Meinertzhagen, 206
Commassie, 182
Committee of Imperial Defence, 191, 195
Conference of Missionary Societies, 227
Congo, *see* Belgian Congo; French Congo
Congo Reform Association, 130–1
Congo river, 140, 160
Constantinople, 108
Coryndon, Sir Robert, 228
Council of India, 18
Coward, Noël, 9
Cranworth, Lord, 69, **69**, **78**, 79–81, 82, **82**, 158, 159, 213, **229**, 239
Crewe, Lord, 71
Cromer, Lady, 143
Cromer, Lord, 16, 23–4, 29–32, **30**, 50, 130, 143, 178, 196, 239–40
Cross river, 199
Cunninghame, R. J., 155
Curtis, Lionel, 218
Curzon, Lord, 11, 15–24, **23**, **24**, 28–9, 32, **32**, 42, 45, 61, 141, **141**, 143, 144, **144**, 157, 178, 180, 194, 196, 198, 217, 218, 220, 240
Curzon, Lady Mary, 28, 29, **141**, 143, 194

Dahomey, 59, 62
Daily Express, 232
Daily Star, 131
Daudi Chwa, King of Uganda, 35–6, **35**
Davidson, James Guthrie, 117
Davidson, Randall, Archbishop of Canterbury, 113, 114
Delamere, Lord, 35, 74–81, **74**, **75**, **77**, **78**, 82, 90, 92–3, 154–5, 157, 158, 213, 228–30, **231**, 240
Delhi, **24**
Delhi Durbar, **170**
Denshawai, 31
Derby, Lord, 218–19
Desborough, Lord, 157
Dick, Tarpon, 155
Dilke, Sir Charles, 130
Disraeli, Benjamin, 11
Diver, Maud, 181
Dominica, 36
Duala, **41**
Dufferin, Lord, 46
Dutton, 177
Dyaks, 46–7
Dyer, Brigadier-General, 221, **221**

East Africa, 22; administration, 35–40, 48; after First World War, 227–30; big game shooting, **142**, 143, **143**, 154–8; First World War, 213–15, 218; military campaigns, 199–206; settlers, 82; trade, 122
East African Army, 164
East African Mounted Rifles, 213
Edward, Prince of Wales (Duke of Windsor), 222, **222**
Edward VII, King of England, **9**, 11–12, **17**, 143
Edwardes, H. S., 58, 60, 65, 66
Egypt, 16, 23–4, 29–32, 50, 178, 192, 196, 218, 220
Egyptian Army, 194
Elder Dempster, 125, 126, 128, 130, 131, 182
Elgin, Lord, 33, 35, 36, 71
Eliot, Sir Charles, 75, 76, 79, 202, 240
Elliot, Lady Eileen, 181–2, **181**
Encyclopaedia Britannica, 42
Entebbe, 35, 36, **37**, 38, **38**
Erroll, Lord, 90
Esher, Lord, 192, 207

Faisal, Prince, 223
Fernando Po, 126
Fiji, 70
Finch-Hatton, Denys, 230
First World War, 22, 58, 84, 90, 114, 164, 187–8, 207–16, 217–19, 220–1
Fitch, Clive, 181
Fitzpatrick, Captain, 226
Foreign Office, 16, 18, 75, 130, 163, 192
Forster, E. M., 46
Foster, Arnold, 191
France, 208, 216
Free Church Scots mission, 104–5
French Congo, 127–8, 129–30
French Seldon, Mrs, 130
French West Africa, 138
Fry, C. B., **167**, 179
Fulani, 52–3, 96, 198
Furse, Sir Ralph, 175, **175**, 188, 226, 231, 232, 240

Gandhi, Mahatma, 222, 228
Gaza, 215–16
George V, King of England (Duke of York), 11, 90, 91–2, 179–80, 218, 233
German East Africa, 209–11, 218
Germany, 114, 130, 209–13, 216
Girouard, Sir Percy, 35, 40, 42, 54, 76–7, 82, 96, 240–1
Gladstone, William Ewart, 14, 18, 23, 26, 33
Glyn, Elinor, 143, 184
Godley, Sir Arthur, 16, 18
Gold Coast, 22, 36, 42, 48, 140, 171, 184, 213
Goldie, Sir George, 125, 127, 134, 139
Goldman, Mr, 38
Gordon, Sir Arthur, 186
Gordon, Lady Idina, 90
Gordon-Cumming, Rouleyn, 150, 154
Gorst, Sir Eldon, 196
Gould, Carruthers, **13**
Grace, W. G., 175, 179
Gray, Herbert Branston, 175–6
Grenfell, George, **91**
Grey, Sir Edward, 157, 163, 190, 195
Grigg, Sir Edward, 90
Grik, 68
Grogan, Ewart, 79
Guggisberg, Decima Moore, 171, 182–4, **183**
Guggisberg, Sir Gordon, 182, **183**, 184, 188, 241
Guthrie, Alexander, 117
Guthrie's, 117, 122
Gwalior, 143–4

Haggard, Rider, 143, 152
Haig, Field Marshal, 215
Haldane, Richard Burton, 191–2, 195, 206, 208
Hall, Francis, 48, 154
Hambantota, 56–7, 61, 66, 83
Harcourt, Sir Lewis, 41, 175
Harrison, Thomas, 139
Haud, 199
Hausa, 94–6
Henty, G. A., 69, 70, 81, 82, 98
Herzl, Theodore, 74
Hicks-Beach, Sir Michael, 12, 14
Himalayas, 16, 97, 98, 101
Hindus, 97–100, 102, 134
Hine, Bishop John, 104, 105–11, **105**, **107**, **109**, 113, 114, 241
Hollywood, 232–3
Holt, John, 115, 123, 125–8, **127**, 129–31, 135, 241
Hong Kong, 34, 46, 116–22, **179**, 209
Hooker, Sir Joseph, 83
Hopwood, Sir Francis, 33
Horn, Max, 131–2
Horn of Africa, 199, 223
House of Commons, 18, 29, 32, 41, 130, 190
House of Lords, 32
Hughes, Thomas, 171

INDEX

Huileries du Congo Belge, Les, 135, 234
Huxley, Elspeth, 157
Hyderabad, 143, 144

Idris, Sultan of Perak, 25, **25**
India, 15, 22, 23, 28–9, 54, 116, 134; administration, 45–6, 223; after the First World War, 231; big game shooting, 143–9, 150; defences, 192–6, 198, 206, 219; First World War, 209; independence, 9; missionaries, 96–102; riots, 220–2; sports, 168–70, **168**, **170**, 179–80, 181–2, 184–6
India Office, 16, **17**, 18, 33, 192, 228
Indian Army, 16, 22, 24, 116–17, 147, 168, 169–70, 192–6, 222
Indian Civil Service, 16, 45–6, 61, 222–3, 224
Indian Forest Service, 145
Indian National Congress, 100
Indian Ocean, 218
Ipoh, 178
Iraq, 223
Irryeni tribe, 202
Islam, 94–6, 102, 107
Ismael, Khedive, 29

Ja-Ja, King of Opobo, 126–7, **127**
Jackson, Sir Frederick, **47**, **77**, 143, **143**, 157, 159, 204, 241
Jaffna, 54, 55, 66, 177, 180
Jaffna Association, 55
Japan, 195, 233
Jardine, William, 118, 122
Jardine Matheson, 117–19, 121, 179
Jebba, 94–5
Jerusalem, **219**
Jews, 74, 218
John Walkdens, 138
Johnston, Sir Harry, 15, 26–7, **27**, 36, 38, 48, 72, 93, 104, 105, 127, 130, 143, 154–5, 157, 159, 234, **235**, 241
Jones, Sir Alfred, 122, 124, 125, **126**, 128, 129, 130–1, 132, 241–2
Jowett, Dr, 16
Jubbulpore, 145
Judd, Will, 155

Kabul, 195
Kaduna river, 95
Kaiama, 61, 65
Kampala, 38–9, 102
Kandy, 56, 83
Kano, 27–8, 40, 94–5
Kashmir, 98–100, 170, 184–6, **185**
Kenya, 16, 48–9, 71–81, 90, 114, 179, 182, 228–30, 234
Kenyatta, Jomo, 234, **235**
Keppel, Admiral, **26**
Kerr, Philip, 218
Keswick, Henry, 118, **118**, 119, 120–1
Keswick, William, 119
Khartoum, 10, 35, 50, **51**, 154
Kikuyu, **47**, 48, **49**, 72, 79, 111–13, 201, 202, **203**
Kilimanjaro, 210
Kings of Bristol, 138
King's African Rifles, 170, 200, 206, 209, 211
Kingsley, Mary, 123–5, **123**, 130, 133, 135, 138, 139, 140, 164, 242
Kipling, John Lockwood, 12
Kipling, Rudyard, 13, 19–20, 22, 44–5, 54, 56–7, 157, 167, 173–4, **173**, 175, 181, 190, 192–4, 201
Kisii, 213
Kisimu, 72
Kitchener, Colonel, 214
Kitchener, Lord, 10, 16, 24, 28–9, **29**, 35, 50, 82, 169, 182, 194–6, **197**, 200, 206, 207–8, **208**, 214, 242
Knutsford, Lord, 18
Koitalel, 204
Kontagora, 65
Korda, Alexander, 234, **235**
Kota Bhara, **45**
Kowloon, 117–18
Krishnamurti, 100
Kuala Lumpur, 25, 67, 68, 84, 89, 178, 180
Kuching, 178
Kwato Island, 187, **187**

Labouchère, 72, 102
Labour party, 224
Lado Enclave, 143, 160–4, **161**, **162**
Lagos, 65, 140, 171
Laikipia Plateau, 74
Lake Club, 180
Lang, Andrew, 172
Lang, Cosmo Gordon, Archbishop of York, 91–2, 114
Lawrence, T. E., 223
Laws, Dr Robert, 104, 105–6
Leadbetter, Rev. Charles, 100
League of Nations, 219, 234
Leeward Isles, 40
Leopold, King of the Belgians, 126, 128–31, **129**, 153, 160
Lettow-Vorbeck, General von, 90, 164, **210**, 211
Lever, William Hesketh (Lord Leverhulme), 132–40, **132**, **136**, 234, 242
Lever Brothers, 134
Leverville, 136, 138
Liberal Party, 14, 18, 20, 29, 32, 54, 121–2, 174, 190, 196, 206–7, 218
Liberia, 138, 164
Likoma, 104, 106–7, 108, 111
Limpopo river, 150
Lincoln, Abraham, 98
Lipton, Sir Thomas, 14
Liverpool, 123, 125, 126, 128, 130, 131, 133, 136, 140
Livingstone, David, 92, 93, 103–4, 107, 110, 113, 150, 232
Livingstone (place), 109–10
Livingstonia, 104
Lloyd George, David, 218
Lobengula, King, 151
Lockhart, Robert Bruce, 86–9, **88**, 188, 231, 233, 242
Lokoja, 28, 51
Londini, 79
London Missionary Society, 108, 110
Lonsdale, Earl of, 157
Loretto, 188
Low, Hugh, 83
Lugard, Flora (Flora Shaw), 18, 28, 33–4, 41–2, 51, 52, 122
Lugard, Sir Frederick (Lord Lugard), 15, 22, 27–8, **28**, 33–4, 40–1, **41**, **42**, 50–3, 59, 66, 72, 94–6, 121–3, 157, 169, 184, 208–9, 213, 224–6, 227, 229, **229**, 234, **234**, 242–3
Lyttleton, Alfred, 28, 29, 33, 175

McDonnell, Sir Schomberg, 24, 28–9, 31
MacIvers of Liverpool, 138
Mackenzie, Bishop, 104
Maclean, Rev. Norman, 111
Macmillan, Northrup, 157
Mad Mullah (Mohammed Bin Abdullah Hassan), 199, 206–7, 223
Mafeking, 149
Malay Civil Service, 84
Malaya (Malay States), 34, 42, 54, 57, 70, 233; administration, 25–6, 32, 43–5, 46, 67–8, 223; after the First World War, 231; military campaigns, 192; planters, 83–90, 122; sports, 178, 180, 188; traders, 117
Malinowski, Bratislov, 226
Malory, Sir Thomas, 22
Mannar, 55–6
Manson, Sir Patrick, 169
Maples, Archdeacon Chauncy, 106–7
Marichchukaddi, 55
Marie-Louise, Princess, 184
Masai, 72, 75, 79, 202, **203**, 204, 213, **215**
Matura, 177
Maugham, Somerset, 90

INDEX

Mauritius, 40, 206
Mayes, 204
Mbuyuni, 213
Mediterranean, 218
Meinertzhagen, Richard, 48, 75, 145, **146**, 164, 170, 199–206, **200**, **203**, **205**, 209–11, 214–19, **216**, 243
Mesopotamia, 218, 219, 223
Middle East, 218, 219, 223, 231
Millais, J. G., **148**, **149**, 151–2
Miller, Dr Walter, **95**, 96, 243
Miller Brothers, 139, **139**
Milner, Lord, 19, 24, 29, 32, 38, 42, 143, 184, 218, 220
Minto, Lady, 169, 181–2
Minto, Lord, **32**, 33, 181–2, 190, 196
Mitchell, Sir Charles, 25
Mombasa, 72, 75, 112, 155, 157, 210
Montagu, Edwin, 222
Moody, Dwight Lyman, 98, 184, 186
Moor, Sir Ralph, 131
Moore, G. E., 54, 83
Morel, E. D., 128–30, **128**, 131, 134–5, 138, 224, 243
Morkill, Alan, **67**
Morley, Lord, 33, 190, 196
Morning Post, 221
Mozambique, 108, 211
'Munshi', 11, 12
Munshi tribe, 190
Mussoorie, 170
Muthaiga Club, 229, 231
Mwanga, King of Buganda, 35–6

Nafada, 58–9
Nairobi, 54, 71, 75–7, 81, **82**, 155, 170, 206, 213, 223, 228
Nairobi Jockey Club, 179
Naivasha, Lake, 164
Nakuru, 77
Namirembe, **103**
Nandi, 82, 204–6, **205**
National Review, 226
Nepal, 145
New Club (Perak), 180
New Guinea, 187
New Zealand, 9, 74
Newbolt, Francis, 175
Newbolt, Sir Henry, 174–5, 188
Newland, 81, 155, 157
Niger, river, 27, 54, 59, **62**, 140, 199
Niger Delta, 123, 124, **124**, 134, 198
Nigeria, 27–8, 33–5, 40–2, 49, 50–4, **52**, **53**, 57–66, 94–6, 121, 122, 134–5, 140, 171, 184, 190, 198–9, 213, **225**, 226
Nile, river, 72, 154, 158, 160, 196
North Borneo, 178
North-West Frontier, 192–4, **193**, 195, 198, 206
Nsenga tribe, 110
Nuwara Eliya, 83
Nyasa, Lake, 104–7
Nyasaland, 16, 213, 219
Nyeri, 81

Oldham, Dr J. H., 114, 227, 229
Ord, Governor, 117
Ormsby-Gore, 227
Osborne House, Isle of Wight, 12
Oswell, William Cotton, 150

Pacific Ocean, 70, 102, 134, 186–7
Pacific Plantations Company, 134
Pahang, 42, 44, 84, 231
Paice, Arnold, 79, **80**, 81, 243
Palestine, 215, **216**, 218, 219
Pall Mall Gazette, 97
Palmerston, Lord, 16, 118
Papua, 70, 108, 186–7
Papua New Guinea, 231
Peel, Bishop, 111, 113, 114
Perak, **20**, **21**, 45, 67–8, 83, 117, 180, 188
Perak Club, 180
Perham, Marjorie, 232
Persian Gulf, 219
Peshawar, 194
Pillay, K. Thanboosany, 180
Poona, 181
Pope Hennessy, Sir John, 121
Port Arthur, 195
Port Elizabeth, 151
Port Harcourt, 139
Port Sunlight, 133, 134, 135, 138, 234
Pretoria, 125
Price, 55–6
Primitive Methodists, 108, 111, 113
Punch, **27**, **34**, 35, 155, **191**, **217**, **219**
Punjab, 220–1
'Punjab Principle', 201, 221
Pusey, Dr, 104

Raffles, Sir Thomas Stamford, 117, 122
Rainey, Paul, 155
Rangoon, 46
Ranjitsinhji, Prince, **167**, 179
Rattray, R. S., 226
Red Sea, 218, 233
Repington, Colonel, 196
Rhodes, Cecil, 18, 23, 70–1, **71**, 151
Rhodesia, 50, 70–1, 82, 102, 108–10, 114, 228
Richards, Frank, 169–70
Ridley, H. N., 83, 116
Roberts, Lady, 169
Roberts, Lord, 195, 196
Robinson, Sir Hercules, 121
Robinson, Rachel, 83
Robson, J. M. H., 180
Rodd, Rennell, 30
Roosevelt, Kermit, 158
Roosevelt, Theodore, 152–3, 157–9, **158**, **159**, 160, 162–3, 190, 218, 243–4
Ross, Dr Ronald, 14, **14**
Rothschild, Lord, 157
Rothschild family, 152
Rovuma river, 108, 211
Royal Artillery, 194
Royal Fusiliers, 200, 206, 211
Royal Niger Company, 125, 127, 134, 138–40
Russia, 195
Ruwenzori mountains, 26
Ryder, Claude, 95

Sadler, Sir James Hayes, 35, 40, 71, 76
Saki, 22
Salisbury, Lady, 29, 196
Salisbury, Lord, 12–16, **12**, 18, 20, 24, 29, 54, 72, 93–5, 122, 154–5, 192
Sankey, Ira David, 98, 184, 186
Santayana, George, 231
Sarawak, 46–7, 178
Scott, Dr Clement, **93**, 104, 106
Scott, Lady Francis, 90
Scott, Lord Francis, 182, 231, 244
Scott, Sir George Gilbert, 16
Scott, J. S., 121
Scott, Thomas, 117, **117**, 244
Scott, Sir Walter, 22
Second World War, 232, 233
Secular Society, 96
Seely, Colonel, 122
Sekondi, 171
Selangor, 45, 84, 117
Selangor Club, 180
Selborne, Lord, 110
Selous, Frederick Courtenay, 150–7, **152**, **153**, 160, 164–6, **165**, **166**, 167, 172, 177, 211, 244
Seremban, 86, 89, 178
Serengeti, 210
The Settlers' Guide, 70–2
Seychelles, 36
Sharp, Sir Alfred, 143
Shaw, Flora, *see* Lugard, Flora
Shaw, George Bernard, 97, 182
Shiré Highlands, 93
Shiré river, 143, 150
Simanggang, 47
Simla, 16, 28, **32**, 180, 181–2, 188, 192, 196, **197**
Sinai, 218
Singapore, 25–6, **25**, 46, 83, 84, 86, 89, 116–17, **116**, 119, 120, 122, 177–8, **178**, 181, 182, 188, 209, 233

INDEX

Smith, Stanley, 184
Society for the Propagation of the Gospel, 94
Society for the Protection of Aborigines, 18–19
Sokoto, 27
Solomon Isles, 134
Somaliland, 16, 39, 70, 92, 154, 199, 206–7, **224**
Somaliland Camel Constabulary, 207, **207**
South Africa, 24, 76, 125, 151, 206; administration, 18; big game shooting, **148**, 149–50, **149**; Boer War, 10, 12, 14, 15, 18, 76, 94, 153, 173, 190, **191**, 198; 'Chinese slavery', 19, **19**, 29; independence, 9
South America, 70
South China Mail, 209
Srinagar, 98–100, **99**, 101–2, 186
Stead, W. T., 97
Steevens, G. S., 230
Stigand, Captain Chauncy, 155
Stone, Daryl, 111
Strachey, Charles, 40, 134
Strachey, Lytton, 54–6, 57, 83, 232
Straits Team, **176**
Strand Magazine, 35, 39
Streeter, W. G., 111–13, 114
Studd, C. T., 184
Sudan, 16, 39, 72, 122
Sudan Political Service, 50, 177
Sudd, 154
Swanzy's, 139, **139**
Swettenham, Sir Frank, **20**, **21**, 22, 25–6, **25**, **26**, 32–3, 34, 44, **44**, 68, 83, 177, 233, **233**, 244
Swettenham, Sir James, 25
Swire, Jack, 119, 120
Swire, John Samuel, 115, **115**, 118–19, **119**, 120, 244

Taikoo Sugar Refinery, 119, **119**
Taiping, 68, 178
Tamils, 54, 84
Tana river, 92–3
Tanga, 210–11
Tanganyika, 90, 114, 210–11, **212**, **217**, 219, 223, 229
Tarlton, Leslie, 81, 155, 157
Tarzan, 232–3, **232**
Taveta, 210
Temple, Charles, 40, 41, 52
Tent Clubs, 147, 148
Terai, 145
Theosophy, 96–8, 100, 101, 209
Thynne, Lady Katherine, 29
The Times, 18, 26, 28, 34, 51, 112–13, 114, 153, 164–6, 196, 233
Togoland, 211, 223
Tonga, 186
Tonga tribe, 110
Tory Party, 13–15, 18, 20, 28, 32, 174
Tozer, Bishop, 104
Tractarian Movement, 104
Transjordan, 219
Travers, Canon, 108, 111–12, 113
Treasury, 14, 18, 72, 227
Trenchard, Hugh Montagu (Lord Trenchard), 171, 198–9, 223, 244
Tripoli, 94
Trower, Bishop, 108
Truth, 72
Tucker, Bishop Alfred, 22, **102**, 103, 105, 114, 245
Tugwell, Bishop, 94–5, **95**
Turkey, 215, 218
Twynam, Sir William, 66
Tyndale-Biscoe, Canon Cecil Earl, 98–102, **99**, **101**, 180, 184–6, 245

Uganda, 26–7, **27**, 35–40, 143, 219, 229; administration, 16, 48; big game shooting, **142**, 154–8, **154**; military campaigns, 192, **199**; missionaries, 102–3, 112–13; planters, 79
Uganda Railway, 22, 35, 48, **49**, 72, **73**, 154–5, **156**, 204, 230
Uganda Rifles, 192
United Africa Company, 140
United States of America, 218–19
Universities Mission to Central Africa (U.M.C.A.), 104, 105–9, **105**, **107**, **108**, 111, 113, 227
Victoria, Lake, 35, 38, 72, 213
Victoria, Queen of England, 10–11, **11**, 18, 33, 92, 118

Wallace, Edgar, 188, 234, **235**
War Office, 192, 198, 206, 207–8, 214–15, 216
Ward, Rowland, 142, 152, 154, 232
Warner, 'Plum', 179
Waugh, Evelyn, 227
Webb, Beatrice, 75, 224
Webb, Sidney, 224, 229, **229**
West Africa, 18, 26, 48, 123–7, 132–5, 138–40, 180, 211–13
West African Frontier Force (W.A.F.F.), 171, 198, 211, **212**
West Indies, 18, 25, 36, 81, 125–6
Westminster Gazette, **13**
Weston, Bishop Frank, 108, 111–14, **112**, 227, 228, 245
Wilberforce, Bishop Samuel, 91
Willcocks, General, 169
Willis, Bishop, 111, 113, 114
Wilson, Woodrow, 218, 219
Windward Islands, 36
Wingate, Lady, 50, **51**, 154
Wingate, Sir Reginald, 50, **51**, 154, 157, 207, 220, 233
Winstedt, Richard, 46, 84–6
Wodehouse, P. G., 174
Woolf, Leonard, 22, 34, 46, 54–7, **55**, 61, 64, 65, 66–7, 83, 115–16, 177, 180–1, 184, 224, 226, 232, 245
Woolf, Virginia, 57, 66, 83

Yangtse river, 118–19
Yao, 104, 106

Zambezi river, 104, 150, 151, 153
Zanzibar, 104, 107, **107**, **108**, 111–12, 113, 114
Zaria, 94–5, 96
Zionism, 74
Zungeru, 41
Zuru, 64–5

Luscious Fruits galore.
The Sun that ever S
SARDINE
Peers's Pills
Dress
Great herds of Game
A few Elephants charging.
The little Englishman with the eyeglass who pots 'em in the eye every time
The usual Lion with menagerie mane
Various nasty creepy
G. Millais del. 1894.